Memories

incorporating

PERVERSE AND FOOLISH

and

MEMORY IN A HOUSE

Lucy M. Boston

MEMORIES

incorporating

PERVERSE AND FOOLISH

and

MEMORY IN A HOUSE

Introduction by Jill Paton Walsh

Colt Books Ltd
Cambridge
with
Diana Boston
Hemingford Grey

Diana Boston

2.10.2002

Colt Books Ltd
9 Clarendon Road
Cambridge CB2 2BH
Tel: 01223-357047
Fax: 01223-365866

with

Diana Boston
The Manor, Hemingford Grey
Huntingdon PE18 9BN
in aid of The Manor Hemingford Grey

This edition first published 1992
Reprinted 1992, 2000

ISBN 0 905899 05 9

Jacket design by Clare Byatt

A CIP record for this book is available from the British Library

Printed and bound in Great Britain by Biddles Ltd
www.biddles.co.uk

Introduction

by Jill Paton Walsh

Lucy Boston's reputation as a writer of excellence for children was already well established in 1973, when she published *Memory in a House* — the first to be written of these two autobiographical books. Six years later she returned to an earlier period of her life for *Perverse and Foolish*, an account of her childhood and youth. The two books are here reprinted together, in chronological order, to mark the centenary of the author's birth in 1892.

Lucy Boston lived an exceptionally long and active life, and she was creative in many spheres. For much of her adult life she pursued music and painting rather than literature, and her achievements include a dazzling collection of masterpiece patchwork quilts and a garden of great beauty and subtlety. She did not begin to write until she was sixty.

In 1937 she bought the Manor House at Hemingford Grey, and restored it, the work taking two years: 'by far the happiest of my life,' she tells us in *Memory in a House*. The war brought its own stresses, and the use of the house as a sanctuary for the young airmen flying from nearby airfields. Lucy's deep and abiding attachment to the house had, however, lit a long fuse, which a decade later turned her into a writer in whose every work (*The Sea Egg* is the sole exception) the house appears, often fictionalised as 'Green Knowe', and her love of the house and its setting shines clear.

According to her own account in *Memory in a House*, Faber would have published *The Children of Green Knowe* on their adult list, alongside *Yew Hall*, her first adult novel, had she not wished it to be illustrated. Peter Boston's delicately surreal woodcut-like drawings had given her real joy, and there was an absurd publisher's anathema against illustrations in adult fiction. Thus as if by accident she found her true vocation, for it was as a children's writer that she attained a world-wide reputation.

Lucy Boston's achievement as a children's writer is a considerable one, and has proved enduring. She wrote twelve children's books in all, moving across the past and present of her house, and peopling it for herself, giving 'a local habitation and a name' to the anonymous past generations whose vanished presence is so palpable there. It is worth noticing that in this enterprise love of the house is matched by love of children; it was their company she called up to fill the void of the past.

Jasper Rose's monograph on Lucy Boston's work, (Bodley Head, 1965) is at some pains to distinguish her from other children's writers; but the truth is more interesting: together with William Mayne and Philippa Pearce, who both began to publish for children at about the same time, Lucy Boston's 'Green Knowe' books caught a wave. To the early fifties, in addition to Pearce and Mayne, belong the first fully mature titles from Rosemary Sutcliff, C.S. Lewis's *Chronicles of Narnia* and Tolkien's *Lord of the Rings*. Although it is only with hindsight apparent that these writers formed a movement, Lucy at sixty was fully in touch with the spirit of the times, and was one of a galaxy of talented writers, exploring and mapping the possibilities of children's books as fully serious literature.

Three aspects of Lucy Boston's writing made her quintessentially a children's writer. First the transparent clarity and limpid simplicity of her prose, which made thought of subtlety and delicacy easily accessible. Related perhaps to her love of music, she had an exquisite ear for the sound and resonance of the language. Second her total lack of condescension to young readers. 'I do not know how anyone can judge of what they write, unless they are writing for themselves,' she has said (*Memory in a House*.) Third, although in her adult novels, and in her poetry, she wrote eloquently of the mysteries of adult love, it came naturally to her as a writer to take up her stand on the large ground which adults and children have in common.

Time, change, memory and continuity were among her recurring themes. Other writers have worked with those, but she has never had her equal at evoking the physical sensations of the fleeting moment — at awakening a rapt attention to the mercurial beauties of the natural world. Speaking to the Children's Book Circle in 1968, Lucy Boston said:

> I would like to remind adults of joy, now obsolete, and I would like to encourage children to use and trust their senses for themselves at first hand - their ears, eyes and noses, their fingers and soles of their feet, their skins and their breathing, their muscular joy and rhythms and heartbeats, their instinctive loves and pity and awe of the unknown...

Besides the beauty of the natural world, at its pinnacle in her beloved house and garden, one other thing fired Lucy Boston's imagination to incandescence. That was her indignant sympathy for all subordinates, for all whose personality is assailed, whom the world is trying to pressure into being other than what they are. The majority of such embattled selves are and have always been children, though the finest example in the whole of her work is the magnificent tour de force with which she identifies with Hanno, the captive gorilla in *A Stranger at Green Knowe*.

Lucy was also a poet, able to give her particular vision — the fusion of personal emotion with context in place and time — expression with lapidary grace. Her 'Poems in Old Age' especially, privately printed with earlier work, in '*Time is Undone*' (1977) movingly testify to her indestructible capacity to feel, and to voice feeling.

The childhood and formative years of such a writer as Lucy Boston are of the profoundest interest, but *Perverse and Foolish*, which exposes the author's character to view with undefended candour, is an exceptionally interesting autobiography in its own right. It is as fine as any of her fiction. 'I was nakedly naive, had no demureness and no boundaries, but I also knew no evil unless pride in one's own honour is evil.' By her own account she retained a childlike innocence well into adult life; the personality laid bare in *Perverse and Foolish* is recognisably the wayward, passionate and undiplomatic person who rescued and loved the Manor House at Hemingford Grey, and turned it into a crucible of the imagination, as recounted in *Memory in a House*; indeed, her innocence and her sense of honour remained with her life-long.

I never knew a person less inclined to manoeuvre to be liked. You took her for what she was; unflinching and amused she responded to your response. She was incapable of emollience. This fearless quality, which made her rather awe-inspiring as a friend, made her a very good autobiographer.

Nevertheless, some grace notes need adding to the account. In defence of her own values, her own honour, her own house, Lucy was capable of a most withering scorn, as passages in *Memory in a House* make clear. But she was not capable of unkindness. She gave love and respect as generously as she hoped to receive it.

In so long a life much that she loved vanished, and much of what remained was threatened and fragile. An elegiac note sounds persistently in these memoirs. What they do not quite convey is how alert and pungently funny she was. And how self-mocking.

'You said you didn't grow any rose later than 1914,' I once had occasion to remind her.

'Did I? Did *I* say *that*? I should have said 1900!'

Or, when we suggested that there might be novels in large type available from the mobile library she said, 'Yes; but those are for dear old ladies!' She was then ninety; as prickly, as upright and as blooming as one of her own rampant old roses. In one memorable conversation she and I joyfully invented a new religion in which you got credit for enjoying yourself, there was to be no worship except walking out of doors and *sensing* the world, and any form of glumness was a sin.

There was no glumness about Lucy, even in her very late old age, when she could no longer see to read or sew. She sat quietly beside the fire in her dining room. The door stood open to the leafy canopy of the great beech tree behind the house. A squirrel crossed the threshold, and the friends who came and went were deputed to feed it cheese or chocolate. A blackbird pecked holes in the fruit, or sat under the table rehearsing very softly the songs he would pour out full volume in the garden in the coming spring. Time stood still, and the world seemed held in a state of wholeness.

Nothing can make good the loss of such a friend; but Lucy delineated herself clearly and honestly in these two books, giving those who knew her eloquent reminders, and those who never met her a chance to know her. It is a great joy to see them again in print.

Cambridge, February 1992

The author, Lucy M. Boston, aged two and a half

Perverse and Foolish

A Memoir of Childhood
and Youth

To Peter and Diana Gunn
who with their curiosity and
expectation — of what? —
positively drove me, unwilling,
to write this book

Foreword

I have no guarantee of what is written here but memory, a known cheat. Looking back from my eighty-fifth year there is much that has faded out altogether, but here and there at random, pictures clear and bright as the magic lantern slides of my childhood stand out, which I must believe. Nobody else need! The chronology has slipped, before and after often get mixed. I have tried to keep a continuous story and to amplify it as little as possible with hindsight. I remember and have put down the thoughts and feelings as they were then, not as later experiences would recreate them.

L.M.B.

1

My earliest memory is of sitting in front of the nursery
fireguard in the evening beside the feet and blue-calico-
covered knees of Nurse, with my youngest brother in a
crib close by. The room was big and full of shadows that
flopped in the jumping fire light. I was seized with a
sudden rash feeling of adventure. I would cross the
mysterious room right to the other side. I crawled as far as
the table and under it, and then the great loneliness of so
much empty shadowed space frightened me and I hurried
back to those familiar knees. This one odd picture in my
mind is dated by the fact that I was still crawling, but I
seem to have been as much myself as I am now. At least
in memory no difference is perceptible.

The nursery was in fact abnormally big. My father was
an eccentric with big ideas, a small, goodhumoured,
dynamic man. I was said to be strikingly like him, though
I can't see it in photos, or in the very unappealing portrait
of him as Mayor that confronted all my youth. It was a
monstrous picture, painted by a cripple (doubtless because
he was a Wesleyan as we all were) *with his feet*. None of
the family portraits were masterpieces, but the older they
were the better. This one, though competent and
immensely present, was repulsive. The sitter was wearing
the gold Mayoral chain of which the medallion rested on
a tight round belly. His trousers also were tight and on
each knee rested, Rameses-like, a podgy hand. I used to try
to feel love and admiration for the parent so presented for
my consideration, grim-mouthed and blankly glaring, but

it could not be done. However, much later on, Stanley Spencer, who had become a close friend of my brother James, greatly admired a photograph of Father and used it for the figure of God in his great Resurrection picture in the Tate.

My grandfather Peter Wood was better represented by a marble bust that, mounted on an apricot marble column, dominated our dining room. This we all admired, and my brother James at the end of his life greatly resembled it. Peter Wood was a physician who had taken up the new idea of sea bathing for health. He chose the safe and sandy beach of Southport, then quite undeveloped, and built a row of charming little Regency houses on the front to be rented by his patients. The sea has retreated from Southport. Even in my childhood it was often out of sight. The Promenade and the Marine Drive were built one after the other to fill the stretch of sand as the sea withdrew. The little houses, if they still exist, are lost in the seething vulgarity of the present town.

I never knew any of my grandparents. On the Wood side they had eight daughters before my father was born, and one son after him — All the family were passionate Wesleyans and their passion gave them dignity. My grandfather promoted the building, on half of his own garden, of a very big chapel, of which the architecture, smell and stencilled decoration are forever imprinted on me, horrible, but redeemed by the curiosity, interest and irrepressible humour of a pewful of children whose legs did not reach the floor. From the Chapel grounds a Gothic arch in the wall gave private entrance to the family residence. It gave also a certain creepiness to that end of the garden as I always imagined coffin after coffin carried through it. In fact, of course, however short the distance funerals would have been carried out in state with hearse and broughams from one pillared gate and in at another fifty yards away.

Grandfather had lived in considerable style in a large house called 'Woodbank' set in about ten acres. As a child

I used to see the family coach in the coach house, incredibly dusty, woodworm- and moth-eaten, standing with raised shafts, too forgotten even to be wanted out of the way.

The house was then inhabited by three unmarried aunts. My father was well over forty when he married, so his elder sisters were old ladies when we were children. One had remained a nightmare figure for life. She was the eldest, known to us as Beady Liz. We used to meet her drawn in a Bath chair by a decrepit old man (doubtless a Wesleyan) round her garden. She wore a bonnet of jet with black antennae, a black cloak trimmed with jet arabesques, and in her pinched face her eyes were jet. She sat upright and rigid in her ludicrous hooded vehicle like an upended coffin, showing no sign of life but hostility, and took the air in this fashion round her own grounds in solitary repudiation of the wicked world. There was also at times a widower-in-law, a tall, tottering zombie who qualified for Monty James' scholar whose eye-sockets were covered with cobwebs. To stop and say, 'Good morning, Uncle Jenkins' to him was more than a child dared.

The youngest of Father's sisters, Emily, also lived there but I do not remember her till somewhat later. She evidently could not get on with her sisters, for when she settled in, they moved out. She had avoided the invalidism of the others and was in fact something of a tartar, with eyebrows flying up into the roots of her hair and a habit of saying exactly what she thought. She dressed sumptuously in purple, and she mocked. The boys liked her. She could and did command the minister to come and pray with her when she wanted company, and having got him there flirted very effectively.

◇

In order to be near the family home and its affiliated Chapel, my father took a house in the street which led directly to the double wrought-iron gates. It was a mean street of small, identical, barely genteel houses. Aunt

My father

Emily's companion Miss Millington lived in one. I never knew of, even less met, any other inhabitant of the street. All the gardens contained privet and laurel. All the windows had Nottingham lace curtains well drawn across, with an aspidistra inside to block the central gap. My father, having bought such a house, began — in which I see my likeness to him — by knocking off the roof and the whole back of the house in order to double the depth and put on an extra storey. He built out a wing on one side and put in outsized bow windows on the whole front and back. It dominated the modest street. All this was in preparation for the family he intended to have. He then got craftsmen — well chosen — to paint all the important rooms to his requirements. The doors were painted in beautiful pastel colours with panels full of delicate flowers such as surround Persian miniatures. On ribbons among the flowers were moral maxims. These doors were done with such perfect workmanship that after thirty years of rackety family life the surface and colours were still most beautiful.

In the breakfast room above the picture rail a passage of Scripture travelled across three sides. It read, 'The lines are fallen unto me in pleasant places. Yea, I have a goodly heritage.' While one was stirring porridge one's eyes turned round the room to read it.

The long dining room had heavily carved beetling wooden mantels for the two fireplaces, and life-sized family portraits of four generations hung round. Above them a painted frieze gave place at regular intervals to mottos such as,

'He that giveth to the poor shall not lack.'
'Honour thy father and thy mother.'
'Thine own friend and thy father's friend forsake not.'
'The soul is not where it lives but where it loves.'

I used to know them all, but these were in view from my usual place at table and have sunk in. In the bedroom one could not stand to warm oneself by the fire without an exhortation to prayer staring at one from just below the mantelshelf, but the triumph of eccentricity was the drawing room. I wonder what my poor mother thought when first she saw it. This was where she was to entertain the Mayor's associates and friends. My father had recently been to the Holy Land and had brought much back with him, his idea being apparently to make a holy and uplifting room, perhaps such a room as Joseph of Arimathea might have had, or perhaps he was just letting his fancy have a fling. The frieze was a continuous painted landscape representing the journey from Jerusalem to Jericho. Under it the walls were divided into recesses by very intricate and beautifully made wooden arcades of the Moorish onion shape, a pattern unknown here. Who can he possibly have found to make them? Each recess was fitted with semi-circular seats covered with a material brought back for the purpose. It appeared to be woven of horse hair and metal and was like a file to the back of children's knees. It never wore out and never could. From the ceiling hung antique brass lamp-holders shaped like udders with glass oil-containers hanging down, such as might have hung in Solomon's temple. There were many beautiful objects made of brass beaten out almost as thin as linen : a life-sized cock with windblown tail feathers, a duck, a coffee jug with a spout like a swan's neck and a bowl to stand it in.

Other rarities were displayed in a glass-fronted cupboard made in the same fantastic elaboration as the recess. It was of natural black wood, very handsome. The lower half displayed a plaster facsimile of the Warning Stone from the temple of Solomon. The translation below read,

'Let no foreigner enter within the paling
Round the Holy Places and its precincts.
Now whosoever shall be taken therein
Shall be found guilty unto death.'

This unexpected room did not look at all like a Kardomah Cafe as you might perhaps think. It looked like a gentleman's enthusiastic and satisfied near-lunacy. My mother had neither enthusiasm nor fantasy nor taste. She was totally indifferent to the appearance of things, but possibly not to the expression on visitors' faces.

As they left the house they would read over the inside of the front door 'The Lord shall bless thy goings out and thy comings in'. ◇

To return to the nursery in which the six of us lived. We were girl, boy, girl, boy, girl, boy at yearly intervals. I was the penultimate, between my brother Frank above and Phil below. Jamie (later known as Jas), dazzlingly handsome with huge brilliant eyes, was the god and tyrant of the tribe, but all were under the governorship of Nurse. It was she who brought us up. She was a big quiet woman, a disciplinarian whose command was never queried, but kind and fair. I can see the nursery table, all present, with Phil and myself in high chairs and Nurse unsmiling in charge. She was not a highly trained Norland Nurse, but a good serious Lancashire native. She had been, before Mother married, in her Sunday School class, and had come with her as a support and help in the new life.

Nurse disapproved of too much laughter at table, and frequently threatened that she would make us laugh on the other side of our faces, but she never slapped us. From the protected piety of my high chair, rather like a pulpit, I watched the way of the world. I saw with interest my sister Frances push the crust she had been told to eat down the teapot spout while Nurse was mopping up Phil. The sin would clearly come to light, and did. Frances was made to stand in the corner. This was Nurse's most severe punishment. I wonder how far back in nursery history standing in the corner goes, and what genius in child psychology first thought of it. I often saw Frances and Frank banished there and once stood there myself. I went defiant and unrepressed; there was an interesting super-cornerishness about the corner at first. One fitted it so neatly, and it offered a different slant of wall-paper to each eye. The pattern was repeated illustrations of 'Goosey,

Goosey Gander', of which the upstairs and downstairs offered amusement as one covered first one eye and then the other. But very soon the corner became the most boring and constricting of prisons. One's back was blind and vulnerable and desolate, and all life was going on behind it. Jamie of course needed severer treatment. He was passionate and spoilt. Still in my high chair, waiting for the others to take their places, I once saw with shocked disapproval, that with his belt, of which the buckle was interlocking metal snakes, Jamie was slashing Frances. For this he was taken down to Father. In the study was kept a swishing cane, ornamented at the thick end with a crimson tassel. No doubt for thrashing his sister it was well applied. Frank was not yet old enough to have been caned, but regarded the implement with awe, especially the ritual tassel.

Nurse was totally loyal to our parents. Daily she told us of their virtues and notability. I do not think she was happy. All her meals were in the nursery at the top of the house, not personally brought her but sent up on a lift. She must have been lonely, perhaps more effaced than self-effacing. She attended the Salvation Army which perhaps less cold than the Chapel where her station was rigidly marked out. She took us there, but did not even share the pew. In the evenings she picked out on a small Jews harp the tunes of Moody and Sankey hymns, a most melancholy substitute for the music she had in her. All the training I ever had was from her, and yet I cannot recall a reprimand or a punishment, though she often looked very grim.

Our parents we saw once a day at Family Prayers, to which we were taken down. When we had all taken our seats on the chairs in front of which we should later kneel, the servants filed soberly in and sat in a row beside the door. Father then read from the big family Bible, sometimes making me stand between his knees while he guided my fat finger along under the words. (He called me his 'little Pige', short for pigeon.) Those of us who were old enough to memorise then said, in turn, a verse of Scripture. Phil at his first effort said with simplicity, 'He maketh me to lie down in still waters', which disturbed the gravity of the occasion, and thereafter he was never asked to try.

Strange to say, I remember nothing of the actual prayers, impromptu of course. Later on I had plenty of experience of very embarrassing prayers. Presumably Father's were short and in Biblical language. After Prayers we followed Father into his study on the first floor where we each received a small biscuit with a twirl of pink sugar on top, and were dismissed to the nursery. Very occasionally Father and Mother would come up to see us before we went to bed when we were larking around on the top landing. They laughed as if at a play, but only stayed a minute and never played with us. On Sundays of course there was Chapel, and after that we all, on our best manners, came down for Sunday dinner, always roast beef and Yorkshire pudding, followed by red and yellow jellies. Before the meal we all sang 'Praise God from whom all blessings flow,' and after it 'We thank thee Lord for this our food'. In between these two verses we ate and absorbed the good words before our eyes on the frieze.

This was all that as small children we normally saw of our parents.
◇

The nursery as I have said was very big, the size of three main rooms under it. Surprisingly it had no texts. Nurse evidently did not count. Of course she was not being brought up. The kitchen also was without, not even 'Blessed are the poor', but over the range in large letters, tersely, 'Waste not, want not'. I do not think that the texts were for ostentation, but rather that Father just felt happy among them.

In the nursery there was of course the old rocking horse, which after travelling round the family nurseries is now with me again. Father had ideas ahead of his time. He had had made a movable, detached flight of stairs as part of the nursery furniture. They were hollow underneath and easily housed all our toys, and provided a useful series of levels for many games. I chiefly remember sitting on the top step with a toy harp being an angel, a game with no holding power. The small wooden harps, with strings so loose they made no sound, were totally unpleasing: I wonder what misguided relative chose them for us. We had special toys for Sunday such as bricks that would only build chapels and Noah's arks. It was a limited range. We might have enjoyed missionaries and cannibals as a change from soldiers, but no one had thought of that. Sunday books were either uplifting or depressing — the New Testament illustrated in colour, very nightgowny, *Pilgrim's Progress* also illustrated, in which Apollyon, and even more Giant Despair, terrified me, and Foxe's *Book of Martyrs* with every kind of martyrdom vigorously depicted. On Sundays too we went down after tea to the crusaders' drawing room where we played 'Onward Christian Soldiers marching as to war' in and out of the small inlaid tables, singing as we went. The Persian carpet trodden by those infant feet is under my feet now. It gave one a shock after writing those words to look up and see it. Five pairs of those feet are gone.

The house was lit by gas which I remember most clearly in the bedrooms where we were after dark. There was a simple jet, unshaded, which gave a flat square flame, blue at the source and yellow at the top. What can possibly have lit that drawing room? I have an uncomfortable hazy feeling of pale blue fluted and flounced glass shades, ludicrous in that setting. Fairly early on a change was made to electric light, an exciting innovation; when I went to boarding school ten years later, they had still not caught up with it. The workmen were in the house a long time. We always enjoyed workmen who are generally so understanding with children. We were, I am sorry to say, provided with sheets of paper printed with texts in a particular lettering made up of broken bamboo sticks, for some reason special to texts, never seen in any other

Lucy

context. These we coloured with crayons and lovingly presented to the men. They were received with grins but never rejected. The electric wires were hidden under strips of wooden moulding up and down and round the rooms. The odd lengths left over we collected to make marble runs. Jamie was very ingenious at this, starting from the top of our movable flight of steps, with different gradients, angles, drops, tunnels and even see-saws. The various speeds, pauses and reverberations could make pleasing music as the marble obediently ran.

For weekdays we had many and splendid toys, especially Jamie, possibly chosen for the first-born son by an enthusiastic father. They added much to his kudos in my eyes. Phil and I, coming at the end, had nothing to compare with them. Mary and Frances too had superior dolls. Theirs were jointed all over, even their wrists and ankles, their bodies and limbs covered with white doe-skin, soft to touch. Their faces were china, not plastic, smooth to a young finger with a slight egg-shell drag. Their hair was real hair, their clothes hand-sewn with doll-sized stitches and tiny buttons, all complete, everything we wore. They were Victorian young ladies who did not smirk. Their eyelids closed over their eyes with real lashes. They had dignity and manners.

Every Saturday we were given one penny to spend as we chose. Nurse took us to the penny stall in the Market, where wonders could be bought, such as a gilded state coach two inches high with two horses, wheels that really went round and doors that opened, showing the seat inside, or 'silver' cups, saucers and teapot on a tiny 'silver' tray. The boys bought cannons, whistles or tops, or more often liquorice 'tram lines' that hung revoltingly out of their blackened mouths as they consumed them inch by inch. When in season I always bought a pansy root with one velvet flower, thrilled with the whole smell of wet paper, soil, leaf and pansy. As the soil of our garden was grey sand, almost nothing grew, but Jamie had a white lupin which I thought a wonder from heaven. My father had made an attempt at laying out the small back garden which had high walls all round and no sun. It had sycamores, laurel and privet and one small rose, probably the old Monthly Rose as I do not remember any scent. This was the only rose of my childhood and I treasured it. It was set among rockery stone of some soft white substance like half-consolidated marble with crystal granulations. With a penknife one could scratch out caves in them and with the sand trickling round their bases they made a thrilling terrain for the mounted toy soldiers of the Boer War. We were Boer War children. We wore on our lapels buttons printed with the face of our preferred General — 'Bob', Lord Roberts, being the most popular. We all knew and sang both the words and tunes of the war songs of the moment — 'The Absent-Minded Beggar' and 'Oh! Listen to the Band'. One may wonder how, without radio or gramophone, a whole nation came to know them; I suppose individually, each from the other like bees in a hive.

The sterility of this garden affected me from a very early age, and until I bought the Manor at Hemingford Grey forty odd years later my most recurrent dream was trying to reform that sixteenth of an acre of disappointment.

We had the run of the garden belonging to the Aunts. They kept two old gardeners and a gardener's boy. The Aunts were invalided indoors behind their bedroom curtains and as far as we could tell never looked out. The garden was kept severely decent. I could still make an accurate map of all its paths and corners. It was interlaced with gravel walks which the gardener's boy on his knees weeded with finger and thumb month after month so that never a pebble had a blade of new grass beside it. The main pillared gates were opposite the end of our road, but inside them was a long drive, under a double row of trees, finally coming to a dead end. Probably, before he sacrificed half his garden to the Chapel, the affluent physician could drive across to a second gateway on the far side. The heavily draped main windows of the house looked over a long lawn in the middle of which stood a pedestalled urn with geraniums. Otherwise there were no flowers. Nobody went into the garden except ourselves.

A doctor, of whom I am sure my sea-bathing grandfather would not have approved, was making a good living by persuading all wealthy ladies to take to their beds at the age of forty and remain there for life, seeing him constantly. My Aunts were therefore permanent invalids, only occasionally feeling well enough to take the air in a Bath chair, as I have described. Usually we had the place to ourselves and when we reached the bicycling age must have caused the old gardeners despair by rutting up the perfectly regulated pebbles of the paths. There was an orchard, the trees planted in naked beds with a path between them every six feet. Further away, screened from the gentry by a long artificial bank twelve feet high, was the kitchen garden, each bed hidden from sight by a dense privet hedge as if vegetables were indecent. In the high bank, as I scrambled up, I once saw a primrose and a cowslip. Someone in the far distant past, before the doctor cast his wicked spell, must have enjoyed this bank and planted it. Also once, by mistake, a tiger lily flowered by the old pump, last unvalued descendant of a living garden.

For us every path, every crossing or corner had a name. We cycled madly round, skidding as we turned. No wonder the withered gardeners were soured. Their tidy death of a garden was nevertheless the best thing in our home life. We were without any supervision and the labyrinth of paths was too extensive to be boring. The day before my schooldays were to begin, I wandered by myself in the Aunts' garden on a beautiful evening, looking at the golden sky and the poplars traced against it and lamenting that my life was now over for ever, never to be free again. I was seven. I think it was then that I began to realise that landscape was what moved me most. A few years later I knew it as both my anchorage and my motive force.

◇

At home we met no other children but cousins. Only Wesleyans were fit company for us and unfortunately Methodism was a religion chiefly drawing tradesmen, except for a few leading families such as ours. The Wood family speech and manners were upper class, arrogant and exclusive. The Aunts' bearing was regal, their language was that of the Authorised Version which was their only reading. I cannot speak for my father because he died when I was six. From what I remember of his presence I exonerate him from all littleness, but the Aunts were snobs. Never were female 'companions' worse treated than Aunt Emily's Miss Millington. She might stand for the most miserable unliberated woman of the period. She was at fifty so outcast, so deprived of self-respect, so hopelessly trodden on as to have become in fact an object of contempt.

In all the houses of our relations there were aged retainers, butlers and nurses, excellent devoted servants who were worked unsparingly and, though respected, ignored. Perhaps sometimes they got a word of recognition, but I never heard it from my elders. I presume these old people stayed because they had nowhere else to go. Old age pensions did not exist and in any case they were, in this feudal way, part of the family. Yet they served with pride and the way my uncle's butler opened the door to me as a small girl, with a courtesy and a welcome greater than I got from my relations, stands out as one of my childhood's great pleasures.

The household served by this butler was wealthy. Uncle Holden, parent of our future guardian, lived in style, He was a big, fat man who spoke broad Yorkshire. His bearded kisses always smelled of soup. His beard was very long and as soft as a girl's hair. His eccentricities were our joy. He was deaf, and in order to save himself the trouble of holding his hand behind his ear he had caused to be made for himself a pair of tortoise-shell ears almost big enough for an African elephant, held in place by a spring fitting over the top of his head. These he wore in Chapel

Uncle Holden

with great effect, and they enabled him to shout 'Alleluia'
or 'Praise be to God' at suitable (to his idea) moments in
the sermon. His wife, having the same doctor as all her
sisters, had adopted delicacy. A whole service was too
much for her, so just before the sermon Uncle in his grey
frockcoat rose and left his pew to meet her alighting from
her brougham at the door, and brought her in on his arm
with imposing gallantry. This gave style to the service, and
as our pew was level with theirs we had a good view of
the little drama. Immediately in front of Uncle was an
elderly lady who by some accident had her head
permanently stuck sideways. To me it always made her
hats look funny, as if she put the hat on to face forward
though she could not. The fact that she was always in
profile to Uncle made her the ideal informant when, in
spite of his ears, he did not get the number of the hymn.
He had only to tap her elbow and with an easy half turn
of her waist she and Uncle were face to face and she could
point with a gloved finger to her hymn book. This she did
with a peculiarly graceful and sanctimonious half bow that
was the delight of the six young Woods. At the end of the
service Aunt was supported on her elephantine husband's
arm down the aisle to the door, and generally one of us
was taken in the brougham back to lunch.

The house was spacious and imposing, handsomely
furnished and worldly instead of cranky like ours. The
food also was like nothing we ever saw or tasted at home.
Uncle was a glutton. My sharp nursery eyes must have
widened when the butler carried in two large plum
puddings, one of which served five people and the other
was lifted whole on to Uncle's plate. After lunch he slept
and snored with a large handkerchief over his face. We
were given toys — not Sunday ones — and told to play
quietly. The favourite was something that may have been
called a mobiloscope. It consisted of a circular cardboard
container like a hat-box without a lid. It spun on a pedestal
and its walls were perforated by high narrow slits every
two inches. You fitted inside it long strips of what we

should now call 'stills' of acrobats or steeplechasers, spun the thing round and looked through the slits. Wonderful! 'The acrobats somersaulted, the cyclists cycled, the horses leapt. This was many years before the invention of the cinema.

It was a liberal house. Even the family portraits could be looked at with long pleasure. Uncle before he aged into gluttony and sleep must have been a lively generous fellow.

◇

To return to our own other-worldly home, Mother was loved by her servants. She was not more generous to them than anybody else — a Christmas present would be an apron — but she was human and helped them in their family troubles. We had a laundry woman to whom I was much attached. I think of her whenever I see a Tintoretto goddess or nymph. She had an Italian type of face, the most beautiful rounded arms and a very soft voice. Her realm, reached down a black hole of winding, underground stairs, consisted of two vast cellars, one for the copper, the wash tub and dolly. Imagine a small wooden stool, or dolly, with four stout legs. Through the seat is set a three foot pole with a cross bar at the top. The stool fits easily into a high tub full of sheets whose folds wrap round the legs of the dolly. It must then be swished about as one holds the cross bar, the weight of the wet linen being quadrupled by the length of the pole. No one who has never used a dolly could guess what cruel work it is. The wash cellar was dark and always awash. It was underneath the eccentric drawing room, but no one there ever thought of it. The ironing cellar was a long tunnel underneath the dining room. It was festooned with clothes lines to take the sheets for twelve people. Rows of flat irons were ranged on the three sloping sides of the stove and a long table stood under the window where a grownup's eyes were on a level with the soil of the back garden. At the far end to which daylight never really reached were racks containing mysterious bales of things once belonging to my father or his father. It was believed by us all that among them was a mummy's hand. From these old bundles came a musty smell that seemed to confirm that belief. However one had only to get in among the hanging sheets for the mummy to be forgotten in the smell of Sunlight soap and dripping linen. Here Mrs Brade toiled alone all the year round. I used to go down, braving the dark stairs and the mummy hand, to have her sweet and gentle company and to iron dolls' clothes. Once she surprised me by saying, 'Oh, Miss Lucy! To be here is my idea of Paradise!' I learnt later that she had a drunken husband who beat her frequently and that as a result, though she had had five longed-for babies, they had all been stillborn. When my mother died and the house was closed, she was the most heartbroken mourner.

◇

Our three maid servants shared a large bedroom. They had no bath, but a wash basin and three large conspicuous chamber pots. The nursery suite had only a child-sized bath like a deep porcelain sink. Into this Frank and Phil and I were dumped together to scrub each other's backs pretending we were scrubbing floors. Nurse slept in the night nursery with Phil and me. No bath was provided for her.

Grandfather, the sea-bathing physician, had refused to consider allowing anything so dangerous as a boiler to be installed in his house. I was never intimate enough with my aunts to know if they had a bathroom or not. Father's, however, was the latest and most expensive that could be had. The bath was constructed like an enormous mahogany cradle of which the hood touched the ceiling. The inside of the hood was semicircular, finely perforated all round to give the 'Needle Spray'. At liver height there was a bruising 'Douche' and from the roof came two kinds of shower, normal or fierce. There was a control panel with many wheel-shaped knobs with their function printed on them and a dial with arrows to show how much hot to cold had been turned on. A mahogany lavatory seat as commodious as an armchair adjoined the bath, but its plumbing, alas, was primitive, being the same in principle as in British Rail today.

◇

Mother's father was a Wesleyan minister who commanded love and respect, especially for his charity. I was told he was the bastard son of a West Country lord by a laundry maid. Apparently the bastardy outweighed the holiness and Mother was received into the family with a coldness amounting to cruelty, from all but one, Aunt Bertie, of whom I never heard as a child. She was never mentioned except once absentmindedly by Mother, who named her as one of a group and said she had been very fond of her. Much later on her death bed, in her delirium she constantly called for Bertie. I remember her laughing with Father, but after his death I cannot remember her laughing again. It was not a love match − she married under pressure from her parents (they had seven daughters) when her inclination was elsewhere, to a man twice her age. Father had had a great love in youth for a wild-spirited girl who was killed in a hunting accident. Mother slightly resembled her in type of feature and was asked for as soon as seen. She was not like the horsewoman in character, but delicate, intensely sensitive and idealistic and without a trace of sensuous feeling. She bore, as Victorian wives had to, a child every year, but had little maternal feeling. Before she died she told me she wished she had never had any of us. She should have been a nun. She was very gentle.

During my father's lifetime she was nearly always Mayoress. She must have had a civic life of which we knew nothing. She may have been very bad at it. Much entertaining of that kind can hardly have gone on without some echo of it reaching the nursery. My mother was not made for that kind of thing, and her idea of food was that it was a sad necessity. Later on she began to think it was

My mother and father

not even necessary and the boys raged with hunger.

◇

It is extraordinary to me how little I remember of my father whose favourite I am told I was. Of his appearance I have no visual memory at all. I might have been blind. I remember the feel of his hand, his voice and laugh, and a comfortable confidence. He occasionally took us bathing in the shallow waveless sea that crawled across the sands to the Southport pier. He and we all wore the horizontally striped costumes that were the standard bathing outfit for men and children of the period. I imagine they were designed for decency, the stripes serving to cut up and conceal the shape of the wearer and produce hideousness. They are as I write high daytime fashion for the under thirties with whom hideousness is a cult.

There were holidays when Father was present. When the family travelled by train we had a reserved saloon and the station master met us at the station entrance, saw us bestowed, and waited to see us off. I remember him as wearing frock coat and top hat if only for such occasions. At any rate he was in full grandeur. The trains of course were those wonderful and never to be forgotten puff-puffs, the fury of whose puffs in the station threatened to burst my infant eardrums.

We stayed at Shap Wells hotel, now I believe submerged in a new reservoir. I walked with Father beside a stream and was shown by him how to throw leaves in the current for boats and run to follow them with joy and wonder. That puts me at about three years old. We walked through herds of Highland cattle, terrifying to me, but I was soothed by talk of God's providence — the soil for the worm, worm for the bird, bird for the table, and in face of these piercing-horned monsters my reaction should be, 'We thank Thee Lord for this our food'.

Father was an obsessive preacher and I suppose he was good at it with his Biblical language and true passion. There was a settlement of miners on Shap Fell to whom he

preached! He had an idea that his little pigeon might be a
catcher of rough souls. He took me often between his
knees and taught me to sing:

> 'Will you meet me at the Fountain
> At the Fountain bright and fair?
> Will you meet me at the Fountain?
> Yes, I'll meet you, meet you there.'

When I had learnt it he told me he would take me with
him to the camp and I should sing to the miners. This
never took place. Probably my mother vetoed it.

◇

Back in Southport he once took me with him to the Town
Hall and the Police Station. Hanging onto his hand I
approved the saluting and respect with which he was
received, and his authority. He said he would inspect the
cells, and I should go with him. Did he mean me to be
impressed by the fate of evildoers, especially of those who
drank beer (he was a teetotaller)? I only remember being
held up to the spy window in each door and seeing inside
simply one of the unhappy Poor, each crouching alone in
a blank cell. I was embarrassed. I still think it was inhuman
to make a peepshow of them. Possibly the intention was
not only that my inexperienced soul should receive a
lesson, but that the hard hearts of the sinners within might
be led to repentance by the face of innocence. But my
father was big-minded and warmhearted and I make him
sound mean.

Once, when in some forgotten nursery squabble I had
bitten Phil's finger, I was marched downstairs by Nurse to
the dining room where Mother and Father were at table.
Their meal was interrupted while my heinous offence was
told, Nurse standing beside me like an indignant constable.
I pleaded in my own defence that I was just happening to
close my mouth when Phil put his finger in it. Father let
out a gale of laughter and I was dismissed with my sin and
subsequent lie unpunished.

Nurse

That is absolutely all I can remember of my father, yet the thought of him always brings reverence and love.

◇

Sometimes Nurse took us all in the horse-drawn tram to visit the Churchtown Botanic Gardens, a place offering a variety of strong emotions. The particular attraction was The Swings. It seems now a long way to go for such a simple pleasure, but they were imposing swings, hung from a height on iron-linked chains that my hands could just close round. I can still feel and hear them. One could swing sky-high whence the return was dreadful and always made me sick. The others would be there for hours, but I was taken by Nurse to find other interests. As one entered the big gates of the Gardens, there was the Museum, approached up a flight of steps guarded at the base by two stone lions crouching and gnashing. I would not have dared to come near them but for my upbringing on *Pilgrim's Progress*. Perhaps like the lions Christian had to pass they were really chained. Sustained by faith I bolted up the steps.

The Museum was full of terrors. First there were two human skeletons hanging side by side, male and female, horribly mobile. These pursued me home and through the night. Beside them was a dead tree wound around by a gigantic stuffed snake, sinister but by comparison bearable. It was only Garden of Eden stuff. There were rooms full of exhibits that have left no impression at all, but the worst things of all were what we called the waxworks. These were two glass-fronted boxes containing rigid doll's house figures. If one put a penny in the slot a nerve-awaking whirring began and things which should not move did so. One box was otherwise pleasing, showing merely bell-ringers in a tower who pulled on ropes while bells rang. The other was an execution scene ending with the gallows drop. But the subject was irrelevant. It was the age-old terror of the inanimate moved by unseen power. It rivalled the martyr's stake as my nightmare for many years, chiefly in the imagination of the wide Museum staircase at the bend of which sat a life-sized waxwork of a man, impudent and tense. All he did was, as one rounded the bend, to turn his head with a mechanical jerk to watch one pass. This was total horror. Emerging shaken from the Museum to rejoin the swingers, holding Nurse's hand I came up to a round bed completely filled with scented, velvety yellow pansies. This was the other side of the medal, a surprised joy that made an impression as deep. I have tried all my life to raise a bed as good, but that young rapture cannot be remade.

◇

As we grew older attendants multiplied. Nurse had an underling, young and lively. Frances and Frank, the two immediately older than I, had an apple-cheeked Yorkshire girl, Eliza, whom we all loved. She came from Whitby and once to my great envy took Jamie and Frank home with her for a long visit. Picture postcards of high seas on that coast so impressed me that for years I collected photos of fountaining surf, though I had never seen or heard it.

On the floor below Eliza's charges was a governess for the two eldest, a Miss Shrewsbury, who had only one dress, of fudge-coloured serge from throat to floor. She never expected or found anything to smile about. Remembering her I sympathise with all the young ladies in Georgette Heyer's novels who fear governess-ship as the final horror, and exhausting and humiliating as Ivy Compton-Burnett shows it my memory of it in reality is worse.

When I was six Father contracted pneumonia, almost a certain killer in the days before antibiotics. During his last days the setts of the whole street were covered deep in sand to deaden the noise of passing horse-drawn vehicles, but visitors came to inquire in a perpetual stream. A bulletin was hung outside the front door. These dramatic signs could be watched from the nursery window. I was as yet innocent of death and had no apprehension. About a year later a tame parrot died before my eyes and the realisation came with full force, but when before my father's funeral I was taken by Nurse and lifted up to put a lily of the valley in the cold hand, the weirdly dressed up doll lying in a box lined with pleated white satin did not draw a tear. We had never been allowed to visit him during his illness and what I now saw was meaningless; simply displeasing.

Phil and I, too young to go to the funeral, were dressed in black and watched from our high windows the long cortege of hearse and carriages. Relatives in streaming black crepe were handed into their broughams by gentlemen, top hat in hand, all in heavy but orderly silence, each vehicle moving away in turn with the creak of tautened harness and moving wheels. When all the chief mourners and civic representatives had gone, they were followed on foot by more people than I had thought existed. My filial pride swelled and I said to Nurse, 'Now I can never be happy again'. But as I said it I knew I was putting it on, and felt at that moment my first real personal shame. I feel sure that the evangelical teaching I had received had never got down to details such as 'Thou shalt not assume appropriate feelings'. Quite the opposite. I have seen one of my infant letters among my mother's treasures after she died. The baby writing obviously guided by an adult hand read, 'Little Lucy loves Mother but little Lucy loves Jesus more'. It is enough to make any adult blush, but I give myself credit for having an innate ethic that disclosed itself sternly at the age of six.

From this time on, as one elderly relative after another died, we were permanently dressed in black, mourning a year for each aunt or uncle deceased. By the time we were in our teens funerals had become an outrageous family charade. I did not get out of black till I was fifteen and Mother was in black all her life. I used to watch her dress for Chapel and groan at the ugliness of everything she put on.

After Father's death our life lost all magnitude. Each

child had been left a small fortune to be spent on education during minority, but Mother in the mean Victorian fashion had only just enough to keep the house together and had she remarried would have forfeited all. She had no dynamism, no practical competence, and she had till now never made out a cheque. She was saved by having no interest in anything money could buy, a natural and extreme frugality and austerity. There were many negatives to her character, but if one awards a negative to each of the deadly sins and adds to that list no vulgarity, no inquisitiveness and no possessiveness, something grand remains.

I do not know how she bore her widowhood because about this time I fell ill and was sent to the Fever Hospital. It was thought to be a case of simultaneous measles and scarlet fever, the latter then a very dangerous disease. The hospital as I remember it was two corrugated iron wards at right angles to each other. At the end of my ward were two 'grownups', probably teenagers, too far away to know, and at the other myself. The nurses made a fuss of me and I enjoyed being there, except for a waggish nurse who scissored at me and said 'I will cut off your nose'. I believed her. It is curious that though obviously very ill I have no memory at all of feeling it. Perhaps children don't recognise a state that is not yet in their field of reference. When I was able to stand I was taken to the window from which one could see the men's ward at right angles. In their window another nurse supported a desperately white and ill one-legged boy, perhaps seven years old, with the face of an angel. I was told to wave to him and got a wan smile in return. That is the whole of my first love affair. Afterwards I was sent home and saw many doctors and was kept in bed in the dark for a time and was not allowed to walk for months. While I was in bed someone brought me a bunch of wallflowers whose velvet and scent was a joyful experience repeated every few minutes. So flowerless was my early childhood that I keenly remember each flower that I met. I also had, sent up from the kitchen to amuse me, a large potato with five knobs (head and four legs) which to me was as an adored puppy. There came a day when Nurse relentlessly removed both flowers and puppy saying they were going bad. I wept for a cruel bereavement and was told 'not to behave silly'. She did not think as she whisked them away that at eighty-five I would still feel it. During my convalescence I was given *Alice in Wonderland,* the first non-pi book, a fascinating delight. I was still dependent on being read to and fought petulant battles with Nurse to make her read it when she was busy. 'What do you want that stupid book for?'

◇

We had been left, as was usual for fatherless children, to the guardianship of a cousin on the Wood side, a very capable man of perhaps thirty years old. He evidently took his responsibilities seriously, perhaps a little too much so, coming as he did in my mother's mind from the enemy side of the family. She flared up and told him to leave her children to her. Nevertheless he was entirely good and generous, never let us see there had been any difficulty and was tolerant, loving and helpful always. From the time when I sat on his knee and blew to make his Hunter watch spring open and chime, I was as devoted to him as if he had been a much older brother. His total integrity and courtesy were an education of the kind that is so profound as to be taken for granted.

In Mother's now reduced circumstances the governesses and undernurses vanished. Nurse was left, as her faithful help, and we all went to school. The boys' and ours were in adjacent streets. The two eldest boys went to 'Miss Clough's'. She was probably a Wesleyan because from their talk their education was more 'pi' than ours. (Jamie at ten became an enthusiastic temperance canvasser and drew us all into it.) We all set off together every morning, at first by horse tram but later on foot, a walk of about two miles through the town.

We passed every day the same gentlemen walking

briskly in the opposite direction to their offices. Cars were
not yet known. If you were not grand enough to keep a
groom and brougham, you walked. These gentlemen all
had nicknames. One dapper little man always had his
pockets full of chocolates for us. These morning walks
through silent residential streets were enjoyable, especially
in spring when every front garden had overhanging
hawthorn trees in bloom.

My youngest brother Phil had curly hair as fine as
cobweb and the colour of polished brass. It came down
nearly to his waist and was considered too beautiful to be
cut off. The poor little Samson was sent at six with me to
a private school of about forty girls. It was run by a severe,
immaculately gowned woman with glossy hair smoothed
back from a marble brow. She was helped by her
monstrous mother, heavily bombazined and with a lace
cap over her white hair. There were also two pupil
teachers, really schoolgirls with their hair up.

My first morning began with writing the alphabet on a
slate. In the lowest class all the work was done on slates,
lovable objects, the pleasant drag of the pencil making a
soft sound and leaving a beautiful line. I could already read
and write, but poor Phil, screened and embarrassed by his
trailing cloud of hair, did not succeed in either until he was
ten, though as intelligent as any. Even at home he hardly
ever spoke, so that the three or four sentences he is known
to have uttered were never forgotten. We were all
astounded to learn from the report of his last year at a
public school, that he was a brilliant debater. I wish I had
known the brother that strangers knew.

The second lesson of the first day at school was reading.
The passage beginners were given was not 'The cat sat on
the mat' which had explained reading to me in a couple of
glances at home, but we plunged straight into the deep
end of literature.

'Remember now thy Creator in the days of thy youth
while the evil days come not, nor the years draw nigh
when thou shalt say, I have no pleasure in them; while the

Phil

sun, or the light, or the moon, or the stars, be not darkened, nor the clouds return after the rain; in the day when the keepers of the house shall tremble, and the strong men shall bow themselves, and the grinders cease because they are few, and those that look out of the windows be darkened, and the doors shall be shut in the streets, when the sound of the grinding is low, and he shall rise up at the voice of the bird, and all the daughters of musick shall be brought low; also when they shall be afraid of that which is high, and fears shall be in the way, and the almond tree shall flourish, and the grasshopper shall be a burden, and desire shall fail; because man goeth to his long home, and the mourners go about the streets; or ever the silver cord be loosed, or the golden bowl be broken, or the pitcher be broken at the fountain, or the wheel broken at the cistern. Then shall the dust return to the earth as it was: and the spirit shall return unto God who gave it.'

This was stuttered and stammered over round the class with reluctance. I had of course heard it before, but it seemed to me now a revelation and a glory in words. I do not think anyone except perhaps my father would give that passage to a seven-year-old expecting it to be greedily received as what reading had to offer. When I see modern reading primers I am aghast at their mean vulgarity. In my day I guess this passage was a moral gesture for the beginning of term. We went on from it to *Coral Island,* and afterwards when we got to 'Literature' we were given the facile jungle of Scott. But on that first day I had taken hold of the real thing.

The grim bombazine dowager, ruler in hand for the rapping of knuckles, taught me to play scales, but for singing we had the choirmaster of the biggest church in the town. (He appears in *The Children of Green Knowe* as the choirmaster of Great Church.) There was no piano in the big classroom but he brought a tuning fork and a linen roller that he hung on the wall, printed with Doh Re Mi etc. As he pointed to each word we had to sing the notes.

Lucy

Squatting on the floor in the front row among the youngest I joined in with the others and sang what they sang. I had no idea what it was all about. We also learned songs, such as 'The Minstrel Boy' and 'She is far from the land' (where her young lover sleeps).

It was while we were learning the latter that the master, holding up the class, pointed his cane at me and told me to sing it alone. I was gratified and piped up to my maximum noise, probably about that of a new-born kitten. He turned away putting his hand over his mouth, having enjoyed his little joke without unkindness.

In those early schooldays I made no friends. There were only two Wesleyans in the school. One was the friend of my sister Frances. They would not allow me to walk with them to school. I had to follow behind. The other I was told by my mother not to speak to 'because she was vulgar'. Otherwise I do not remember the face and name of a single child in my first years. Probably we were oddities and tended to get left out. We never went into any of their homes nor had them to ours. The text we were brought up on was 'Come out of her, my children,

(Babylon, the Great Whore) *and be ye different'*. The only party I remember from that time was in the house of a cousin of my parents' generation. I had not been there before and was shy and frightened as Nurse dressed me in unlikely party clothes.

We had no carriage. The only form of transport was the horse-cab. There was a cab rank at the end of our street where the cabbies had a shelter provided by my father. The cabbies and their drooping horses were a familiar feature of our life. The cabs were old, rickety and smelly. The smell was extraordinary. I always presumed that somehow both horse and driver slept inside. The feel of the dusty upholstery under one's fingers was repulsive. There was a current legend that once when one of the Aunts was being driven, the bottom had fallen out of the cab, forcing her in her long skirts and elastic-sided boots to run along inside keeping up with the horse. Which would not be difficult.

The silliest of our middle-aged cousins, who at fifty had a face like a highly coloured Dutch doll, wore forget-me-nots in her hair and cooed like a woodpigeon. She ran a mission for cabmen. I don't know what she offered them. My brother Frank added to the standard bedside prayer which was 'God Bless' (all our relations in order) 'And bless the cab horses and keep them warm tonight'.

To return to my first party, it was a large and overpowering party. I sat at the long table beside an unknown, mischievous not to say malicious-looking boy a year older than myself. He made one remark, pointing to an elderly man at the head of the table, 'You see that man over there holding up his knife? If you don't behave he'll roar at you and have you sent out.' Had I known it, this was his father and my host. I ate in misery and silence. Twenty years later I married that boy, malice and all.

◇

The teaching in school was very simple: for arithmetic we learned the multiplication tables and weights and measures. For history we learned by heart the dates of all the kings and queens of England, one dynasty a week. For literature we learned a simple poem such as Wordsworth's 'Daffodils'.

Learning by heart, even when, like the mere names of kings, it was meaningless, I found quite as much fun as, say, Ludo or Snap. It was something to do. But the bulk of the class seemed simply to sit through every lesson without the slightest interest or effort. Simple (if idiotic) questions such as 'And what happened to Wordsworth as he lay on his couch?' went round the class and found no answer. No one seemed to mind, neither pupil nor teacher − who expected it. This attitude continued right through the school. None of these girls was going to earn her own living. There was no pressure at all, no Eleven plus, no 'O' or 'A' level. They saw no point in learning. They were there to be kept out of mischief till they grew up. Three years of this uneventful life have left no vivid memory but the sickly scent of privet in the school playground and the way a pretty pupil teacher did her hair.

◇

At home we now saw more of our mother. Relieved from her Mayoral duties she turned to us. She had also acquired a friend, the only one she ever had, but she was one in a thousand, and being single spent most of her time with us. Her name was Patty Ashton. In appearance she was as like a pullet as a human being can possibly be, though her eyes were blue in a wattle-pink face. She was therefore very funny to look at, and spinsterish to the last feather. One of the family jokes was her woollen combinations, seen on the clothes line, long-sleeved and long-legged *and* with a knee-length skirt added for decency. The trade name was Modesta. She claimed to have only five of the seven layers of skin, and it may well have been true, she was so available. She was the most loving and understanding person I have known, in all family acerbities equally sympathetic with all, with a merry sense of humour that

Father with Frank and Lucy

had no edge. I took all my bruises and fears to her and was always comforted. None of us took her seriously, but she was my mother's sole support throughout their lives and her comic goodness gentled everything.

◇

If my father's religion was personal and passionate, my mother's beliefs were 'received' and were as certain as tenets never questioned. Every word of Scripture was literally true, including the creation of the world in six days. But to the ten commandments she added four more:

> Thou shalt not drink alcohol;
> Thou shalt not go to the theatre;
> Thou shalt not play cards;
> Thou shalt not dance.

These were held as stringently as those given to Moses. She was also anti-Catholic without any qualification, as were my aunts, one of whom was heard to tell her companion to draw the curtains as two nuns walked past in the street, so that 'those *devilish snakes*' should neither see nor be seen. In Foxe's *Book of Martyrs* the martyrs are all Protestant and we as children were taught that the stake was a likely fate for us. 'The fires of Smithfield will be relit.' I do not know how much the rest of the family was affected — none of them ever said anything to me that reflected my fears — but night after night in my dreams I recanted at the stake, I only, all the others being burned — off stage, I am glad to say. My imagination was not equal to witnessing it. I always woke terrified and totally ashamed. During some domestic shift or other I shared a bedroom with my brother Frank, to whom I confessed that I was afraid to go to sleep because of my dreams. He rose tenderly to the occasion and with talk and riddles kept me awake as long as we both could hold out. So great was my terror of burning that it made me shake even to burn a piece of paper. Fire phobia pursued me into my thirties.

During Hitler's time when hideous martyrdoms were a daily occurrence I wondered whether I ought to be grateful for such an unflinching upbringing which was after all not out of date but very actual. Yet I doubt if terror in childhood is a help if the moment comes. I was practised in recanting.

Another night pastime Frank and I shared was to stand side by side behind the bedroom curtains to watch the windows of the houses opposite. They were separated from us by our back garden, the lane for the back gate, and their back gardens. The occupants must have thought that with so much space and two high walls between, they were not overlooked. A whole street of back windows was lit up for us to watch. On the ground floor were the kitchens, on the first floor several dentists' surgeries where nothing was going on, and above that bedrooms. We never saw anything traumatic or even dramatic, but it was a fascinating peepshow. Even the passing up and down stairs, the private conversations snatched in empty rooms, the order given and obeyed at a run, were sufficiently mysterious and the whole thing toy-like and pretty in the surrounding dark.

◇

From the fourteen commandments the forbidding of music was by some oversight omitted, probably because, except for hymns, it had not been heard of in my mother's family. I can't believe my father was indifferent. Not only was he distantly part Jewish, but in our generation music broke out all round. However, all I have to put to his credit musically was a collection of delightful musical boxes, beautifully veneered and decorated, playing Scotch airs in a very sweet tone. There was also a large square box on legs. Into it one put discs the size of a modern record covered all over with sharp wire bristles. It gave out a displeasing sound like a harmonium. Quite recently there was a talk about these on the radio, and I heard the old queezy sound again.

2

A great change came when, for Mother's health, we all moved into Westmorland for a year. We lodged in a large house beside the river Kent at Arnside and my real life began at ten years old. The village was small enough for us to know every inhabitant, and in any case we were well known because our maternal grandfather had lived there. The steep little cliff path that led to his house was known by his name, Garrett's path. My mother's unmarried sisters still owned it.

The house where we were installed was kept by two sisters, Annie whom we all loved and her cross elder, known to us as Flop-legs. It was furnished much better than the usual lodging house, with handsome, farmhouse mahogany and beautiful china. There were big oil paintings of horses ploughing or returning at dusk which I much preferred to our ancestors at home. They must have had some merit for I looked at them constantly, never disappointed. The sisters must have come down in the world a long way. We occupied the house not only for that year but for many summers afterwards. It was a second home. It stood on what was called The Promenade, a macadamed cul-de-sac fronting eight or ten houses. It was wide enough for a char-a-banc to turn round and was edged with a sea wall along the river. From our windows we looked across the wide estuary of wet sand to Grange on the far side with Cartmel Fell behind. Upstream we saw the real fells, blue or sandy-coloured against the sky. What brings all this and the sharp smell most vividly and nostalgically alive is the sound of swifts, who built under the eaves and screamed and looped for ever in a weaving host round the bedroom windows.

The estuary of the river Kent was glorified twice daily with the drama of the 'bore', the tidal wave. All my days pivoted upon the time of its expected arrival, the waiting stillness of the shining expanse in which only a small shallow channel of the river remained, hardly enough to float a rowing boat; the expectant cries of the gulls forestalling what must be, and at last at an incredible speed the heaped up waters of the Irish Sea poured in, headed by a low but tearing wave churning and eating the sand as it went till in no time there was deep water, a mile wide with a dangerous undulating force along the centre, making for the viaduct where it eddied in tumult among the piers. The viaduct at that time was entirely wooden. The small steam-powered trains crossing it made a most musical muffled thunder, louder when the tide was out, but always delightful. Later on it was rebuilt in iron and lost all its magic.

We quickly knew all the boatmen, and were welcomed in the boat sheds where small yachts were made. All the boats on this stretch of the river were locally made and we knew them all by name. The boatmen were very tolerant of us, perhaps for our grandfather's sake. They taught us the risks of the bore and how to deal with it, and at what distance it was safe to follow it in a boat, and even how one might meet it head on, but that was for Jamie only. They allowed Frank and me, with our thin childish arms, to row about as much as we liked. When not in a real boat, a toy one, stripped of its mast which always toppled it over, was my Argos, drawn by a string round dangerous reefs, in and out of tiny bays along the bank. The imaginative pleasure I got from this over-spilled into pure happiness, blue sky, gulls' cries, vast distances and wet sand between my toes. It strikes me now as interesting that a small child can at the same age play with a risky tidal wave than which nothing could be more objective, and

Lucy, Frances, Frank, Mary, Phil and Jamie

draw a chip of wood by a thread, feeling that to be the more complete experience.

The valley is closed in by hills and fells rising behind them, whose outlines were my constant reference and grounds for confidence. The river, whose every mood, current, sandbank, curve, rock, cliff and cove I came to know intimately, was by far the biggest experience of my early life, an in-built way of thinking.

Besides the river there was the wooded hilly country all round, as yet completely natural and open to us in every direction as far as we could go, and we roamed far. There were no cars, no buses, nothing that we now would call a road, only larger or smaller lanes. We travelled on foot, but if we really wanted to reach a town, such as Kendal, we could cycle, sure of meeting nothing worse than a milk float or pony cart.

There were two schools in the village, both much better than those we were used to. The girls' school was a converted country house, very pretty and beautifully situated. There were teachers with whom it was a challenge to learn, whose discipline was admired and whose approval was a quick joy. There was only one classroom, smaller groups used the living rooms of the old house; no assembly hall, no gymnasium, and the hockey field was a lop-sided valley with a goal post at the top of each of its hills. Nobody thought this was a disadvantage. In this school I was happy every moment.

The boys also were content. Phil with his hair at last cut short could go with Frank and they were taught by real men, one of whom was an idol whose name was forever in their chatter. Jamie, hereafter referred to as Jas, was away at boarding school, Rydal Mount.

◇

The eldest of us, Mary, was the physical scapegoat of the family. She embodied all weaknesses and diseases and the rest of us were totally healthy — she was plain and her figure was almost deformed, but she had elegant hands and feet. She was at sixteen intelligent, dignified and able. Under other circumstances she could have done much, but her handicaps were so great that nothing else could ever happen to her. She was lonely and reserved, but amiable with the younger ones. Jas the dominant male, demanding and receiving homage and admiration and imitation from all, but especially from me, for I adored him. Frances I saw little of. Though so near in age and almost identical in appearance, we had nothing in common. She had a mother fixation and was always hanging on to her skirts. Frank was self-effacing but my constant companion. Phil – handsome, silent but laughter-provoking – was everyone's favourite. Patty Ashton and Nurse were there to support Mother.

◇

I particularly remember the snowy winter of that year. We went to school in the morning and returned at night in the dark, carrying swinging lanterns that held a candle. There were as yet no electric torches. The way was up Garrett's path, a steep footpath up the edge of a rocky bluff. It was fenced on both sides and for some reason had a kissing gate every twenty yards or so. The falling snowflakes were caught by the candlelight as they danced past and if I swung my arm the golden circle met white wadded fencing on the left and then on the right, still there though constantly disappearing. When my feet told me we must by now be approaching a gate, the exploring light would find the friendly landmark magically transformed and kissed again and again by the flakes that came in from the surrounding blackness. Each gate told me exactly where in the obliterated universe I stood, in my little circle of candlelight. This treasured adventure was entirely private.

◇

Now came my first spring in the country. Hitherto spring had only meant the double red or white hawthorns along the town streets. The idea of a front garden as status symbol had not come in. I do not remember seeing a daffodil even in the park, the soil of Southport was so deadly poor. I cannot remember when I first smelled lilac though the thought dilates my nostrils and in memory fingers still small enough to match the single florets hold them in wonder. These tiny experiences have the size of revelation. The world opened wide, to let in what?

My mother, penny careful (she gave a tenth of her income to charity), never had a flower in the house. Now at Arnside I received the full impact of the returning sun. Every inch of that earth responded. There were fields of wild daffodils, those slender little flowers with white haloes and primrose trumpets, infinitely more beautiful than the dandelion coloured giants of today. For sixpence the farmer would let us pick till we were tired and could not hold any more. In the open country and across the commons primroses and violets were everywhere while the smell of the earth itself was intoxicating. The scent of a bunch of primroses must be one of the sweetest things in childhood. Walking across the 'near common' on springing turf kept smooth as a lawn by rabbits, we came to Newbarns Bay, a big scoop of wet, grey sand only covered at high tide and smelling violently of river. There was a farm here providing delicious home-made meals served by a severely reserved fifteen-year-old lass who was Jas's first infatuation. Here too there were woods carpeted with lilies of the valley and wood anemones.

Beyond Newbarns came the 'far common', larger and still more beautiful. The footpath across it was little more than a rabbit track, hardly visible. I do not remember ever meeting anyone else on it, and litter was not yet invented. It led ultimately through a limestone stile to another bay called Whitegrate, surrounded by a limestone rock face ten or twelve feet high. Unlike Newbarns this cove was floored with a shelving bank of white limestone pebbles which occurred nowhere else that I know of in the course of the river. They not only gave off a rainbow light that surprised the eye, but also a clean chalky smell. This was a favourite picnic place, magical to the senses. From here one looked more down the estuary than across it — an immense area of sandbank, and wandering channels, growing ever wider toward the imagined horizon and reputed to have stretches of deadly quicksands.

Above the miniature cliffs a track ran through an oak coppice, scarlet-leaved because rooted in limestone, giving off an exciting aroma. Primroses rioted in the oak roots. The path was overgrown and hardly passable for an adult but it was then and for twenty years afterwards my particular and secret kingdom. It led ultimately through a deserted village, (abandoned perhaps in the Black Death?), a cluster of half a dozen ruined cottages, built of stone but now hardly higher than a ground plan, overgrown with brambles and nettles, ferns rooting in what was once a window sill, a room full of tangled growth and a butterfly passing through. I haunted it. How could desolation have happened in what seemed to me the most perfect place in which one could ever live?

◇

I have taken the reader a long walk with my ten-year-old self round the base of a hill called the Knot, having the estuary on our right hand all the way. After the Deserted Village one came scrambling down to another bay and then the path turned inland to a wide, green valley in which stood Arnside Tower, a square ruined Peel tower such as were dotted about the district. The romance of the great desolate walls with windows to non-existent rooms and corner spiral stairways ending in space was the seed that burst into life when I found my present house.

From the Tower, a path led through the larch woods of the Knot, and finally down an undulating hillside clothed with bracken fronds of another unforgettable scent, back to the village. The impact of such rich, varied and vital experience, on an imagination reared on sterile sand and Foxe's *Book of Martyrs* was explosive. Suddenly I was myself. What chance have children who grow up in a tower block and walk, if at all, in streets smelling of diesel, who have never heard a robin in his own woodland singing his happiness in that lively stillness?

The joys of Arnside were wide and inexhaustible. A long walk inland took us through oxlip woods and cornfields full of wild flowers (no weed killers yet!) to a farm where I was once permitted to see in his stall a bull as huge as a steam engine but with every inch of his hide charged with danger. He had an eye like a smouldering furnace and a head and neck heavy enough to demolish anything. He was tethered by his dribbling nostrils.

Beyond the farm was a hill covered with limestone, at the summit of which were the Fairy Steps, the object of our excursions. We went through a wood where the trees grew out of crevices between horizontal limestone strata. The crevices were full of ferns and mosses and of unguessed depth, very mysterious. The stone was a pale bluish silver, half polished, which gave a curious light to the wood. The Fairy Steps, small, regular and absolutely natural, wound up through a crack just wide enough for children to pass, almost impossible for buxom Nurse, on to a plateau. This was before the era of trippers and there was nothing to diminish the magic. Only a rabbit track led to the steps and all about on the turf sprawled lichen-covered boulders that to my finger were clearly alive. Sitting up there on one of those warm stones that felt akin to me, as it were ancestral, the view comprised everything that I knew and loved, bounded by the familiar outline of the distant fells. This acknowledgment superimposed again and again, accumulating depths of recognition, cannot be traced back to a first time, but it works there, the basis of all that came after.

◇

More accurately placed in time are the pleasures of the Three Springs. Out of the tree-crowned bank of the river there gushed, overflowing a stone trough, a stream that ran down the sand. Here in the holidays all the little

Woods busily made a series of dams to hold up the stream, one basin below the other, with turf gates to control the flow. To be spade in hand became second nature – and still is. Often now when amateur gardeners offer their help and I give them a spade, I see instantly that they have never used one. They have no idea how to handle what to me is as simple as walking. With so obvious a tool it is still possible to do everything awkwardly and inefficiently. Then I remember the Three Springs, the first wooden spade thrown away as silly, the tin blade which bent backwards if you asked too much of it. But as we were always barefoot, the final satisfaction of the slam of the boot must have come later.

◇

Summer brought another range of flowers whose names my mother taught me. The grass of the hillside was closely interlaced with rock roses in an endless spread, you could lie on them in the sun, and 'I know a bank whereon the wild thyme blows' became afterwards a passionate personal avowal. Here I met harebells, a flower of such delicate under-statement that it almost seems the most beautiful thing ever.

Autumn brought blackberrying, and the highest tides, boats moored on the shore being dragged under water because their anchor ropes were not equal to the depth and the Irish Sea was awash over the small inland promenade.

◇

This glorious year came to an end and we were back in Southport. Every night in bed I wept in tearing grief for all I was now parted from. I wanted instead of pavements the feel under my feet of the worn rocks along the shore, of the sweet turf of the hills where every gradient was a muscular pleasure. I wanted the night sounds of the river life, flocks of sandpipers in flight, curlews and solitary gulls. The promise of next year w as too remote to mean anything. For children NOW is inescapable. Not to have that boundless joy NOW was despair. I think I felt as much then as later on I felt for an absent lover.

◇

About this time also my brother Frank went to boarding school at Rydal Mount. Mother and I went with him to Colwyn Bay. He was upset and to my astonishment and pleasure held my hand in the train. I could hardly believe it. We had never been taught to kiss our brothers and sisters and had never done so. This was the only physical contact I ever had with any member of my family, bearded uncles excepted. Mother and I stayed the night at Colwyn Bay, and the next morning at the hour of the school break we went to see the poor boy in the playground where he stood alone by the fence. We gave him a bun, as sad as if we had left him in a zoo.

Frances and I went to the same school as before. She was going through a period of malicious teasing, of being aggravating for the sheer pleasure of it. We now shared a bedroom where there was bitter friction about nothing. Any little thing will serve a child to show spite, and it never fails to find its mark. However, Fortune now sent me a friend. A new girl came to the school who was unlike anyone I had met before. Connie was an Irish Catholic and came from a cultured family. She had long fair hair and magnificent blue eyes set in very full upper and lower lids. She might on account of her little animal nose have been called Piggy, had not her expression been both so proud and so voluptuous. She was as unathletic (hockey was our game) and as lithe as a young cat, with hands and feet almost as small. Even when adult she took size 2 in shoes. We paired up instantly. If we were the opposites of each other we were both unlike all the rest.

Connie's parents lived halfway between the school and our house. It was probably on the day of our first meeting that I went home with her. It was a house where everything pleased the eye and it had its own very pleasant smell. Her mother was elegantly simple and made me welcome with a sweet smile. Thereafter she never inquired what we did.

On that first day we went straight up to Connie's room. She had a wooden bedstead that I thought marked her out as one of the élite. Ours were all push-bike iron. More surprising still, Connie had a bookcase by her bed. We had only one in the house, except in Father's closed up study, and few of what filled those shelves could be called books. They were sermons, treatises on engineering and papers. Mother's few classics were in the breakfast room — *Cranford*, Jane Austen, Dickens, Meredith. Connie had a wealth of books, including everything illustrated by Rackham or Dulac. Her whole room also was frilled and deliberately charming. Her mother couldn't go wrong.

Connie introduced me to the pleasure of blowing bubbles. She made this an outlet for her whole personality. When the trembling distended iridescence was loosed from the pipe and mounted like a balloon, she watched it with greater concentration, seeing more than anyone else could. Everything she did was filled to the brim with vitality and imagination.

Another feature of this household that was a revelation to me was the position of the servants. There were two, both very old, white-haired and frail. They had served the family through two generations and were treated with love and reverence as if they had been grandmothers. When they came into the room, they came smiling as friends, not as servants. I looked on at this and saw that it was good.

Connie had a passion for poetry. Our chief amusement together was learning by heart. If at school the class was asked to memorise (though that word was not then used) a famous passage from *Marmion* or *The Lady of the Lake*, Connie and I would have privately learned half the book simply for pleasure. This we did on long walks together, often on the desolate marshy sands stretching between Southport and Lytham, which had a horizonless steamy beauty and the song of larks. We chanted *The Ancient*

Mariner. Connie, who was as morbid as she was sensuous, particularly loved 'the nightmare Life-in-Death . . . who thicks man's blood with cold', but my favourite lines were 'Softly she was going up, And a star or two beside'. Not very long ago I was working in my garden when I heard a small boy high in an elm which overhung the river. He believed himself to be alone, and in his high clear voice, as loud and carrying as a thrush, he was chanting, as if hanging in the shrouds,

> 'The sun came up upon the left
> Out of the sea came he!
> And he shone bright, and on the right
> Went down into the sea.'

Verse after verse rang out, and I 'blessed him unaware'.

Connie also introduced me to Omar Khayyám, which my mother would certainly not have allowed, and that also we learned. It precipitated all those discussions about time and eternity that I suppose all twelve-year-olds thrash about in. She claimed to have abandoned all religious belief. Only one thing mattered — never to hurt anyone or anything. She was therefore a vegetarian and I became one. I remember to Mother's credit that she neither resented nor argued against this tiresomeness. She quietly let me get so hungry on apples and bananas that ultimately I gave way.

It was not only poetry I learned by heart, there is prose that anchors itself in the memory, pre-eminently the Authorised Version of the Bible, of which I could quote great parts without having intentionally learned it, notably Genesis, Job, the Song of Deborah, the Song of Solomon, the Gospels and the Book of Revelation. There was also *Pilgrim's Progress.* I knew *Alice in Wonderland* word by word, the Jungle Books, and of course *Uncle Remus.* Prose should be memorable. To go right down the age groups, *Little Black Sambo* (now it seems colour-barred) is a miracle of memorability, perfect prose.

I spent a great deal of time in Connie's house. There was nothing to attract her to mine and we omitted it without a thought. Her mother put me up in the great curtained bed of the spare room where Connie and I talked the whole night through. How do children find so much to talk about? It bubbled happily on non-stop.

It was a regular practice in those days to sleep two in a bed. Even the boarders at school shared double beds. But when I ultimately at sixteen got to a Quaker boarding school, though the Head mistress had not yet caught up with electric light, she had caught up with other notions in the air, and any girl found in bed with a friend was expelled. Nowadays all is different again.

◇

My mother had only one fear, and that was sex. While we were too young for it she never questioned what we were doing and was very tolerant of our fads and enthusiasms and let them run their normal course. I doubt if she knew Connie by sight. Certainly she never opposed the friendship, perhaps because I was very much alone.

Frances was ill. She had the newly fashionable disease, appendicitis. It was decided she should have the operation − then large and serious − at home. The schoolroom was cleared, stripped of its wallpaper and disinfected, all while the patient waited, so the operation cannot have been urgent. Two trained nurses were brought in and Frances was operated upon on the schoolroom table. The operation, if it had ever been necessary, was presumably successful, but owing perhaps to the difficulties of surgery in a private house and the lack of routine, four hot bottles were placed against the patient's legs without covers and four serious deep burns resulted. The surgeon was for dismissing the nurses at once but Mother showed her essential goodness by refusing. Their careers would have been ruined, whereas it was certain they would never make this mistake again. They remained in the house a very long time as Frances was suffering from shock and in great pain. The dressing of her burns was agony twice daily. She was given a wooden penholder to bite on so that she would not scream. I watched with awe and reverence, as if she was bearing it in my place, as it were for me. I felt exactly the same sixty years later when she died with fortitude.

In fact, her health and nervous system never recovered and she became more than ever a 'mother's girl'.

◇

While Connie was widening my horizons on one side, on the other my evangelical background was fighting its last battle. There was a yearly event called the Convention which was spoken of at home as of great importance. It may even have been held in memory of Father or financed in his will. In a field beside the Chapel a tent was erected as big as a circus Big Top. As far as I was concerned the tent was the Convention. It had a splendid looping shape and a strange subdued but lively light. The edge of the canopy where it met the upright walls was decorated with semicircular flaps that shifted and whispered and let in flying sunrays. Many tall masts leant this way or that supporting the roof. The whole thing creaked in the wind and took huge breaths. I so loved the tent that I went to meetings willingly and often during the week that the Convention lasted. It was run very much on Billy Graham lines, but without his organised showmanship. Emotional speakers pleaded with us to be saved and described their own experience of the bliss and certainty that followed. They implored us with every hysterical or hypnotic trick they could command to stand up if we were 'Saved'. Who should be saved if not I, brought up as I had been? I stood up. No feeling of bliss followed, only of doubtful embarrassment. Clearly I was not saved.

I brooded over this for some days and returned to the fascinating tent to watch and listen to its secretive moving and breathing. The orators turned on the pressure again and I thought, I was not saved last time. I will be this time

definitely and for certain. I stood up again and even went
so far as to follow the other would-be saved to the foot of
the platform, to be received and congratulated by the
orators as new members of the heavenly club, or as tricks
they had won. I went home even less confident than
before, feeling that if this was all, at least I had done all I
could. As I entered the house I heard my sister Mary burst
into Mother's room and say, 'Lucy's been saved again!'
And Mother and Patty Ashton and Mary all laughed.
Rooted to the stairs, I realised that all this about the
Convention was hypocrisy. They encouraged me to go and
really thought it was silly. From that moment all my
mother's teaching was invalidated. Of course I was
emptying out the baby with the bath water, but some
hypocrisy there certainly was, also what at my present age
I dislike even more, the snobbery of dealing out vulgar
religion for 'the others'. The Convention was again
nothing more than a flapping tent. To give credit where it
is due, Mary never wasted words and her brief rebukes
cured me of many things. 'It's silly to say Nobody loves
me' stopped that silliness for ever, and when I talked too
much she said, 'Don't be so ebullient'. I had no idea what
the word meant but it was all the more efficacious for that.
I ceased to be a babbler.

◇

I must have been about twelve years old when our
guardian married. The bride was a lady of wealth and
great civic standing in Manchester. She was spoken of with
awe and some apprehension. When he brought her to see
us I was dumbfounded. She was an immense woman with
ginger hair, to my young eyes ludicrously overdressed,
over-hatted, overveiled and scented, sweeping round like
a tidal wave. She was much older than he and I couldn't
understand it. However there he was, his eyes starry with
pride and gratitude, running after her, carrying her
voluminous wraps and parcels. Frances and I were to be
bridesmaids and for this were dressed in rose pink silk in

tiers of frills from neck to hem. To me, accustomed to the plainest black or white, this dress was admissible for a charade like a wedding but an agony of overdressing for later occasions. I had to go to school concerts dressed like a Christmas cracker. Fortunately the death of Beady Liz put me back in black.

Our new cousin-in-law took us on as part of her marital opportunities for organising. She invited me to tea. Her house was the best run establishment in the town, nothing in it but the most luxurious and modern. Her maids were trained and starched to perfection. I took in everything with interest and surprise. In spite of what seemed excessive splendour, it was both comfortable and effortless.

After tea my hostess got to work on me. She had decided that I was to be a medical missionary and outlined to me, as if it were a known certainty, what my education was to be, in order that I might go to Oxford or Cambridge or London. I wriggled in embarrassment, having no intention of being a missionary, but what can a young guest do when so overborne and overlooked, with a proud guardian watching his wife's dynamism so approvingly?

I listened politely to all congratulations on my future and shuddered. Presently she sent her husband out of the room to fetch something, and then said to me, meaning I believe to flatter me with a suggestion of being all women together, perhaps a practised manoeuvre, ' I can't help laughing at him. He's like a little boy.'

My rage at this condescension to my loved guardian was so great that I was fortified for ever *not* to be a missionary.

◇

There was a day when the first car appeared in Southport. Those who had seen it rushed home to say so, but this sign of the end of our world was less important to us than the new Helter-Skelter tower in the fun-fair on the sands. It was some time before I was actually taken for a drive. I found it far less pleasurable than the two-horse wagonette

or char-a-banc in which we went for school excursions. If
I was quick enough off the mark, I usually managed to get
a seat on the box beside the driver where besides being
high above the hedges with a good view of the country, I
could enjoy the rolling rumps of the horses and the
piston-like movement of their stifles, together with the rich
smell of horse and leather, the jingle, the tossing and the
musical clip clop. One could not of course cover great
distances, but every minute of the progress could be taken
in, caressed by the eyes, breathed in, smelled and
remembered. We did not merely see things whiz by, we
moved along as a natural part of the country, we arrived,
as it were, all the time.

The motor car was not the only innovation. About this
time Frank and I saw our first Moving Picture. The theatre
was forbidden us because of the supposed immorality of
actresses, but there was nothing about the camera to lead
Mother to guess at the lives of future film stars. Indeed
nothing could have been purer than our first film. It was
called *Our Glorious Navy* and showed battleships putting
out to sea in a technical hailstorm and sailors cheering. We
came out happy that our navy was so glorious. This must
have been a freak show put out for propaganda. It was in
the Town Hall, there were not yet any cinemas. I do not
remember going to a Moving Picture again until some
years later when *Hamlet* was filmed, played by the ageing
Forbes Robertson. It was shown in the local theatre and I
was allowed across the guilty threshold to see it. I was so
moved by the play that on the way home I walked slap
into a lamp post, hurting myself considerably, but not
enough to come out of my trance, for I did it again a
hundred yards further on.

Jas, Frances and I were developing a talent for art.
Connie also, but while I was being trained at school in the
Ablett's System which confined us to drawing deck-chairs
in every position with exact perspective, she was free and
brilliant and expressionist. She and I spent days modelling
in bas-relief in plasticine.

Phil had a passion for music. An upright piano was put into our mad drawing room which had also acquired some cheap modern armchairs and so had become senselessly ugly. There was a harmonium for him in the dining room and he practised every spare minute. I was learning the piano but never could play anything however hard I tried. But from now onwards till near middle age I had so much purely physical energy that I was driven to spend most of my time just getting rid of it.

My outlets in Southport were the gymnasium, the hockey field and the swimming baths, the two latter providing me with a kind of bliss — even the hockey field! I suppose a yearling foal galloping about its meadow feels something of the same. The delights of the swimming bath are more understandable as they foreshadow the glories of the sea. I had picked up a slim little girl who was a Junior Diving Champion from Australia, whose arrow-like flights I tried to imitate with my much broader and heavier body and splash. I was never elegant but was ambitious enough to scorn the top diving platform and dive off the railing of the gallery.

The bath had its poetry. The domed glass roof collected and re-echoed the screams of young voices in a sound that was the quintessence of excitement. As one entered the turnstile and started down the long salt-smelling corridor, the sound was heard rising in the distance like a choir of ecstatic angels. The smell of coconut matting soaked with brine was unique, and coming out at the end of the corridor one saw the shaken pale green water that was always trying to restore its broken surface. The shallow end was a thrashing mass of young bodies, but the deep end was less used and there was a pleasure in waiting for it to smooth out before one pierced it with a dive. If, as often happened, I was the last to leave the water toward closing time, I could watch the whole water of the bath slowly settle. The green tiles and white pointing of the bottom would reach toward a restored pattern, wildly feeling at first through jig-saw disturbance for their missing lines, quivering as these found their place, then showing a kind of placid breathing before absolute stillness held them. With what loving reluctance I left that immaculate calm!

In the summer we were back at Arnside, and there we swam daily in the river, but as the currents were so dangerous we were always accompanied by Mother sitting most anxiously in a boat with one of our boatmen friends holding the oars. Nurse waited on the shore with towels to wrap us up as we came out blue with cold. Jas used to swim far out on the deadly tide and just had to be trusted to live. Except for her troubled face Mother showed no sign of worry. It may have been her heroism, but she did not know the river as I did.

◇

In the house at the top of Garrett's path owned by Mother's family were our cousins on her side. Their mother was so unlike ours that we never thought of them as sisters. It was impossible to imagine them in the same nursery. None of us took after Mother in any way. It is a wonder how she could have given birth to so many without passing on a trace of her blood. She was as much a stranger among us as she had been among Father's family. This feeling worked both ways. As we grew up she looked at us with disappointed rejection. The cousins on her side were even more alien to us. We were like black and red ants. Many of the Wood cousins were very odd but we accepted them all as our natural kin, loving many and laughing with tolerance at the freaks. Mother's many unmarried sisters were kind and good to us, but the relationship never took root. Mother was incomparably the best of them. She had a great and gentle dignity.

The cousins were inescapable holiday company. We had grown up practically without art or music but we were not Philistine by nature. The cousins were, though with one exception. They were large, fair and brawny. The three girls, older than any of us, were hideously prudish over bathing, hideously hearty in organising sports and picnics. In the evenings they had sing-songs when they sang the music hall hits of the moment of a vulgarity that shocked both my innocence and my ear. They were all rather condescending to our freakishness, to the way we dressed, to the way Mother let the household run itself. They endeavoured to 'help' us.

Fortunately there were too many of us to keep count of. I was off by myself in the woods most of the time, absorbing what has lasted me all my life. For a time we had Connie to stay with us. She and I lay together on the flowering turf or roamed at large. There was on the hill a grove of ancient yew trees well away from all paths. Here we took off our clothes and played Dryads for the pleasure of the breeze over our whole skin, and of watching the sun spots and leaf shadows playing over our smooth bodies. It was the most innocent thing imaginable and no Acteon burst in upon us and no shocked female reported us.

It was in this summer that a car entered the family circle. Till now none of our relations or friends had had one. My sister Mary, known to us as Grumps, startled us by becoming the first private owner. She bought a small car and somehow learned to drive. There were no schools nor driving tests. Probably this burst of enterprise was because horses gave her asthma. Early cars were open, and the hideous 'motoring cap', the least practical wear imaginable, was considered almost as essential as the steering wheel. Mary did not take any of us out with her. Mother used to say, 'Isn't Mary brave, alone with her car'. I used to enjoy the word 'with', as if the car were a personal enemy. I infinitely preferred a pony trap along narrow lanes between the blackberry hedges.

◇

To counterbalance the joys of Arnside, holidays ended with visits to the dentist, always a place of torture in those days of crude instruments and no painkillers. As an example of the barbarities practised, Mary, whose front teeth projected slightly and rested on her lower lip (a frequent feature of Victorian faces and I imagine all Dickens' young ladies with it), instead of being fitted with a gold band to draw her teeth back, returned from the dentist with her front teeth sawn off halfway up and their still projecting thickness plated with gold. How she must have wept when she saw the ruin of her smile and remembered the agony she had endured! I think it was considered a blunder, for we changed our dentist. There were now two to choose from. Frances went to a handsome young man whom she found charming. He had protective ways, cradled her head and caressed her cheek, even perhaps kissed the pain better. (We always went alone.) I felt contempt for this kind of thing and preferred a grim disciplinarian called Mr Fitch. The very name suggests the action of that horrid little hooked tool. He was tall with enormous black eyes and an expression of icy bitterness. My eyes were enormous and black too, but they got no reaction from him. I was there to have my teeth seen to and inexorably that was going to be done. When after an eternity of pain the tears ran down my cheeks, he turned away for another implement saying contemptuously, 'What are you crying for?' At the end of the session by way of a come-back, I asked him if he could recognise his patients with their mouths shut? He passed over this impertinence, merely remarking that my teeth had a formation interesting to dentists and he would like a photograph of them. Released from the chair and the ordeal over, I returned home very cock-a-hoop and boasted to my mother that Mr Fitch wanted a photograph. She fell into a predictable panic and wanted immediately to push me into the arms of Frances's cuddler. To avoid this and keep my self-respect I had to explain he was interested in nothing but my teeth — didn't want the face they belonged to.

Frances, two years older than I, was given to kissing in corners and running away with girlish laughter. Connie had the same dentist as Frances and also a more amorous doctor, but her body was developing into a lure for men, a rounded sinuosity that Venus cannot have bettered. She took advances lightly and contemptuously, but without offence. I was still a young Touch-me-Not. Yet for Mother Frances could do nothing wrong. She was an ordinary sweet girl doing what real girls do, but with every year that I grew Mother watched me with growing concern. I was something she neither understood nor trusted.

3

When I was fifteen all the family were at boarding school except myself and Phil. He was wholly occupied by his music and even raised Mother's heart to the skies by playing the big chapel organ during the service. She longed for all the boys to become Wesleyan ministers, but to be an organist was new and welcome.

About this time, when I was much alone, my guardian's wife died, after barely three years of marriage. I could not bear the thought of his grief, and as his house was near my school I often looked in to see how he was, and found him quite desolate. He welcomed my young and unexpected sympathy and we became near to each other in a personal, not merely a family, relationship. I used to go to Chapel with him simply to be beside him so that he should not be alone in his pew. But the evening service breeds emotion as an overheated railway carriage breeds germs. We held each other's hands.

Ever since Father died, Mother could not bear to sleep alone. When we were all little we slept with her in rotation. There was a kind of promotion in sleeping in a big bed with French curtains and in a grownup's room. As the boys grew it had to be Frances or me. Now I was the only girl at home. It was no longer a ritual honour, 'Whose turn is it to sleep with Mother?' but had become a trap for scenes. To be held in someone's arms in bed for a scene is intolerable. Also Mother was neurotically nervous. Though all the house was locked, she still locked her bedroom door inside and had six-inch-long screws that fastened the sash windows, and a police whistle under her pillow. All for what? There was nothing to fear at all in those orderly days. I hated being locked and screwed in.

Mother had begun to brood about the White Slave Traffic and was sure Frances and I would be snatched. She warned me constantly till I was reduced to looking right and left if I even crossed our little street to the letter box, not, as moderns might think, for the traffic, but lest there should be — a nun! Nuns and parsons were the bogies in disguise, NEVER to be spoken to.

Mother had taken up 'rescue work' and was the only woman on the board of the workhouse, where her particular interests were the Children's Home and the young women who left their illegitimate babies there when they themselves came out. The Matron had been chosen by the all-male board and was a heartless painted Jezebel against whom Mother's black-clad quietness was powerless. I saw this creature once and was horrified that any children should be entrusted to her.

Mother took the emergent 'fallen' girls into her care. She even in reckless generosity took them into her house as servants hoping in that way to keep them straight. She had perhaps not thought that in the holidays this would involve her in a constant fear of her own sons, now nineteen and seventeen years old. She felt compelled to keep watch. There was a particularly sweet and attractive little thing polishing brass stair-rods throughout the house, who could not fail to smile at two handsome young men, who themselves might naturally think they were backing Mother up by behaving with kindness. But alas! Before long she told Frank she would rather see him dead than having anything to do with 'these girls'. This resulted of course in endless family mirth. The boys were outraged and all their jibes were directed at Mother, so tragically well meaning. Frances and I, not being under suspicion, had more sympathy with her and with the unfortunate girls. Frances in fact took on a protégée, a very lively red-haired girl of her own age who adored her, and who did afterwards 'go straight'. Mother explained to me the value she put on conventional behaviour. The strong must protect the weak. The strong must never do what for the weak would be dangerous. I rebelled entirely against this attitude. The term 'levelling down' had not yet come into use, but a socialism not in material things but in morals and behaviour I would not have. 'Nothing venture, nothing have' was more my ambition: flights, not canary cages. As time went on Mother's incomprehension of us increased; derision became our normal attitude in private, and in her presence silence, sometimes broken by an outburst of choking laughter. Jas was cruelly witty. Only Frances understood her, but she could never get on with the boys. For me on the contrary they had become the most important and loved persons in life, and I was now old enough to be received into their exclusive circle. Jas at Cambridge had become an aesthete, not yet a painter, and a great dandy. His good looks devastated any visiting girl. Frank was nervous and vulnerable but a very determined character. Phil was a charming mystery to whose mind the only clue was sudden engaging laughter.

Connie was still my special school companion (quite indifferent to the boys). She introduced me to *Tess of the D'Urbervilles* and *Jude the Obscure* which she loved for its pessimism but I hated. Both books were considered by our elders quite unfit to read. She was usually away in the holidays. After one such long absence, she confided to me that she was in love. The father of the family with whom she had been staying was, she told me with as much approval as any Georgette Heyer heroine, a notorious rake. He had made love to her, now sixteen, and without him she could not live. I listened with keen interest and sympathy as if to a novel, but was too young to guess that her love was a final and ferocious fact. I left her looking forward to their next meeting. I myself at last was sent to boarding school.

The school, Laleham, at which Mary and Frances had been till now, was described to me by them as a kind of heaven from which I was excluded. There were many things from which I was excluded, such as visits to friends or relatives. When I asked why, my sisters replied, 'because you don't know how to behave'. As I didn't know how, I did not know what they meant, and still don't.

However, Laleham was now closed. Frances was to fill up two terms with me in a new school before going on to Paris to 'finish'. Such a liberal and worldly idea as Paris can never have arisen in Mother's head. It must have been suggested by the retiring Headmistress. No member of our family on either side had ever done such a thing, nor any Wesleyan of our acquaintance. In the meantime for Frances, to move to a new school at nearly eighteen was hard, especially as through ill health she had missed so much schooling and would be placed below her age, but it was not so desperately hard as it would be now. There were still no exams of any importance to our future life, but looking back I am surprised that Mother who loved Frances so particularly should not have guessed to what unhappiness she was sending her.

The school chosen for Frances and me was a small private one of sixty or so pupils run by a Quaker lady, therefore safe for our morals. It was in Sussex, where we might hope to correct our North Country accents.

We made the long train journey alone, crossing London, where I had never been before, in a growler, and then taking a stopping train, full of strange girls, to our destination. I was always a bad traveller and sat miserably beside an open window. The old trains had such luxuries as windows that could be let right down, out of sight inside the woodwork. There were notices saying IT IS DANGEROUS TO LEAN OUT OF THE WINDOW. One's head might be knocked off by a passing express. Nevertheless children always hung out as far as they could. The disadvantage was that we got covered with soot and the carriage seats all smelled strongly of it.

We arrived exhausted, and were relieved to find we were to share a small bedroom and not be in a dormitory.

This had been arranged because Frances, ever since her operation and burns, had terrible nightmares in which she screamed so that I could hardly bear it.

Next day we were shown round by a girl whose kindness was at first reassuring to the lost, but she turned out to be Marcia, that dreadful do-gooder in Ivy Compton-Burnett's *A House and its Head*. She was another Wesleyan and would therefore accompany us to the penance of the local Chapel on Sundays. The Chapel was like a small lecture room and the minister thought the sermon the most important part of the service, in which there was little to inspire devotions. His boring rigmaroles were always divided into five parts, firstly, secondly, thirdly, etc. with recapitulation, and were counted off before our eyes on his fingers, of which one was missing, so the Thirdly was always tapped on the remaining stump, waited for with revulsion.

The kindness shown by the do-gooding girl had been a surprise, but real life soon intruded. Among the elder girls there was one Dorothy, who by her snobbish style, ruled the school. I wonder how she came to be in a Quaker establishment. She was well dressed and groomed, with family bracelets and an exquisite wrist watch. She wore hand-made shoes on her elegant feet. She had a face that would command gallant attentions from members of the Hunt at a Meet, and an exaggerated accent of the kind we had been sent south to acquire. She was always surrounded by her satellites. On the first evening Frances and I, unselfconsciously dressed in home-made mistakes, sat in a corner of the classroom with our embroidery. Although totally unlike in character we were considered identical in appearance. Frances had a better complexion and blacker hair, and she had a smile whereas I only had a grin. We were of the same height and build and were instantly taken for twins. The dazzling group of senior girls led by Dorothy approached and sat round us. In my naiveté I mistook this for kindness and gladly answered all the questions she asked, however impertinent. Many of my answers got an encore ('Say that again — so-and-so didn't hear') and were received with an alluring smile by Dorothy and nudges and giggles from the rest. Frances, older and wiser, remained mute. I was ebullient and feeling that I was being some sort of success. 'Where did you get your nice embroidered dress from? The embroidery on it is rather like what you are doing.' I answered all questions without embarrassment and my answers continued to lead to more. Finally the inquisitorial group broke into open mirth and began to repeat to each other my pronunciation of such words as ask, basket, path, bath, faster, etc. which had been carefully elicited by Dorothy. I now realise that a North Country accent had never been heard before by these Southerners (no broadcasting in those days) and was infinitely ridiculous. I found I rather gloried in it and was not at all put out. Later on we heard from our Chapel-going companion that Dorothy had given out that we were 'charity girls'. I now thought as little of Dorothy as she did of me, and was undisturbed. Consequently I was little ragged, but Frances became the butt of the crudest element in the school and was jeered at cruelly and lived in one long blush. We found ourselves much in the company of the other outstanding oddity who, like us, had no choice. She was the daughter of a diplomat in Constantinople, and gave the impression of being half Turkish; something of the harem hung about her, as if reared on Turkish Delight. She was tall, fat and stupid but utterly good natured. She had one brown eye and one blue, in a long melancholy oval face. She was mad with loneliness and received us with a surge of relief that was irresistible. She never learned to distinguish us one from the other. She liked to be stroked like a cat. Stroking was very fashionable that term, originating from the abominable Dorothy, whose satellites queued up for the privilege of stroking her arms and shoulders. When she left the school the practice vanished.

We were both homesick every minute of every day. When Mother came to see us at half term it was for us rapture. She was as wildly loved that weekend as she ever could have hoped to be. After that we ticked off the days till we could go home, the cramp of the heart lessening day by day till floods of relief began to dizzy us.

At home again, the school uniform discarded, I rushed off to find Connie. She had written to me some time before to say that her mother had forbidden her to go to her cousin (whose father she loved) for the holidays, so I knew she would be at home. A shock awaited me. Her mother looking very strained let me in, saying only that Connie was in the drawing room. I wondered that she did not come to meet me, but went in. She lay inert on the chesterfield, looking into space. She neither smiled nor moved nor looked at me. She might have been in a coma except for the look of pain that stiffened her face. I tried to talk to her, but there was no response, I did not even know if she heard.

I stayed about an hour looking with fright and incomprehension at this wreck of a friend. Her mother sat by her like her fate, helpless to do otherwise, frozen into patience. When I left she did not say, 'Come again'. She said nothing. It was obvious that this state of affairs was accepted as permanent as far as one could see. It made no difference to Connie if I was there or not. She wanted only one thing in the world and without it was as good as dead. I never went again, nor heard from Connie or her mother for many years, for they left Southport. I do not remember how we got in touch again, but at thirty Connie was still living with her mother 'so as not to grieve her'. She was beautiful, attractive and more remarkable than ever, but quite joyless. She told me how often she had tried to kill herself as if by convincing accident, but had always failed. When her mother died, Connie committed suicide by gas, not out of grief but because she could at last do so without causing grief. I have been ashamed all my life that when Connie was broken I found nothing to do for her. ◇

Our guardian continued always to do every possible kindness. He now suggested that Frances and I should take it in turn to spend the weekend with him. He still had the two devoted servants trained by his late wife and the house was kept up in its previous style. It was a great change from ours, now so lapsed and as shoddy as Mother's indifference could make it. Her meals were meagre. I remember my shame when we had a friend of Patty Ashton's to dinner. The food set before her was yellow haddock stewed in milk in a brown pie dish, followed by another identical pie dish containing yellow-skinned baked custard. I remember too the boys' angry muttering when the midday meal was one small pot of potted meat for seven people with thin bread and butter, followed by milk pudding. Mother may have been hard up, but money was never mentioned in the family. At our guardian's every meal was a work of (Dutch) art, ample and perfect and served with the style it deserved, presented to us with reverent ritual by a silent waitress, herself an august figure. Probably these weekends gave us some idea that social manners existed. At home there was only Mother's severe simplicity to copy. When once she invited a lady of importance on some committee to dinner and finger bowls were actually put on the table, Phil, taking his place and reviewing the scene, said in his broadest Lancashire, 'What's them basins?' The meal was, not surprisingly, a calamity.

◇

Though Mother had no friends of her own except the faithful Patty Ashton, she welcomed any of our cousins and they loved her for her gentleness. They all had more difficult parents to suffer from. For instance, when Aunt Emily reigned alone at Woodbank, Father's younger brother, Uncle Peter Fred, used to bring his family to Southport for Christmas. In him, all Father's dynamism had turned into passionate neurosis. His wife had been tall, elegant and very kind, but she died early and

Patty Ashton

thereafter all his crankiness rioted unchecked. His family all spoke of him with frustration and despair. They were half a generation older than we were and Peter Fred was a blight on all their lives. One daughter had been turned out and cut off absolutely for becoming a Roman Catholic. The eldest daughter who kept house for him had become a physical wreck, but she had such an explosive fund of feeling that she never stopped talking and could not speak at less than the highest pressure. She thus made a perpetual joke of herself, but never resented laughter.

There were three sons: the eldest, Norris, was very tall (his implacable father hardly came up to his breast pocket) and as beautiful as his mother. He was a scholar and an aesthete with a passion for the military, which in those days was not at all incompatible. When he bent from his great height to offer a cheek to his young cousins, Frances and I agreed in this at least, that we received an overwhelming honour. He was the paragon of the family. Alas, in the First World War at Gallipoli those splendid legs were shot away, and he died with serene dignity in the presence of his brother Wilfred. In my early school days Wilfred was a young doctor. He was not good-looking but had great charm, especially with children. His yearly arrival was looked forward to with ever increasing interest as we grew older. The youngest son, about Jas's age, was a merry tragic-clown with a passion for music.

Aunt Emily, so much more regal and expansive than her sisters, gave a Christmas party yearly for the assembled Woods. There was no Christmas tree, nor Christmas presents other than a florin each, but things were done with a kind of ritual splendour. Although she lived alone in the big house, she somehow kept up a standard of food worthy of the previous generation. She gave us a splendid evening feast with all the family silver in evidence down the long table. Uncle Peter Fred, whatever his domestic faults, had warm formal manners in family gatherings, and he did not forget his nephews' and nieces' names.

After the feast we went into the library for prayers,

taken by him. We sat round on Chippendale chairs whose red leather seats may have been original. They were so worn and crumbly that the colour came off on my party frock of white broderie anglaise. Unexpectedly perhaps, the reading of the Christmas passages of the New Testament was for me the greatest joy of the evening. Peter Fred had a thrilling personal voice and read superbly, looking down at the Scriptures through pince-nez set crookedly on his nose and his chin thrust out in affirmation. It might have been actually happening as he read. Every year it was exactly the same and always I trembled. Even today whenever I hear 'Now when Jesus was born in Bethlehem of Judea in the days of Herod the King' it is Peter Fred I hear, and am back in that gathering.

When the reading was over, we turned to kneel in front of our chairs, all except Mother and Aunt Emily who allowed themselves to bow their heads seated. I was unhappily aware that I presented, if only to heaven, a bottom dyed rosy-pink. Peter Fred had also his own fascinating style of prayer compounded of the Authorised Version and his own imagination. Who but he would have thought of voicing, 'May thy church prosper O Lord, and *do exploits*?' [Daniel XI, 28-32] In what other context do these words occur? They have come down the years with me, and now when I come in exhausted after too much digging in the garden I think contentedly, 'I have *done exploits*'.

On a much later occasion, as Wilfred and I knelt at adjacent chairs, we were publicly prayed for with ominous foreboding, ending 'Let them not lean unto their own understandings'. The shudder of Wilfred's knees on the floor boards was relayed to mine and bound us together.

Our other cousins were the Boston family, where as a small child I went to my first party and met my future husband. They had a very big house at the far end of the town so that we only began to see them regularly when we were old enough to walk there on our own. The father had five children by his first wife, and after her death he married our cousin (on the Wood side) and had seven more. It was again an Ivy Compton-Burnett household (with what fiendish accuracy she describes the family life of her youth!), with the tensions between the two families and all the hierarchies of age groups, ending upstairs where the two youngest were segregated until in their teens because their mother could not endure an empty nursery. It was a hotbed of aggravation and unbridled laughter, mostly directed at the parents. The father emerging from his study, or at the head of the table, sang out his musings, moralistic or apprehensive, with a burst of false amusement at the end. He had a trick of puffing out and deflating his cheeks after speaking as if simultaneously to apologise for what he was saying and to approve of himself. I do not see fathers doing this now. They have all been put in their place by their children, but it was a period trick. It would be impossible to read aloud the sayings of the father in Ivy Compton-Burnett's *Men and Wives* without this deprecating self-puff. There was nothing so silly this cousin would not say it, and his outbursts were the joy of his family. Perhaps less the joy of his second wife. She was a very odd character. She was stout, but her very handsome features had never thickened, they were as finely cut as if sculpted in wood, and as immobile. However in this set face her great eyes blazed. She took no part in anything and seldom spoke except perhaps a short burst of irritation that nobody took any notice of. She had no influence on what went on except to oppose change. It was an inertia that went far beyond indolence. She wore the same clothes for every occasion as long as I knew her and the same comfortable old shoes. She had strong prejudices and kept to all the rules of normal good manners — where at a Christmas party of thirty everyone should sit, which uncle should be asked to say Grace, which to carve etc. — and though sympathetic was terrified of showing it; her thoughts never surfaced. I now think that perhaps she was entirely made up of passions, imaginations and fears so contradictory

that all movement was cancelled. At any rate she produced
a vital and handsome family far more intelligent than their
father. When the latter was more than usually outrageous
she reddened and tore at the neck of her blouse. There
was a family legend that whenever a child was being born
to him, he paced the house in a frenzy lamenting, 'Never
again! Never again!' But promptly a year later there was
another, and the remorseful vow was repeated. He had a
lugubriously tolerant sex mania and seemed to expect
incestuous goings on. When Hide and Seek was being
innocently played he patrolled the bedrooms intoning,
'Beds again. Beds again.' And if he had a bad day at the
office, he would look down the long tea table stretched
before him, lined with young expectant faces, and
prophesy that he would live to see his daughters on the
streets. In such a house one could count on tumult and
humour all the time.

I do not know how this big handsome house was kept
going. Most likely it was all done by their old family nurse
(who also brought me into the world). She was a tiny
withered person of iron will and much tolerance. At the
age of eighty she still worked there, assisted by a dear old
butler of the same age, who carried in trays of thirty plates
above doddering legs. The nurse, among her other uses, in
term time slept on eight mattresses to keep them 'aired'
under her old bones, a typical idea in a house not run by
reason.

The children of the first family were unlike their
gypsyish siblings. Three girls came first. The eldest was
perhaps six when her mother died, and I suppose much
can be implanted in a child by that age. Otherwise they
were all brought up in the same household as the second
family. Nevertheless they achieved as it were out of
themselves, a grace, a culture, and a dignity all their own.
They were Tennysonian. I loved them all dearly, as did all
the second family. They were wholly good in the biggest
sense and with it had both humour and charm. I have met
only two others I could put beside them. Their kind does

not happen in the modern climate. Harold whom I was later to marry was the youngest. His mother had died at his birth, for which reason his father disliked him and always treated him unfairly. He resembled his sisters physically, but he had a dæmon of his own among the excellences.

◇

The next term Dorothy and her cronies had left, as also our *faute-de-mieux* harem cat. There was room to expand. More important to me than all the drawbacks of school was that I was at last in contact with the real sea (heard all night in the bedroom), that savagely demolished the groins built in close rows down the pebble beach. The infinitely varied clamour of inrush and ebb is to me the most comforting sound one can hear. A trout stream has more grace notes but it lacks the fugal strength of the sea. Inland were the smooth downs where in summer the chalk showing through the grass gave the earth a luminosity which on a blue day made it akin to the sky. Sea and downs were the great and real benefit of the school to me. It had no other, but these were inestimable. As our education was paid for out of the money we each should inherit at twenty-one, no extras were denied us. We rode over those uniquely beautiful downs, still unspoilt with their ancient dew ponds and tracks bordered with gorse. There was nothing military about the riding lessons. The old man who escorted us had outlived any keenness he ever had. We could on a fine day dismount and tether the horses while we stretched and lazed at ease in a place of equal secrecy and vista, and imagined what we would. There was an old race course where the overworked horses could gallop flat out if they had it in them. I had big bones and puppy-fat, so I was always given a strong roan, good to ride. We all of course rode side-saddle, but no style was expected of us. Long streaming hair added to the pleasure of a gallop, echoing the horse's mane and tail. It had of course to be plaited and tied up again before the decorous trot back through the town. The old man willingly helped. Then there was sea bathing. Over the steeply shelving beach big waves sidled along the groins and in retreating dragged shoals of pebbles across our shins. Trained as I was in the strong currents of a tidal wave, I was happy and reckless in this cleaner and more exhilarating rough and tumble. When in singing class we had Kipling's 'Sussex by the Sea', I was wholly at one with him.

Sometimes on fine Sundays the school was allowed to take the long walk across Hindhead to the little church at Alfriston. Chapel girls were allowed to pocket their presumed prejudices and join in with the others. Alfriston was then a tiny medieval village with one half-timbered inn and the old church. I do not remember its architecture, but under the central tower the bellringers pulled and swung in full view of the congregation, a splendid start to what to me was an eye opener. It was my first experience of an ordered ritual, no impertinently familiar, sentimental impromptu prayers, but all in majestic English. The psalms were exactly what one would wish to sing, the General Confession what one needed to say, the Litany not a word too long for me. Why must they now alter that masterpiece and make it 'everyday' and for 'the common man' when to a young person used to current commonplace and coming across this for the first time it seemed overwhelmingly beautiful? I nursed it in my heart.

◇

At school on Sunday evenings the Headmistress took a kind of abridged Evensong. This took place in the dining room with the tables pushed to one side and the chairs in rows. The dining room was bare and bleak, its only decoration two very small prints of Burne-Jones' 'King Cophetua and the Beggar Maid', and Turner's ' Fighting Temeraire' *in sepia!* (If any art was taught in this school I have no recollection of it. My only educator was Jas.) Nevertheless, perhaps because we had all spent the afternoon writing home, Sunday evening managed to have that creepy, soapy, Now-the-day-is-ended feeling inescapable from all 'observed' Protestant Sundays. We sang the fixed psalms and also the psalms for the day in full. We also said the Creed. It so happened that one evening a girl whose conscience had perhaps been troubling her, or perhaps she had just decided where in the dining room the East lay, turned and bowed during the Creed to the surprise of the school. The following Sunday before the service the Quaker Headmistress announced in a grimly disapproving voice that the worship of the heart was quite sufficient and she must ask her pupils not to indulge in unnecessary gestures and automatic practices. Nevertheless, in the Creed, the same girl repeated her bow and the girl beside her half did so. In three weeks the whole school was turning and bowing, including myself. I heartily approved, quite apart from having been bred to be a martyr (though on the other side). Surprisingly there was no reaction from the Headmistress. She accepted defeat.

It is just possible she consulted the head girl, whom I will attempt to describe.

The leader of the school was now Eileen. She was tall and graceful with light blue eyes and a high brow topped with baby curls. She was potentially intellectual had there been any scope for it. She carried herself superbly and unselfconsciously. There was nothing dominating about her face. Her chin retreated just far enough to allow her pretty teeth to rest lightly on her lower lip in that smile that the dentist had so cruelly sawn off poor Mary. Her manner was entirely playful, her snubs final. She was intriguing, very secret, very selfish and utterly charming — a Millamant. I, her junior, admired from afar, astonished by so much presence and *savoir faire*. Eileen could do what she liked with the Headmistress. An approving school watched her at it. The Head was bewitched but did not see it. She proudly doted on Eileen. Whenever in my long life I have heard or read of an intriguing Court lady or irresistible enchantress I see Eileen as the only imaginable incarnation.

Although so popular, Eileen had only one friend, the next most attractive girl in the school, much younger than herself and of the opposite type, a sort of elfin gypsy, very magnetic, with the delicate limbs and huge black eyes of a gazelle. Though in a different dormitory she was often in Eileen's bed against the most stringent rule. Every girl knew, nobody censured. These two were of a quality to do what they chose. For my part, I thought nothing of it, I had never heard of lesbianism. I knew beds as the best place for friendship and confidences, and perhaps the younger one was homesick. Perhaps they were old family friends. Was Eileen good or was she wicked? She could have been either, or both,which is much more frequent. She was then eighteen, and I have never seen or heard of her since. I here acknowledge her.

Many years later I met her gazelle again. She was dance hostess with a travelling jazz band and was as sad as an old shoe.

◇

Frances was soon removed from what must have been for her a place of torture. She went to Paris from where she wrote me rapturous letters. I now slept in a dormitory with eight beds. We had curtained cubicles and were not supposed to enter each other's. Under each bed was a shallow enamel bath. It was the rule that we must pour cold water over ourselves every morning. There was a fat lazy girl who never combed her hair though it was very fine and long. Some instinct for bullying persuaded me I ought to keep up the standards, so every morning I poured water over her shrinking baby-soft flesh, cheered on by all the others, and I set about her hair that looked as if mice were nesting in it. Before it was sleek half of it was out. After that it was less trouble. I do not think she bore me any illwill. Probably at home it had always been done by a firm Nanny.

I was going up in the school, soon to be captain of games and head girl in place of Eileen. I enjoyed all to myself a sixth form. The Headmistress had yielded to the ambition of sending a pupil to the university. It was still an ultra-modern idea. When my brother Jas, himself a convention breaker at Cambridge, heard of it he was appalled. 'It must be Oxford. I couldn't live down a sister at *Girton*.' I had no ambition. Formerly they had tried to make me a missionary, now it was to be a 'blue-stocking'. However, I did not mind the idea of Oxford. I liked Latin and loved Greek. The mistress who had this unexpected job given her was not, I think, quite up to it, but there were only the two of us and we sat in the sun and read the *Odyssey*.

The Head, perhaps intoxicated by the grandeur of being able to say on the prospectus 'Pupils prepared for the universities', also introduced a Master to give history lectures. The school was assembled and crowded into the large classroom. When we were all seated and expectant, in strode a young man in cap and gown. I suppose he might have been twenty-one, but to us he was adult, a large MAN, brawny and not bad-looking. Confronted with sixty pairs of unwavering female eyes he soon broke into a sweat and his hands shook. Throughout his lecture, on the English Constitution, delivered with eyes desperately unfocused on the middle distance, he continually mopped the large drops of sweat running down his brow. At the end — or perhaps before he got to it — he turned and stumbled out, only not running, all dignity lost. As he left the room a roar of chatter broke out which he must have heard as he fled. Once was enough for him.

There was also a young woman new on the staff. (There were seven resident teachers in all.) She was very plain and therefore extra vulnerable, and pathologically shy. She taught the juniors, not me. Her class was always in an uproar, their object being to make her weep, in which with horrid ingenuity and co-operation they succeeded. This is the only time in my life when I have seen mass female cruelty in action. They looked forward to it. Wretched young woman, like the hen all the others peck and the cock never notices!

I was a poor successor to Eileen. I was too fat for beauty, too ill-dressed and too uppish. I had a quick eye for homesickness and with the young and the lost I had a loving relationship, but I was never popular either with the girls or the staff. I asked a mistress whom I met after I had left school, why the staff from top to bottom had such a down on me? She said, 'Because you always looked so defiant. It was very annoying to us.'

Many people complain now of the hostility of teenagers, but I had no consciousness of any such feeling, only of the need to protect something not yet clear to me. Perhaps there was a natural arrogance, but of that I am not able to judge. I suppose arrogance is always unconscious. In my last term I made a few friends. Probably the head girl, even if she has no special charisma, always has a few adherents.

The entrance examination for Somerville took me to Oxford for the first time. Of course I was bewitched. The only towns I had been in up to now were Southport and Bootle! The entrance paper appalled me when I read it through. It was at once clear that I had received no education. There seemed to be nothing I had ever heard mentioned, let alone knew anything about. The only question I now remember was, 'What was Shakespeare's idea of Woman?' which struck me as so silly that I said so, and wrote quite a lot with vigour. I wrote some rubbish on other questions since one had to cover a few sheets. Normally I had enjoyed exams. I liked the quietness and tension, the extreme orderliness and the piles of new inviting paper. It was like a good parlour game and often I have minded the results of these more. I was not much troubled in this case. I had no personal feeling involved. I was only obliging other people. However, in those days there was no competition and greatly to my surprise I was accepted.

4

There was a year to wait before I could go to Somerville, during which time I was to go to Paris. It was in the summer holidays after leaving school that my gentle and nervous mother became Public Enemy No. I. Every summer now she rented an empty school house at Arnside where there was room for any school friends or cousins. Nurse was now acting as housekeeper and fed us abundantly. She took on all the work, which must have been heavy. Mother never suggested we should do anything to help. It was never thought of. Mother was only interested in the morals of the serving class, not their comfort. In the Aunts' house nearby were all the cousins on Mother's side.

Wilfred Wood usually stayed with us at Arnside. He had in previous summers taught us young rabbits to play tennis — a great test of good nature. He took us all for long moonlight walks through the woods and chilled our blood with stories of were-wolves. When he was with us the conversation at meals was lively and preposterous for he had a bubbly sense of humour and mimicry. Patty Ashton's slender pink hand was folded over her nose to contain her shaken giggles. All the girls, in both families Wood and Boston, loved him and almost any of them would have married him, but it took him nearly twenty years to decide. Perhaps at this time Frances and I were in the lead. Frances was rather delicate which gave me a further advantage. Wilfred liked twenty-mile walks over the fells which the boys seemed not to want; that left me as a possible companion. Before he came I had been in the habit of climbing out of my bedroom window in the early dawn to go for long rambles by myself, coming back at breakfast time before anyone noticed.

Wilfred and I spent long days together walking over the map. One does not talk much while climbing uphill, and going down it is the sheer exhilaration and the new view that takes one's attention. The day's exertions were on the whole silent, friendly and detached. One hot day, resting on the turf of a high point, overlooking Windermere, Wilfred lay with his head heavy on my lap. I took this as a great honour, accepted in silence and surprise; but once home again I succumbed to the desire to confide my pleasure. I chose Mary whose grumpy reserve seemed safe, to whom I said, 'Wilfred lay with his head on my lap. I think he must like me.'

It would be difficult to imagine a more innocent confidence, but Mary hurried to Mother with dire warnings. Could it have been jealousy? She was so disastrously plain it never occurred to me she might have romantic feelings.

The next day Wilfred told me with embarrassment that Mother had asked him not to take me for walks again. This was monstrous and wounding. Wilfred was the safest company imaginable and the understanding between us was perfect. I blazed, speechless in fury. Why had Mother spoken to him behind my back and not to me? What reason had she for such stupid, unfair interference?

Worse was to come. It had for a long period of hot weather become a family habit to sleep out of doors, all of us, girls and boys, in serried ranks on the small back lawn, each of us on our ground sheet with what bedding we chose to take. The garden was closely surrounded by oak trees and hazel, leaving above our heads a circle of sky of that wonderful blue which cannot properly be called dark because it is star-lit all through to as far away as one can imagine, luminous and illimitable, across whose face shooting stars flew in curves. Or was it we on the earth who sped? My pallet was next to Wilfred's and on his other side the eldest of the Boston girls, now perhaps thirty, and a special friend of mine.

Before settling to sleep, Wilfred was pointing out to me the stars overhead. He knew them all, and I till then had hardly known they had names, except the Pole Star; they were just 'The infinite shining heavens'. It was thrilling to know that every one of that receding hugeness was named.

While my lesson was continued in whispers so as not to disturb the dormitory, poor Mother was peering through her bedroom window seeing evil where none was, even disturbing Patty Ashton, who never thought any evil, to come and see for herself.

In the morning stern words were said. I was told I must never put myself next to Wilfred again. I must sleep as far away as the garden allowed, or stay indoors. Disgust and contempt were my reactions. Did innocence not exist for her? My rejection of the insult was violent enough to set me on a course of outrageous and defiant unconventionality whenever opportunity offered. I have no doubt I left her with a real teenage flounce, and sought the company of my brothers, with whom I shared a world of candour, trust and decency. We had no fears for each other's behaviour.

Rain prevented me from having a chance to flout the embargo and Wilfred's holiday came to an end.

◇

Mother must have retained from her early married days an unconscious hostility to and suspicion of the Woods as a race alien to her. At Arnside now her sister and family were in the other house a few hundred yards away. She preferred her walks with Patty Ashton and Frances. She can have had no special affection for this sister.

A short cut to the river was down through the cousins' garden. I undressed there for bathing and raced down the zig-zag woodland path in my 'bathing dress' which was very decent, an all-over garment and even skirted. Bikinis were two world wars away.

Our girl cousins in this athletic family were square, muscular and manly, but they went down to the river wrapped in long cloaks of towelling which they dropped only at the water's edge and instantly immersed themselves up to the neck however shallow the water. They were grievously shocked by my upstanding immodesty. They did not stand on the bows of a boat to dive, even less could they have considered the undignified climb up into the boat with its moment of bottom upwards. They tried to teach me decency, something Mother had never thought of till she found her little ones grown into dangerously sexed creatures.

When these rather horrific female cousins had staying with them a baby girl one year old and were giving her a bath, a brother coming into the room was driven out with screams and would have been beaten had he persisted. Such dirty modesty is perhaps the result of experience.

Jas liked, admired and laughed at the father of this house for his rolling self-confidence and gusto. He had the twinkling little eyes of a porker. They now took notice of me. After a few displeasing signals of his intentions, he one day caught me on the landing and carried me fighting like a bull-calf into a bedroom where he flung me on to the bed and his twenty stone on top of me. From this extremity I was rescued by one of his sons calling his father to order. The old man was not put out of countenance. 'Ah well. All right, my boy.'

Neither man seemed to think it out of the ordinary.

A few days later when Mother wished to send me with a message to her sister, I refused to go, saying Uncle was too dangerous. He wouldn't let me alone.

'Nonsense, you silly child,' she replied. 'It's only Uncle's way.'

This was her side of the family and therefore perfectly conformable. But she was right— it was Uncle's way, and there was to be no help from her.

That autumn I went to Paris. I did not find it the paradise described by Frances, but she had made a great friend there whom she brought home, an exquisitely dressed girl with a dramatically sensuous face, suitable I thought for a Borgia. Her skin was as white as a camellia and her full curved lips rose red. She had a fascinating stammer and a snobbish background. It was probably our long deprivation of anything but dressmaker-made black that made Frances and me fall so deeply for sophisticated style. This girl was an exotic flower in our sterile soil at home. While Frances and I admired her strange beauty, she fell for Jas like Salome for John the Baptist, and failing him for Phil. Jas's taste was for simple uneducated beauties. He and Phil fled from her. Not surprisingly, she also had parent trouble.

I was less lucky in Paris. The other girls were amiable enough but not noticeable. There were two wealthy Canadians interested only in the shops, a plump little suburban puss and a lean pallid Anglo-Indian. The others, if any, have faded right out. Mademoiselle, who took us in for a living, was small and sour, porridge-skinned with blackcurrants for eyes. Her pension was in Neuilly near the Porte Maillot, where horsedrawn carriages waited instead of taxis. Imagine Paris without a taxi! In the morning piping shepherd boys came up the avenue with their goats, but in the night there were noisy sewage pumps, for these handsome houses had no proper main drainage. A stinking shaft ran down the centre of the house, with a closet and seat on each floor, without a flush.

We had halfhearted French lessons in the morning, obligatory but un-considered, and every afternoon Mademoiselle did her duty by taking blank English misses round the museums and monuments. I was breathless with excitement in the Louvre, but no guidance or information was offered. Paris made its mark on us according to what each one was prepared to see. Sometimes instead of Mademoiselle, we were chaperoned by a wan young widow drooping under the weight of her voluminous black crepe. Her spiritless misery failed to rouse any response but impatience. I wonder now if perhaps it was that cold biting Hell that I have known since. At the time I judged it a weak misery, a feeble despair. She never spoke, but merely followed along with us. Mademoiselle, on the other hand, though without taste or intelligence, was not weak. She and I had disliked each other at first sight and it grew to detestation. Had my mother written to her about me, or was there something about me that enraged? True, I was nakedly naive, had no demureness, and no boundaries; but I also knew no evil unless pride in one's personal honour is evil. One day I had bent to stroke a friendly dog in the park, and had exchanged a word with its owner, a little man rather like it. Mademoiselle was scandalised. Thereafter whenever we walked, as we left the garden she gripped me by the wrist, holding me in leash as if to announce to all the men we passed that I would be after them if she let go. The humiliation was an intolerable wrong. Between us down our arms riveted at the wrist ran in both directions currents of hatred. We could have murdered each other like rats.

My letters home were full of complaints that no one was teaching me either French literature or French history, except at lower school level; but in spite of the fact that neither Mademoiselle nor the other girls thought these subjects any reason for a stay in Paris, I managed to get a fairly good grasp of the language. Even Paris did not teach me to dress.

◇

In the Christmas holidays I was glad to be back again with my brothers, though Jas's affection took the form of cruel criticism, doubtless well deserved. His name for me was Bouncing Lulu. I thought the three of them the beauties and wonders of the world, though their manners especially to Mother shocked me. Jas was always derisive, but openly, which allowed her to feel it was backed by affection. His pet name for her was 'Mrs Foul'. It shocked Frank profoundly, but not me, because there was a sort of tenderness in his tone. The boys would have nothing to do with Frances. They said she was Mother's spy. I couldn't see it. There was nothing to spy on. The boys were indeed very good-looking, and as most girls at eighteen have at least a brief blossoming into beauty, and as there was a strong family likeness, especially between me and Jas, it is probable that I had my share of good looks. Phil was fair with light green eyes. He was more lightly built and his features were more incisive. He was still so silent that we knew no more of him than what we could see. He resembled a Byronic great-great-grandfather of whom we had an admired engraving.

As Frances and I were now physically grown up, we were allowed to share the bathroom with Mother. We learned with surprise that she had a beautiful body. She was taller than we were. Her skin was smooth and honey-coloured like the inside of a ripe melon. She had small breasts and long simple lines with never a crease. Who could have believed that under such graceless, ugly clothes there was such a delicate creature? It was a shock, and my affection for her instantly increased.

I spent the weekends with my guardian whose stable adult company and formal but warm manners were always a pleasure. Everything about him — his chapel-going, his relation with his mother, his county cricket, his deer-stalking, his salmon-fishing, his business (of which I never heard a word uttered, but it was wool) or his house — was controlled with easy precision. Nothing was out of order and his temper was perfectly equable. It was all superb. I loved the rich tobacco smell of the house, the quietness, the discreet gong. I loved the details of the furnishing, such as his great wardrobe in three divisions with shelves that slid out like drawers, with brass rails for rows of boots and shoes all with trees in them. It was as polished and ordered inside as it was out. My brothers' clothes were hung over chairs. There was no provision for a man in my mother's house, no trace left of Father's presence.

I liked the bathroom with its shining metal paraphernalia and its wealth of clean matching towels, its enormous perfect sponge. I enjoyed seeing him come out of it in the morning in his bathrobe with his hair wet and rubbed up on end, looking so lean and fit. I was getting very free in this house so different from our own. I'd never had a good morning kiss from a sort of Hector in a bathrobe before. I'm sure I gave every sign of a girl happy and at ease and without reserve. The inevitable happened. One evening his goodnight kiss was trembling and tender and my thoughtlessness collapsed into fright. What had I done? I was up against every woman's unsolvable dilemma, how to rebuff a man she dearly loves, how least to wound him. The very thought makes one tenderer and that again makes it harder. Forgetting in my trouble all Mother's previous incomprehensions I told her what had happened, hoping for advice, not realising the inexorable cruelty of the situation. She said nothing, was neither sympathetic nor helpful, but a few days later she said she had told my guardian he was not to have me to stay alone again. I was getting too old and must have a chaperone. This again behind my back. It seemed an unexampled treachery after a confidence. She should of course have told me, but I see now that she relieved me of much embarrassment, and that he, being old-fashioned, would have thought it right and maidenly that I should talk to my mother. At the time I was as angry as wretched. I imagined he would think I had *complained*, a thought so unbearable that I could not again meet his eyes. I longed to rush to him and say, 'Anything whatever you could ever do is forgiven you in advance. ' But he hadn't done anything. I was the silly fool. But I had no opportunity, and in fact seldom saw him alone afterwards, though years and years later we wrote to each other in terms as loving as before.

◇

When I returned to Paris, this time it was with Jas. We went to a retired school teacher and his wife who took in young lodgers. It must have been one of my mother's ill-judged arrangements, for Jas of course if in Paris should have been at an art school. He and I shared a large private sitting room, but he got angry if any object of mine, such as my sewing, was visible in it. He couldn't live with other people's things. There were two other young men in the house who took lessons in French with Jas. The bad-tempered and ill-mannered teacher showed the greatest contempt for his pupils, as if they were the small boys he had formerly taught, but stupider, being English. It was a puzzle to me then and still is, how Jas came to be there and to put up with the insults. I on the other hand was perfectly free and could jaunt about as I wished, learning and loving the streets of Paris, though, except for museums and churches, what lay behind the façades was unknown. We never went to theatres or the opera, or restaurants or concerts, only to organ recitals at St Eustache or St Sulpice, One would think that a term in Paris with a brother such as Jas, then twenty-two, would be the most vivid and exciting period of my life. In fact it was constricted and quite unmemorable. I lived as young girls live from whom nothing is expected, aimlessly enjoying every minute of just being alive. Of the two other young lodgers, one was my age, very shy but agreeable company to share my long rambles. On cold, dark evenings we bought chestnuts roasted on braziers in the streets. The other was a gentlemanly half-wit who was Jas's chosen company. When I asked what he saw in him, he replied, 'He's like a China tea-pot that's perfect only that it doesn't pour'. The wife of our irritable host was good to me, even motherly in the accepting way my mother was not. We knew nobody outside the pension, no French friends ever dropped in on our hosts, no other French house was open to us. I had dropped overboard any ideas about education, was not conscious of missing anything. I ran round like a dog let off the leash. Nobody

bothered me, nobody noticed me. Paris seemed without
danger, just a lovely place to be in.

◇

After this improbable interval I returned home and stayed
there for another half year, leaving Jas in Paris where he
had found for himself a studio to study in, I think with
Braquemont, but can no longer be sure.

While I was at home, Harold began to visit us more
often. He told me afterwards that Frances was the original
attraction, but we took a cousinly interest in each other.
Circumstances put him in our way. His father still resented
him because of his mother having died at his birth.
However large the second family grew year by year,
revenge still had to be taken on the motherless boy, and it
showed. He was cared for as an infant by a spinster aunt,
more sentimental and possessive than a mother and
irritatingly pathetic because she had not that elemental
relationship. All her life Harold took it out of her for
wanting to be loved as if she were his mother. At two
years old he had a stepmother, who accepted him with
kindness but immediately began to produce children like
blowing bubbles. His father took him away from school at
sixteen and put him in the family tannery as an ordinary
workman to learn from the bottom. This was not thought
necessary for any of the later sons who all went to the
university. Tanneries have an indescribable stink which
permeates everything and the hauling of hides out of the
pits dyes the hands a permanent mustard tan. It was as
this kind of young labourer that Harold visited us at the
weekends, stinking and unglamorous, but he took it all
with high spirits and no rancour. He was at this time in
my story very immature, but his later characteristics
showed. He was a little above average height but looked
taller because of a small well-poised head of delicate bone
structure. His hair was the colour of golden bread crust,
silky and straight, his hazel eyes wide set and of a
hawk-like alertness. His smile could be wicked or very

sweet or both at once. He had a fiery, mobile and super-sensitive face. All his movements were highly personal, a curious mixture of secretiveness and eccentricity. To give an example of secrecy in movement, later on when I often waited for him in some hotel, I would watch the stream of men who pushed one after the other through the circular swing door, never taking my eyes off it in the anticipation of seeing the loved head. Yet I never did see him enter; suddenly he would be beside me. Though so individual he had the faculty of disappearing in even a small crowd. With an ordinary education he could have been a literary eccentric. He loved language and wrote the liveliest letters. But having had so little schooling, his originality was channelled into a savage sense of humour. So ill-treated a young man was naturally received with warmth.

About this time the phonograph found its way into the world. Harold and I shared Schubert's Unfinished Symphony, wheezed and scratched out on the primitive machine. I was deeply moved, but Harold only said it was enough to make a dog flute.

◇

I was in trouble again at home. The time had come for me to be formally received into the Wesleyan community. To Mother's horror, I refused. The last nail had been put in the Chapel coffin for me by a friend of Mary's at a prayer meeting.

There is always at such functions a horrid silence at first when one begins to wonder what will happen if nobody prays at all. The embarrassment was courageously broken by the young lady saying in a prissy voice, 'Lord, make us winsome for good'.

I don't know how the rest of the family got over this stile. Perhaps they all went through it automatically at their respective Wesleyan boarding schools, with the whole of their class. I was subjected to all possible pressures. Mother's grief was unremitting. In bed at night she clasped me in her arms and wept, 'How can I meet your father on the other side when he asks me "What of the children?" How can I say to him "They are all safe except your darling, your little pigeon. She is lost"? ' I endured it with misery and revulsion. Who dared say I was lost? It was of course sad that she was tormenting herself, but it was idiotic. I was sent to regular private sessions with the minister. He used Mother's sorrow as his main argument, but also reasoned, coaxed and threatened. To his credit he did not try loving charm. Throughout my youth, as I was always interested in religion, I suffered from parsonical squeezing of knees and waist. Nonconformist, Anglican and Catholic all astounded me by this approach. The last was a priest officiating in a French Hospital in the war. I had asked him to explain the mass to me. He got out all the holy vessels, and with the chalice on his knee, for which I, an outsider, felt great reverence, he got down to cuddling.

Now at home I would not be moved. Yet as I stepped out of the fold into the unknown I repeated privately to myself, 'He shall keep my soul until that day'. I knew I was in search, not in denial. The abandonment of one's father's faith is a deep fear and sorrow and I felt an outsider.

5

The First World War broke upon us when we were all at Arnside. Jas, who had moved from Paris to Munich, had to return. Frank was a medical student at Cambridge, Phil had just left school. Harold was with us this year. He had become my natural companion. Cars were now in. They were the new thing to have. All the boys except Jas, who in all his life never learned to drive, had motor bikes which competed with the opening war in the excitement and stir. Mother took the war gallantly. She was buoyed with uncritical patriotism, swallowed all propaganda — as did I — and was prepared for the brave death of her sons. Otherwise her daughters might be raped. Her sister, with one son more to lose, was what Georgette Heyer would call a watering pot. The tears ran down her face all day and every day. Village patriotism decided that the wooden viaduct must be guarded day and night. From what? Bombers were in their infancy, not yet heard of, and parachutists not invented. The weeping mother saw her youngest set off to spend a night on the viaduct (unarmed) as if she would never see him again. There was no wireless, we only had the daily paper. All enlistment was voluntary, but good mothers did not doubt their sons would go. In our house there were no tears, but considerable tension and the inclination to roar about on motor bikes for tomorrow we die. Frank, Harold, Phil and I made long excursions up and down the Kirkstone pass or anywhere that offered engine tests rather than ease. I travelled in Frank's rickety sidecar, which meant my

getting out to run up the hills after him as the engine
would not take the weight up a gradient, or sometimes on
the carrier of Harold's bike, which afterwards became my
normal transport. Later still he gave me a superseded two
stroke model and I buzzed around by myself, an
incompetent and unthinking menace.

After a fortnight of merrily postponing the war, Harold
announced that he was going to join up instead of going
back to the tannery. His family were in Wales, where he
would go to say goodbye to them. Frank and I decided to
go with him. Mother strongly objected. It was too far, we
might not get there in a day. We might break down on the
way. Where in that case would we sleep? Thoughtlessly I
replied, 'Anywhere. On the beach if it isn't raining. One
can sleep anywhere.'

'*On the beach?* Oh no, no. What if you were seen?'

'Well, what if?'

There was a paralysed silence, then she went on —
'There is something — I often wonder whether it wouldn't
be better to tell you, but I don't know what is best to do.
Something very dreadful once happened in the family.
Something — I can't tell you. I am afraid it might make you
worse. '

Worse than what? I thought. What am I supposed to
have done? I guessed she must be referring to that Auntie
Bertie of whom there was never any mention, nor
photograph, who apparently never lived and never died,
but who was the only one who had been kind to Mother.
It would of course be the most generous one who went
wrong.

Wringing her hands, which she often really did, Mother
rushed from the room. She had of course gone to seek out
Harold. He came to me looking dumbfounded. She had
made him promise not to let me go with him 'because, she
said, you can't be trusted'. Oho, I thought, I can't, can't I?
To him I said he couldn't promise for me behind my back
and I was coming with him in Frank's sidecar. So off we all
went. The white dust off the unsurfaced roads was so

Lucy at the age of eighteen

smothering that my eyes were red and watering for days afterwards, but we arrived safely with the Boston family. Harold left the next day, seen off on the road by his eldest step-brother and myself. We watched him on his motor bike diminish in size and sound along the coast road. I shed no tears, but his brother did, turning to me confidingly with blurred eyes. I was grateful to him for weeping in my stead. I didn't go back with Frank to Arnside but stayed with my cousins.

◇

That autumn I went up to Somerville, having got myself for once almost well dressed as I can see from photos, but my evening clothes were wild. My ideas were all à la Scheherazade. I bought luscious silks and chiffons and had them made up to my own design or made them myself. I remember them well but can't imagine what I looked like in them. Mother must have been startled by the unlikely things I wore, but she never said a word of criticism or advice, whether out of heroic tolerance or because she never noticed anything so unimportant as clothes, I do not know. She serenely let me make an ass of myself. It was Jas a little later who remarked cryptically, 'If you would only dress like a tart everyone would see you weren't one.'

At Somerville I was fortunate in being given a beautiful room in the new Maitland building, on the ground floor opening on to the garden. A room of my own was bliss to start with. I arranged it with care to my liking, with Islamic covers found in tin trunks of Father's in the ironing cellar at home, added bright silk cushions and hung a terracotta drawing done by Jas. I bought myself a 'Minty' wicker chair, copious as a small bed and of an elegant shape. They were the coveted thing, excellent and durable. Do they still exist?

The first evening was rather overwhelming. The whole college assembled outside the dining hall. It was the rule that senior students must always take in a junior. Some fourth year girl offered me her arm. Was this meant to be manly? It was always ritually done and we all crocodiled in. We addressed each other as Miss So-and-so. Among one's friends it was shortened to the surname only, as among men. Two by two we went in and took our places. For the first time my ears were affrighted by the violent treble vibrato of a hall full of intense females talking for dear life. I never got used to this detestable sound.

The second disagreeable impression was the earnestness that pervaded the place. I was two years older than the other newcomers who were straight from school and seemed to me like silly pretentious school-girls. Those of my age, the third year students, were already lined, haggard and spotty, terrified of their approaching finals and the possible collapse of all their earnest hopes. They all looked ready for a breakdown. The fourth year were more stable but had almost ceased to be human.

Of the girls in my year the most unhappily earnest by far was Miss Ellis Fermor, later to become Principal of the college. She was less lucky than I, having an ugly room in the old part, ill-lit and furnished with what might be described as discarded brown. In this she sat, nervously tensed up. On the other hand, in the room next to mine was a girl whose chief interest was the personal aura. She believed hers to be blue. She therefore covered her room with blue chintz and fitted blue bulbs into her electric lamps. On entering one swam into a sort of cobalt tank. I could not stand it. My aura must be orange. She later became a gossip writer. We all gave each other tea parties. One of the fourth year students gave such special teas she must surely have become a political or diplomatic hostess.

I had decided my Lancashire accent was perhaps not an adornment, so did my best to control my a's into ah's, with the result that at the end of a week it was known that I was Spanish and it was thought that under the circumstances my English was good. I soon learned from my first friend that there was more to a North Country accent than the a's. She pointed out that I clipped all my vowels, as mi book, th' door, etc. So I gave up trying. Twenty-five years later when I was living in Austria I discovered that Lancashire had filtered through even into my German — that the hitherto permissible short a's of man and can must now be mahn and kahn.

There was a sprinkling of black male students in Oxford, but few whites except foreigners, medical students and the unfit. All the rest had joined up, a whole generation. When my brother Phil, just out of hospital after an operation, came to visit me and we were walking across the college grounds, the Principal, Miss Penrose, was seen approaching. She was a tall Carnival figure, that is to say she looked as if her head and shoulders were being held up on a pole which tilted forward. She stopped as she was passing us. I introduced my brother and she replied, 'Young man, why are you not in uniform?' and moved on. That finished her for me. In any case I had no intention of keeping any of the protective rules. We were supposed to go about outside the gates in twos and threes, the years to add up to four. I preferred being alone and ran round Oxford as I had done Paris, loving every stone. I went to Evensong in Christ Church or New College nearly every day. If you can imagine Oxford when it was still the university and hardly yet a town, without car traffic and without the seething life of its young men, it was indeed as miraculously quiet as a noble dream.

I was doing classics and quickly learned how badly I had been taught and that I should never pass the first exam, but I still loved Greek and with it the shrewd humorous Scottish don who tutored me. If we had that vicious creature a MAN to tea in our rooms we had to ask a don to come and chaperone us. When Harold, in uniform, came my tutor was the one I shamefacedly asked. It seemed too tiresome for a don to have to do this. She came willingly and was very charming, but afterwards I spared her and simply let him in through the window. He had joined the Suffolk Regiment and was in training in Cambridge, only paying me a short visit.

I had not been in College two days before I was called upon by a member of the Oxford Christian Union, counterpart of what I knew in Cambridge as the Kickyou. A young woman whose type I knew all too well desired to know if I was saved. I had had too much of being saved and my religion now had an opposite orientation. In the happiness of my own room I was reading Spinoza, though I could not accept determinism.

Next Margaret Murray, a great charmer, tried to make me a social reformer. This was earnestness to the nth and in the full swing of modernity, but it seemed to me that all this earnestness was second best, it was incompatible with the shock, the bombardment of new sensations and the emotional vistas of merely being. Then there was the war. It had not yet shown what it was to become, and was still expected to be short, but it knocked the earnestness out of exams, or so it seemed to me, since I did not guess that after the war seven women out of every eight would have to earn their own living.

The violation of Belgium was the propaganda used to rouse idealists. The city of Oxford was to receive a train load of refugees. Some organiser of the proper-thing-to-do decided that Somerville College should greet them at the station with their national anthem. We were all drilled in this and learned the words, which in our pronunciation could only have underlined their feeling of exile. The gesture passed unacknowledged by the wretched arrivals and it was all we ever had to do with them.

◇

The Christmas holiday was nightmarish. The top floor of our house had been requisitioned for billeting troops. Frances and I cooked mountains of bacon for their breakfast but otherwise saw nothing of them and they were quiet and orderly. The streets of Southport were full of marching men, the air re-echoed with their tramping. The Lancashire Regiment seemed made up of identical, rickety near-dwarfs, all showing off and as to tough they were stunted. I could not believe my eyes. Were these the average men of my proud county? Where did they come from — the cotton mills or the mines? It was pathetic and horrifying, and also impressive. Nowadays at least there is no physical difference between richer and poorer, but I had no doubt that these were grinning ferocious fighters. Their jokes as they tramped past me in the street were frightening, aimed at me.

At home Mother was in only just contained hysterical despair. She believed, as did I , every word of propaganda about the holiness of the war. Jas, who in Cambridge had become a close friend of C. K. Ogden, was sceptical and derisive, firmly believing that the war was a fraud and had nothing to do with him. He had just returned from the studio in Munich and saw nothing wrong with the Germans. The chief objects of his bitter humour were the British fathers who 'gave their sons'. I thought this callous and stupid of him, since 'gave' only meant accepted that they must lose, and that is clearly a terrible grief. However, there was Jas at home making us all laugh. I remember when the boat carrying Kitchener was sunk and he went off first, Jas's rendering of the scene was so outrageously funny that Mother ran out of the room weeping. Frank was finishing his medical course at Cambridge which absolved him from joining up, but Jas, her eldest and most promising son, was refusing to serve his country. She was like a Roman matron and suffered corroding humiliation.

◇

During my second term at Somerville I grew increasingly restless. The Trojan War? I wanted to be sharing the experience of my generation. I was now twenty-one and had come into my money, a totally free agent. I often heard the other girls complaining that their parents would not allow them to travel or to study something as unremunerative as Art or in any way to follow their own inclinations. I seriously suggested an Anti-Parents Society and offered to finance my friends. They were intensely shocked. They could not possibly displease their parents, and in our generation it was unthinkable to receive money. I had only offended them.

I decided to leave college and go to the war as a nurse. The Bursar had French connections and promised to try to find me a place in a French hospital. Meanwhile a relative who had been a Sister at St Thomas's hospital arranged for me to go there for two months as a free-lance V.A.D. Frances was working in a hospital in Southport; her job was cleaning the lavatories. Heroic, but I aimed at France where it was all going on.

St Thomas's was a major experience. I thought it superb. It ran like a perfectly adjusted machine. The high standards, the practical routine, the ritual style and hierarchy of authority, the total devotion and medical skill delighted me. This was something really good. It was entirely supported by charity and independent. The National Health Service was not yet thought of. I was in a surgical ward for men, not the war-wounded, but traffic accidents and major operations. My jobs of course were unskilled, but I could watch and we were taught by the Sister. I absorbed all I could, like taking deep breaths.

I lived in lodgings by the Marble Arch and crossed London by bus morning and evening. I knew nobody in

London except a friend of Jas who had stayed with us at home. As it happened he was in the same lodging, but all the time I was there, he never spoke to me. I felt it inexplicable and cruel. I was, outside the hospital, so lonely that it hurt. Sundays were a misery. I went long bus rides in every direction to learn my way about London, or took trips on the river steamers. I was pursued by hateful men if I dawdled. Harold sometimes promised to come and I waited all day in vain. Once he explained casually that he had been out with another girl. He told me about his lady loves as naturally as my brothers did.

Consequently all my interest was in the hospital. Any free time I had in the week I spent in the gallery of the operating theatre, watching with interest and some nausea what went on there. The nausea was cancelled out by the unexpected beauty of the scene, the mirror quality of all the shining machines and equipment, and the composition formed by the circle of white-clad and veiled assistants, each dependent on a junior to hand or take, all grouped round the central figure of the surgeon, and the light focused on one small, bare patch of the shrouded body. It was a Giotto to watch. I also appreciated the clown's humour of the lowest in the hierarchy who after the operation cleared away the legs and other discards. No emotional quick change could be more theatrical.

Otherwise from sheer loneliness I had to live for my patients. There was among them a very decent elderly man who could not sleep for worrying about three little girls that he had left alone at home. I went off in the evening to visit them in the East End, taking sweets and toys. The eldest was eleven. She was a capable little thing, well able to look after her sisters. She got the little ones out of bed and they were all delighted to get a message from their father. I stayed with them perhaps an hour and then went back to St Thomas's.

My ward was now under the night Sister who did not know me, but took me for a relative. The anxious patient, having had reassuring news, with love and kisses from his pretty ones, settled down to sleep and I went back to my lodgings.

Another patient was a young policeman, a Highlander whose speech I could hardly understand. I washed his splendid neck and shoulders every day with pleasure. There were no snags here such as a beard or bald head. I never knew whether to wash a bald patch. It seemed a little officious. My Highlander, coming from so great a distance, never had a visitor. It occurred to me that it would relieve both his boredom and mine if I acted the part. On Sunday afternoon I dressed up in my all too eccentric summer best and laden with grapes and flowers sailed into the ward. I made my way through the crowd of visitors to the one unvisited. It was a calamity. The Sister pounced on me like a hawk on a sparrow and hustled me outside where she lectured me with a rage like snapping shears. No nurse must ever visit a patient except on duty, still less ever show friendship for any particular one. She was there to attend to an injury, not to a person, What I had done was the unpardonable thing.

No one had told me of this rule, but perhaps a more modest girl would have invented it for herself.

I was removed from the men's surgical and put in the women's medical. It was a dreary change. Here there was no drama, no laughter. An underling like me was never told what any listless patient was suffering from. In a surgical ward the mood is of recovery, in the medical it was of lingering and despair. However, the two months allowed me for training were nearly up, after which I returned home to await a call to France.

Meanwhile I went every day to Liverpool to the out patients' department and there learned that St Thomas's was an ideal not reached in the provinces. The doctor in charge of out patients was a brute. He was surrounded by medical students, and the patients were brought in like animals for the students' practice, not for their own benefit. I remember a modest and frightened young woman being forced to have her body fumbled and pressed by all the students, to harden their embarrassment, never mind hers. Perhaps students have to learn to be inhuman in order to survive the stress. I had to see a reluctant student make his first unsure incision in the groin of a six-month-old baby, unanaesthetised. There was nothing for me to do but look on, and I felt I was being shown how everything shouldn't be done, not how it should, besides being shocked and made to feel sick every day by the doctor's behaviour.

I quickly removed myself from the Liverpool hospital and resorted to Cambridge, where Frank was at St John's, Phil at King's doing music, Harold in camp and Jas in lodgings on King's Parade where I joined him.

The war was growing in deadliness and was the undercurrent of all thought. Nevertheless, or even because of it, this period of my life was intensely happy. I had the company of the four people with whom I was most at home, a closed circle. With my brothers I was at all times, dressed or naked, entirely at ease. The difference of bodily formation seemed to make no difference to thought, feeling or reaction. All was clear and open between us. We were of the same kind. This gave me a simple attitude towards men that later caused continual mistakes. I thought they were natural friends.

Our landlady, Mrs Palmer, was a motherly woman never out of temper with us. She cooked all our meals and carried them up from the basement to the first floor. She did her very best for us, but it was not always appreciated. One 'special' pudding made for some occasion was found uneatable. We recklessly threw it out of the window on to King's Parade, not having the wit to realise till it was sailing through the air, that it would be very conspicuous. In the early morning as I looked out of my window to see how much it showed, I saw the policeman on his beat unselfconsciously carrying away some of our pudding on the toe of his boot. We thought this blissfully funny. Our silliness was not the high spirits of intoxication. Our whole family on both sides was teetotal. I had not yet tasted wine or spirits, but Harold in the army was learning fast, and Jas had lived in the Quartier Latin. Nevertheless no wine had reached our table.

It was summer. I spent my days on the river which I had almost to myself. Cambridge was empty during the day but crowded with young officers in the evening. The old Red Lion was like an officers' club. Its ancient waiter, Plum, with warm civility and aching feet did his best to serve the milling and voracious crowd. I dined there once or twice with Harold, but felt like a cat among a hundred dogs. Harold had made friends among the officers of whom he talked constantly. His life as a workman in the tannery had brought him in company with no one of his own kind. Now among his equals he was expanding with joyful excitement, surprised that the world had such goodly people in it. He made friends never to be forgotten. He introduced none of them to me. They all roared about on motor bikes, and Harold, now enjoying officer's pay, bought himself the latest model. It was then that he gave me his cast off two stroke. When Nora Hughes, a friend from Somerville, came to stay with us on a visit, I doubled the hazards of my driving by taking her on my carrier. I wonder that either of us survived.

Harold found time to take me on his carrier now and again. We went careering off on a very different high-powered flight to his favourite woods and hills. There we sat among hay-stooks in the moonlight and looked out at the wide view and listened to the owls, but never touched each other even though the stars came out over us. I lived in fact much like a swallow or a bat, enjoying river and sky and space and buildings, and finding that more than enough; but I also went every evening to Evensong in King's College Chapel, then as yet un-embellished and overwhelmingly beautiful. The sound of the King's bell at 5.15 calling us in is still to me the most evocative sound I know, bracketed perhaps with that of a mountain stream tumbling over stones, the one Christian, the other pagan, one going in and in, the other spreading out and out.

Jas in Cambridge had always been very good to me, inviting me when he was an undergraduate to come for all the special musical events, the first production of Handel's *Semele* by Dr Rootham, *The Magic Flute*, the B minor Mass in King's which was an awakening of explosive importance. He also told me what was currently important to read or see. He now spent most of his time with C. K. Ogden, whose rooms were above the fishy smell in Petty Cury. With I. A. Richards they made a close trio. Jas, unlike Harold, would always introduce me to his friends. He took me into Ogden's sanctum but I was unimpressed. He may have had a brain whirring like a computer, but in himself struck me as a silly old woman with no values but giggles. Many years later when I had become interested in palmistry, being eager to see how these famous brains would be shown, I asked him to show me his hands. They were soft and white and had *no lines at all*. I have only seen this astonishing phenomenon once since, and that was on the hands of a girl living on her beauty, having and needing nothing else whatsoever. Perhaps Ogden had nothing but his computer.

◇

There was always a room for Harold in our lodgings and there were nights when he did not have to sleep in camp. On one such night — I do not remember at all what preceded it — I woke up to see him in my room. I would not have been startled by this, except that he was more real than reality. Perhaps that is the special quality of hallucinations and explains why they are so obsessive. If this was a hallucination it is the only one I ever had. I saw that he was not there. To investigate the phenomenon I left my bed and went up to his room. I slipped into his bed as naturally as I would have joined him in a punt.

'Were you in my room just now?'

'No, I was here.'

'Funny, I saw you there.' He received me without surprise, embarrassment or misunderstanding. I was virgin

Jas

as Shakespeare's heroines are, as were his own three sisters, but when I felt the length of his body against mine and the thudding of his heart under my head, it was something I hadn't bargained for at all. I isolated the shock of it from my behavioural consciousness, retarding it for future evaluation. We spent an amicable night without the hint of a caress, but without sleep. It was rather like being in a rowing boat following a spring tidal wave at Arnside, confident but aware of the cosmic force we were riding.

In the morning Mrs Palmer came in with the daily tin saucer bath and water cans that she carried to each room. Cambridge lodgings did not run to baths and in 1977 when I was house hunting for a friend I was amused to find how many well-built, well-proportioned houses still had no more than a loo in the garden. On this morning Mrs Palmer, having placed the bath and cans on the floor, turned to the bed. 'So that's where you are, Miss Lucy, ' she said, surprised but not upset. I just grinned at her, thinking, 'This is better than Mother'. I was less pleased when her old husband popped up from the basement as I went out and leering called up, 'So Mr Boston's a lucky man!'

Twenty years later when I returned to Cambridge from abroad, an old woman caught my arm in the street. 'Miss Lucy, don't you remember me? Mrs Palmer.' I greeted her warmly, being at that time almost friendless. She went on, 'I've so often wondered about you. Did you marry Mr Boston?'

'Yes, I did. But he has left me.'

'Oh, Miss Lucy! How you did love that boy!' (What a voice from the past.)

◇

My adventure into nonconformity I celebrated with a short poem. I showed it to Jas from whom I had no secrets nor he from me. I know he had done the same with a chorus girl whose beauty in a photograph seemed to me almost unbelievable. Young people brought up as closely as we were, with no contacts outside their own family, are liable when they find themselves in the unexpected world to launch off in gauche and idiotic courses. Jas's chorus girl, he told me, was taking to drink, and he was trying to cure her. Did he think that by showing her that he respected her, he would coax her to keep off drink? It seemed to me that if she loved him, as she surely did, his cure was likely to make her worse. I did not consider myself in love with Harold, but I had grieved sympathy with Jas's girl.

It was no doubt with the intention of pleasing me that a week later Jas showed me the *Cambridge Review* with my simple and explicit poem printed in it, and another of even less value. I was outraged and told him so, after which to revenge himself on my ingratitude, the two poems, which he had arbitrarily caused to be printed, were referred to as Lucy's bilious attacks. That put a stop to my poetry for fifteen years.

◇

Throughout the summer while the war grew ever less imaginable, I stayed on in Cambridge. I took to sleeping out in a punt up by Byron's pool, where Harold could slip out of camp and join me for an hour or two. Once waking up alone in the dawn I saw a kingfisher perched on my wrist, a portent surely. Or, I went by canoe along the rapidly diminishing upper river until even a canoe could be forced no further. Canoes are not good for sleeping in, but if they are well mud-grounded it is possible. Coming back into Cambridge in the early morning still full of wonder, I was amused to hear an early riser on the bank say to his companion, 'Gawd! She's come from the mountains! '

However, I had not forgotten that I meant to nurse. As I still heard nothing from the Bursar at Somerville about an opening in France, I signed on at the old Addenbrooke's Hospital for the time being. It was hard after the boundless freedom I had been enjoying. I had to move to the nurses' lodging where I shared a room with a good-tempered V.A.D. She had a sober steady disposition and thick black hair down to her ankles. What a weight and responsibility to carry on your head in the ward! I was fascinated to watch her disposing the long rope-like bands in such a way that a nurse's starched cap could be perched on top. She accepted me very tolerantly.

I was to begin on night duty. There was a very attractive Sister over me, who was having a happy time with the doctor on night duty. She told me, as if out of pure kindness, to go off, to go to sleep, or read. Or perhaps do a little polishing, perhaps the candlestick and inkstand. She would call me if she needed me. I had nothing to do until the 5 a.m. washing and bed making. Every night was wasted and this was the only time I could see Harold. I was allowed out in the afternoon and used to go and sit disconsolate in the sitting room in King's Parade, where Mrs Palmer lovingly cosseted me and listened to my laments.

Luckily after a month I was changed to day duty in a ward full of old women and teenagers.

There was a pretty girl with severe St Vitus' dance; she might really have been possessed of the devil. She was kept curtained off from the ward because any movement set her off. She twisted and sprang in her bed like a newly caught fish in the bottom of a boat. Her contortions were frequently violent enough to fling her out of bed. We were forever picking her up off the floor. Her midday meal was always and only kidney beans which I had to administer as best I could to the involuntarily side-stepping mouth. Sedatives if they were invented had not yet reached Cambridge. Again St Thomas's put the provincial hospital to shame. All the red tape was here, but it had become obstructive and lost significance. I liked nursing and still thought the patients were the important part, but the ward Sister was sour and hostile. If a sheet was caught on a wire of the bedstead, she would deliberately rip it in half in order to blame me. It shocked me very much to have to scrub out the bed pans in the bath used by the patients. Also, instead of curtains that could be pulled to screen patients when necessary, the nurses had to carry three heavy bamboo screens the length of the ward and back. My feet cried to high heaven for relief.

After work we had to return to our lodging and stay there. It was not long before the landlady came to tell me there was someone to speak to me at the door. It was Harold of course.

'Ho! It's you. I *am* glad. Come up to my room.'

The landlady interposed her rigid body. 'Certainly NOT,' she said.

'Why not? This is my cousin. We must sit somewhere and there's nowhere else.'

'No visitors are allowed in the nurses' rooms. Certainly not men.'

She made the word sound very dirty. We both burst into laughter. 'Oh well, we'll just sit on the stairs.'

So we sat on the stairs and made great merriment for an hour or so, the landlady's grim face appearing from below every now and then, hoping to see worse than she did.

We made an appointment for Sunday afternoon when I was free, and then I let him out.

When the happy day came I discarded the starched cap and knife-edged belt and put on what were then called 'gladrags', probably, and most unsuitably, a dress of apricot silk. We mounted the motor bike, and clutching my young officer round the waist I waved derisively at Addenbrooke's as we roared past along the Trumpington Road.

On the Monday I was summoned to the Matron's room where my sins were enumerated before me.

She had seen me wearing a ring when on duty in the ward. (It was a small signet ring inherited from my father. I looked on it as part of my hand. Even St Thomas's had not objected.)

Secondly I powdered my face. Who could have guessed, untold, that these were sins? Thirdly, my landlady complained of my trying to introduce men into my bedroom and of improper behaviour on the stairs.

And lastly, I had been seen riding through the town on

the carrier of an officer's motor cycle. Unfitting conduct for a decent girl. I was dismissed.

I was too contemptuous to be hurt. I finished my day in the ward, said goodbye to my patients and was warmed by the regrets of the old women whom I left behind uncherished in their beds.

I returned bouncing with release to Jas and Phil. I wrote to Mother telling her casually that I had been dismissed, and thought no more about it. She of course, as I should have known, took it as total disgrace reflecting on the whole family. Little as she thought of my morals, she travelled down instantly to Cambridge and went to see the Matron in my defence, a painful act of loyalty. I cannot imagine the scene, but Mother's quiet manners and grief, even perhaps her tears, had overcome the starch of the Matron. After all, they really saw eye to eye. Mother returned to us triumphant, to announce that the Matron would take me back.

Nothing was further from my intention. Of course I was not going back. I had had no idea Mother was cherishing any such hope in her mind. I thought she was just clearing the family name. I hope I thanked and was kind to her, but I don't remember feeling anything but offhand. I was not going to be managed by Mother or the Matron, both of whom had ideas of behaviour that I found insulting. Mother saw that there was nothing to be done with me. She travelled home the next day and I did not even go with her. ◊

Soon afterwards the Suffolk Regiment was to be moved further south. Harold came to say goodbye to us. His behaviour was odd. Every few minutes he made sentimental lurches toward me with 'I say, Lucy - ' which never got any further. It was a little time before I realised he was drunk, and I might never have understood if Phil had not been choking with laughter. He had not seen one of his family in this plight before. It certainly makes for domestic hilarity. This was the last time I ever saw Phil. I was pleased with even drunken advances from Harold, never having had any sober ones.

The next day I went home to Southport, but I had no sooner got there than Harold's sister rang up to tell me he had had a bad road accident on his motor bike and was in hospital. The Suffolk Regiment had gone off without him. I went to the Bostons' house to get more details. He had crashed on the Newmarket road, had broken a knee, crushed a hand and a foot, and had concussion. How bad was he? Nobody knew. His father, that very silly man, was pacing round the house puffing out his cheeks and blowing his moustache upwards, in gusts of self pity.

'I am the most unfortunate of men. I have no luck. Fate crushes me again and again. Here's my eldest son, nothing much to be proud of perhaps but still my eldest, and he's a cripple, good for nothing. A miserable cripple good for nothing at all.'

Fury filled me. I took the first train back to Cambridge.

The military hospital was set up in the fields behind Queen's Road. I had to get permission to visit from the officer in charge. I was embarrassed, having understood by now that my appearance was not reassuring. The Colonel looked me up and down and turned away to suppress his amusement. He gave generous permission.

I found Harold in a private room, a small wooden cell. He was in great pain and, in the excitement that follows shock, wound up, noisy and difficult, but also desperately funny and taking it all with high spirits. His elderly nurse already doted on him. A face screwed up in equal degrees of pain and laughter is irresistible.

◊

Autumn was upon us. Each enclosing evening, a time when the smell of fallen leaves increases, I walked to the hospital across Garret Hostel Bridge, then a slender iron span. The Backs, with double avenues of vast elms and deep shadowy spaces, were unlit and empty. Cambridge was soundless except for the college bells ringing for

Phil

Evensong. I walked in full consciousness of what closed me round or opened above me, awed to be so small, moving among so much.

Harold had no other visitor. His dear friends in the regiment had all gone, his sisters were unable to come, Phil was already away at a Flying School. Jas perhaps was just leaving it to me. I was well received. The devoted nurse accepted me with kindness. Harold lay with one leg attached to an extension, the foot considered irreparable done up in plaster, his right hand strapped out on a wide splint. He was helpless, but a spluttering jet of passionate humour.

I went regularly for every possible minute, taking anything I thought might relieve him. I chose a Medici reproduction of Velasquez's Captain Bartolomeus Borro to break the enclosing monotony of his wooden walls, a boisterous portrait that could make one laugh. Once sitting at the head of his bed I had constituted myself as his prop and bedrest. I was wearing a rose red silk blouse on which his head rested. This was the evening chosen by the Matron for an inspection. Rattling with starch and pendant accoutrements, scissors, pens, note book, keys, she appeared in the doorway flanked by her underlings. She gave me glowering looks and withdrew under my grin. It was the woman who had dismissed me from Addenbrooke's. I daresay the aiding and abetting nurse was scolded, but perhaps officers were allowed visitors from the demi-monde. Who else would they know, so far from home?

In time, Harold was on crutches, one of his very personal and dynamic hands deformed but fully usable, his foot lacking several bones still in plaster. The surgeon had told him he would never walk again.

I think we must both have gone home for Christmas, but the next thing that I remember is that Jas, Harold, Nora Hughes and I were up at Llyn Ogwen, at what was then Mrs Jones's cottage. Here I met for the first time I. A. Richards of whom I had heard so much from Jas. He was standing outside the cottage, obviously not expecting us. I got the impression of a very unfriendly man, embarrassed, moving himself whenever we moved so as always to face us squarely, as if on the defensive. He edged nearer and nearer to the cottage till he could back into it. I admit I was very disappointed. However, a little while later he came out again all friendly and at peace, but now with a very large patch of sacking tacked, probably by Mrs Jones, over the seat of his trousers. Next day he began to initiate me into simple short climbs over nearby boulders and a small chimney, in which Harold, to disprove the surgeon, joined us, discarding his crutches. That heavily plastered foot was dragged up through the snow after its fellow and one and a half clinging hands. No mention of that foot was ever allowed again. He forced it to do everything he wished, though I think every limping step hurt to the end of his life. However on this occasion to my relief, having proved his point, he climbed no more, but crutched along the valley with Jas instead. Jas had brought into the wilds of Wales a crate of claret and after supper we all got very convivial. I drank too much and disliked it.

We must have returned to Ogwen in the spring, taking Nora Hughes with us. Ivor was there again and he took Nora and me slab climbing. I was more agile and quick than she, but I could never look downward or outward, so that while she was fumbling in her agonisingly slow way I had to stand on my ledge with my eyes shut. After she had left I spent some days scrambling about with Ivor, but could not enjoy descending the steps of a small waterfall sitting in the water. Later Jas told me Ivor had said I was uncivilised. I recognised this as true and was much discouraged.

It was at Ogwen that Harold had the greatest sorrow of his life, the death in the trenches of his friend Ian Claughton. This grief he never lost.

6

Early in 1916 I got my offer of work in a French military hospital, so long waited for. I collected the outfit recommended, fortunately not so miserably starched and Victorian as for English wards, but comfortable white overalls and a large square of lawn to cover the hair, perfectly natural and rather becoming. Mother urged me to buy pyjamas instead of nightgowns because they would be better for escaping from pursuing Germans. In fact throughout the war I never saw a German.

Before setting off I spent the last evening with Harold in London, probably at the Alhambra, a fake-Scheherazade shrine of romance that entirely filled my needs. Few people with less than my age will now remember that beautiful and to me mysterious haunt of youth and high spirits, balcony above balcony all with Moorish arches, the whole vast crimson space excellently proportioned and softly lit. I hope if I could go back to it now I should not find it tawdry and vulgar. It remains in memory as an enchantment in the middle of London.

We must on this occasion have missed my train, for I remember us bundling into a taxi with much laughter and saying casually to the driver, 'Take us to Southampton.'

'Yessir. Southampton Row.'

'No. Southampton.'

'Yessir. Southampton.' He slammed the door and off we went.

I was wearing a very saucy hat with a veil drawn tight under my chin, perhaps chosen for travelling. Somewhere between Leicester Square and Southampton docks Harold broke into the conversation with 'For Christ's sake take off that bloody veil', and I received a first kiss, possibly his very first, for it was abrupt and of the hit or miss variety, hopelessly inexpert. I was grateful for the intention and we may even have completed the journey arm in arm. I am quite sure we had not got as far as hand in hand.

I went on to the boat alone, seeing no other passenger. Perhaps they were already in their berths. I stood a long time on the deck looking at the great pool with its circle of reflected lights. Beside our steamer there were only a few smaller boats, their masts very slightly swaying against the sky.

It was a still, dark night. No sound came from the open water outside, but the call of the oceans brooded insistently. No one could have told there was a deadly war being fought across the Channel. There were no searchlights, no blackout, no convoys, no aeroplanes overhead. It was a Channel crossing like any other, nor did this strike me as strange, having no prophetic foresight.

◇

I spent the next day wandering round Le Havre by myself, then crossed the rough mouth of the Seine in a tossing cockleshell of a boat to the Normandy coast and finally arrived at my destination, Houlgate, late at night. I reported at the bureau and an orderly showed me to my room, which was large and luxurious. The volunteer nurses were housed in one of the best hotels in the resort, all of which had been commandeered by the army. I opened the tall french windows and could hear the sea rolling gently on a beach close below me.

My luggage had gone astray. I did not wish to sleep in the underclothes I had already worn for two days of travel, so, still Scheherazading, I shawled my naked self in a yard-wide red chiffon scarf I had worn round my neck. It was delicious on the skin, light and warm. I slept serenely.

What I had not expected was a knock on the door next

morning and the irruption, before I was quite awake, of four other English nurses come to welcome me, with coffee and croissants. They were taken aback at the sight of their new acquisition lying there so voluptuously in a spread of dark hair and all too transparent crimson chiffon. One, a genteelly reared Surrey girl, burst into laughter and thereafter became a friend. Another, by far the vulgarest woman I ever knew, withdrew muttering. She was a trained nurse, probably dismissed from her hospital, though it is not for me to say so. The third was an elderly Scottish nurse, very trustworthy, and the last the daughter of a bishop, educated and charming and correct, but like me untrained. All were living in the same hotel. Downstairs were wards large and small. The view from my window along the coast was splendid, and the nearest building was the Casino, also a hospital.

My luggage arrived after breakfast, so I was able to dress and report for duty. The office was a small room in the Casino, presided over by a fatherly but very gross sergeant and a slightly lame young aristocratic assistant whose lands were a few miles inland. I became in time fond of both of them. They were a standby in a world turned upside down.

I must explain that French military hospitals, if this one was a fair example, did not consider nurses necessary. There was in France no profession of nursing, only nuns. There were orderlies, rough untrained types who dealt with the bed pans and took round the meals, served in the tin cans of the trenches. No beds were remade once the patients were in them. Nobody bedridden was washed. No rooms were cleaned, no charts were kept over the beds. The dressings of all mobile patients were done in the *Salle de Pansements,* and here voluntary French ladies came to help. There was no one on duty at night except officially the orderlies who, as they worked all day, were naturally sound asleep. There had originally been volunteer nurses at night, but as they were too often found in bed with the patients in the morning, night nursing had been forbidden.

The nurse whose place I had taken, had, in sweeping out a ward that offended her, found under a bed a kit bag containing a German's head. All these horrors were told me over *déjeuner* the first day.

The English nurses had taken over the wards as a matter of course and were carrying on according to their English lights, two of them actually rustling in starch. Their officiousness must have caused some surprise, but they were considered harmless by the indifferent authorities and appreciated by the patients. There was nobody over us, no one to whom we were responsible. We were simply allowed in.

I was appointed as assistant to an American lady who had a small ward of her own adjoining the operating theatre. She was a gaunt woman of sixty or so, with the face of a bothered sheep. She had all the generosity and idealism of Americans but no sense at all. She had given untold money to buy equipment for the hospital theatre, and so was well in with the *Médecin-Chef*, himself a totally insignificant, trim toy soldier. The theatre was not used for big operations in this type of hospital, but it was used. It was served by a middle-aged, evil-looking woman under the protection of the *Médecin-Chef*. She had the wide open empty blue eyes of one who uses speech only for lying.

The American lady presided over her ward of six beds, for slight operation cases. I would not be surprised if a few incisions had been made to keep her happy. She was fussy, muddle-headed and self-important. She had come over to make a difference to the war. Her French was of the kind one hears assayed in Paris shops.

Predictably she disliked me at sight. Her patients did not go to the *Salle de Pansements* but their wounds were dressed and bandaged by her. It happened that I was a good bandager. I had taken the trouble to acquire this neat and amusing art. Later on in my nursing days when there was much ragging of a patient, '*Sans Fesses*', who had lost his buttocks, I was the only person in the hospital who could criss-cross him comfortably in such a way that it would not drop off. But now I was merely an assistant. The American Nightingale was unhandy. She could not get the hang of this business of changing the roll from one hand to the other as you circled the shoulder or waist of a standing man. She *walked* round him, nearly always dropping the bandage before she got back to the starting point so that it rolled away across the ward floor. As I retrieved it, perhaps from under a bed, and began the slow process of rolling it up again to replace in her hand, watched by the boys with lovely grins, it was difficult to remain solemn and not to act it as a comedy. Why in fact should one be solemn? I did control myself, but she sensed a lack of respect.

The function of this hospital was to take from the casualty clearing station those men not too seriously wounded to be moved. It was for *soldats* only. The officers presumably were better treated. The men came in train loads, filled up two hotels and the Casino and remained a few weeks, till they were all moved on and the place was got ready for the next batch. When I got there, the majority of the patients were on their way to recovery. Those who could walk were free to go out and get drunk with their friends in the bistro. It was considered a sure way to make your sepsis active again. One of my six men was still bedridden. Alone in the ward when his mates were out, he was bored and homesick. I acquired a draughts board and sat on the side of his bed to play with him. The American Nightingale coming in unexpectedly in the evening shrieked at me.

'Nurse! Get off that bed at once! Don't you know it's unprofessional to sit on a patient's bed?' I could have said it was unprofessional to roll surgical bandages across a dirty floor, but I said mildly, 'We were only playing draughts'.

'Never do such a thing again. I feel I hardly dare leave the ward.' I left the ward in a rage and almost bumped into the arms of the anaesthetist, who considered a kiss but thought better of it. He was an excellent, well brought up young man. We had a long amused conversation and I forgot the insult I had received.

Next morning I heard that the American Nightingale had seen the *Médecin-Chef* and asked to have me sent home. Dismissed again, and so soon! Luckily for me the *Médecin-Chef* had an eye for laughing girls and couldn't bring himself to do it. With a cynical wish to please all he sent me word instead to take over two upper floors of the biggest hotel, in all two hundred men. They were almost all up and about, but had to report each day to the *Salle de Pansements*, to which I now had entry. It was a large gilded room, one whole side of which was windows looking on to the sea, probably once the dining room. From the ceiling hung chandeliers enclosed in holland covers thick with dust.

There was a doctor in charge and four French ladies assisting. Half a dozen men at a time stood round stripping to show wounds in various parts of their anatomy. One of the French ladies was a mad, bitter creature who with her probe deliberately made each dressing as painful as possible, saying as she did it, 'My brother was killed in the trenches. Why weren't you? (Jab) I'll see to it there's no malingering here.'

Another had her sixteen-year-old daughter beside her, a slim, snow-white, baby-faced Botticelli Madonna in hospital overall and cap. Here was the *'jeune fille bien élevée'* that I so little resembled. She was so suppressed by upbringing she could neither risk a word nor a half smile, only modest, mute docility. Her mother kept a sharp lookout and if any male body was likely to be uncovered anywhere between the armpits and the knees, Mother tapped on the floor with her heel and the untainted maiden slipped out of the room. Heads, arms and feet only were polite enough.

The other two French women were duchesses with awe-inspiring historical names. At *déjeuner* they shared a table with the oddly assorted English, but did not mix with us. They did not expect us to understand French, and I was the only one who had any real grasp of it. They were talking about *'un pauvre blessé'* whose state was so disgusting that it made them sick. They had had to abandon him. *'Le pauvre, c'est trop écoeurant'*. I asked them then where he was, and learned he was in a single room somewhere in my two floors. I went in search, and presently found him. He was not young, a slight bottle-shouldered man with an undistinguished bald head and the eyes of a dog in a trap. He had lost all his lower jaw and much of the upper. He could neither speak nor eat. Such disfigurement cut him off from his fellows. He was in voluntary hiding — whenever I saw him, standing alone there in awful despair, unable to ask for anything, unable to think of his wife. I at least could dress his horrible wound, could see it and not reject him, could smile at him and bring him writing paper. There was no radio, no library, nothing day after day but silence and a view over the great empty sea and empty sky.

Before long he was moved off with all the rest, I hope to somewhere where faces are remade. It was beginning to be done. Soon after the war I met a man who was intriguingly handsome because his face gave no clue to his personality. It was a surgical face made for him after a disaster similar to that of my patient. From the latter I had a letter which pleased me very much. I had not been able to form any idea of what kind of man I was tending, his class or his intelligence, but his letter was written in a cultured hand, beautifully expressed and warm with thanks. He did not, alas, tell me what they were doing for him.

No doctor regularly visited my floors. Those needing dressings went down to him. Searching through the rooms I found others who needed attention. There was a man with a temperature of 104-105 whom I watched over at night in spite of the ruling but as nobody was looking after him, nobody knew. Considering how little training I had had, it was a wonder if I did not kill anybody by mistake. I did perhaps let one die by oversight. There was one room with five ribald, lively men confined to bed for one reason or another. Many Rabelaisian jokes were made about me, an entertaining risk for them as they were never quite sure how much *argot* I understood. I never minded what they said and could take a pinch in the behind as nothing to worry about. We were all young. In this larking ward there was a boy who lay without joining in. He had an impassive face rather like warm carved stone, a strong piece of sculpture. He left his food untouched, but when I asked him if he was all right, if he wanted anything, he looked away and would not answer. He did not toss or cough, or show any sign of pain. I asked the man in the next bed about him, but he just shrugged and said, ' *C'est le cafard'*. Certainly the memory of the trenches was enough to leave one like that. However when the next day he hardly seemed even to hear me, I reported him to the doctor. He was found to have advanced double pneumonia. Antibiotics were not yet invented so double pneumonia was almost always fatal. The boy was moved to a sort of cupboard that might once have been the housemaid's closet, which was where they now took patients to die. I feel sure this boy was dying on purpose. He had sensed a way out. By the time they had carried him to this secret hole he was as good as dead.

The priest was brought, and the doctor stood by to register a death. I knew nothing about Extreme Unction and was now overwhelmed by the beauty and rightness of this send-off. They then closed his hazel eyes, and I think he was dead. I bent and kissed his forehead, thinking, 'I do this for his mother', and at once was seized with fear that I had done yet another unconsidered act, and perhaps cancelled out the Unction. Nobody said anything. They had finished with him.

There were three priests on the staff. One, in charge of food, was a gross bestial sinner who offered me his bed and afterwards persecuted me with vile abuse. He was later dismissed for peculation and disorderly behaviour. Another was a cultivated Jesuit, whose face struck me as enjoying a higher form of wickedness, but I have nothing against him except the sanctimonious cuddling I referred to before. The third was young, thin, ill-favoured, bespectacled and deeply unhappy. He could look nobody in the eyes, perhaps because he could never be one with the hell-seasoned boys whom he served. I could not but respect him and it was he who administered Extreme Unction. I would have hated to offend him though I cared nothing for the opinion of the duchesses.

Now I had got the measure of it, nightly before I went off duty I went the rounds of two floors and said Goodnight to my one hundred and ninety-nine men.

Letters from home were as regular as in peacetime. They were stuck up on a board in what had been the entrance lounge of the hotel, now a sort of common room for the staff. Here on the green baize overlaced with diagonal white tapes I would find lodged letters from Mother, as if I were still at school, from Jas, now roped into an Officers' Training Camp, and if I was lucky, very funny pages from Harold.

◇

As we were entirely voluntary and there was literally no one over us, we could have leave whenever it suited us. I must confess that as far as I remember, none of the other English nurses took any. I decided to go home for Christmas. I merely told the bureau when I was going. Frances was at home. She was having a gruelling time as a regular V.A.D. in the local hospital, not allowed any of the comi-tragic licence given to me. Mother was very proud of her. Harold was at his home, now able to wear two shoes and walk with a brisk but heavy limp. He had bought a small open car, in which after Christmas we set off together southward. We were overtaken by a heavy snowstorm. The car of course was unheated, the windscreen blocked with snow. To see out we had to open the windscreen and take the snow in our faces. There were as yet only carbide lamps, giving a poor light, and no roads had been improved to meet the future car traffic. The occasional car, a little less freakish than the very first, was not worth worrying about. So, no road clearance. We inched our way along narrow roads with only snow-heaped hedges to mark the way. At Huntingdon we could go no further. We put up at the old George Hotel, then pleasingly old-fashioned even to our eyes. Our bedroom had pictures of the Crimean War and a large iron bed, where our well-mannered intimacy was screwed up a turn tighter. I had almost a disease of honesty, and being unable to pass over the deceit of signing ourselves in the obligatory wartime visitors' book as Mr and Mrs, I confessed in the morning to the manageress that this was not so. She couldn't have been less interested. For a little thing like that she was not going to alter her visitors' list, war or no war.

Harold, impatient at being out of the war, had succeeded in being taken on as chauffeur to a specialist who toured the English military hospitals in France, so in future we would both be on the other side of the Channel though attached to different armies.

I went back to France alone. There were still no difficulties, formalities or precautions. One simply booked and walked on to the ship for Le Havre. A great many people were going backwards and forwards about their business, whatever that was. On this route there was no sign of the war.

There had been changes at Houlgate during my brief absence. The *Médecin-Chef* had been discharged for pocketing the money so liberally given by the American Nightingale for theatre equipment. She herself had left in indignant disillusionment. When I arrived the hospital was empty, waiting for a new train load. Meanwhile someone in the upper hierarchy of administration had decided that the wounded were to be classified according to the part of the body wounded. When the first lot arrived in the middle of the night there was pandemonium. They were all wounded in the feet. The hospital had only five pairs of crutches. No warning had been given. This lot did not stay long. It is to be hoped there were crutches where they were going, but if our hospital succeeded in laying in a supply, it was in vain, because the next lot were all eye cases. There was no eye specialist on our staff. Where both eyes were bandaged, the patients had to be fed, washed and guided about. There were not enough of us to feed them all and it is not a job one can do with brutal speed. These also were moved on fairly soon, to make way for hands and arms.

I was now in the main Salle of the Casino, a lovely place with a wide terrace over the sea. It held perhaps fifty beds. The old Scottish nurse was in charge. She looked grim but treated me as if she had been our family Nanny. She might have said, 'Miss Lucy is rather wild but she will grow out of it.' She knew her job and I served under her very willingly. We got on easily, perhaps because we both had Nonconformist backgrounds. The Casino was filled with the elaborate brass bedsteads that had furnished the hotels, with knobs large and small and loops and uprights like the sides of the Forth bridge. My Nanny had been taught that brass is to be polished, and to this she rigidly adhered. She bid me take all the lacquer off the fifty bedsteads and keep them polished. What a wartime job to come out from England to do! I did as I was told. It was better than slovenliness. The doctor for instance in charge of this ward made his occasional rounds in mid-morning unwashed and unshaved, wearing a long military overcoat beneath which pyjama trousers showed, and unbrushed shoes on bare feet. In St Thomas's he would surely have been struck down, if not by lightning from above, then by the ward Sister. He greeted neither patients nor nurses, asked no questions. He had a cigarette hanging from his lip and merely walked round and out again, perhaps signing his visit in a book. It is true that no one was seriously ill in the ward. Their wounds were dressed. The era of pills for everything had not dawned and nobody expected personal attention. Perhaps he was just a realist, un-interested in style.

Daily I laboured diligently from bed to bed, chatting meanwhile with the amused occupant. In Nanny's time all those rail knobs and balls twinkled and flashed like a myriad Christmas tree decorations, or like the sun on the wrinkled surface of the sea outside. The new *Médecin-Chef* used to look in at the door occasionally to admire this English fantasy.

◇

Spring revealed the beauty of the Normandy countryside. It was not dramatic. The cliffs were made of black mud constantly slipping down, not beautiful in themselves but giving a grand view of the sea from the top. In every cove along the coast there were hotels and little towns but they were confined to the edge of the sea. All behind was purely pastoral, a rolling endlessly varied panorama of half-timbered farm houses in fields full of wild flowers, of orchards and woods and open hillsides, unlimited and unbroken by anything we should now call a road. I had enough free time for walking to explore round about, and almost immediately found I loved it as if I had been born there. Perhaps some distant ancestor had bequeathed me some thin nerve of racial memory that stirred. The only other place where I have felt immediately rooted is my present home, also Norman.

At first my walks were troubled by vagabond children pursuing me with Anglo-phobic balls of mud and pebbles, but in time I made friends with them and instead they brought me stolen flowers. I suffered the loneliness of all young people who feel themselves to be freakish, and these small adherents were a comfort to me. The two I liked best were sister and brother aged nine and seven. They had no home but lived in a collapsed shed on the shore. Their mother was a fat, drunken syphilitic, lying on the bare ground. I used to bandage her legs with hospital equipment. She seemed unable to move about and I have no idea what she lived on. The children, unlike Italian children, did not beg. For a time I fed them with hospital left-overs but the brutal *curé* stopped that. I used then to take five or six children out with me in the early morning to farms where meals could be provided. Along the cliff top, the farmers' wives in peacetime provided exquisite food for wealthy visitors and now they thought this crazy Miss was a godsend in a dead season, vagabond children and all. There was a delectable place perhaps six miles away, run in great elegance by an ageing, painted actress for the most discriminating clients from Trouville. Here I had the nerve to take my ragged gang at an unearthly hour, knocking till the old person got out of bed. She always received me with ready courtesy and served us the best coffee, butter and croissants I have ever eaten, under striped sunshades on neatly raked gravel. Who would blame her if she overcharged? My ragamuffins, being French, knew what was good and I never had any trouble with their behaviour. The hospital food was wretched, but food in Normandy was copious and unrestricted, war or no war. In the end I got my little girl housed in a good farm, and the little boy in a Catholic charity school in Caen. As I left the little creature with a sour old monk, my heart suddenly smote me, but alas, not hard enough to make me snatch him back. I have blamed myself ever since for a piece of interfering ignorant cruelty. Poor little devil, never free again and parted from his sister. I have never done a worse thing.

The hospital *curé*, my enemy, made my concern for the children another opportunity for abusing me. He said to me of them, '*Ça, c'est de la viande*'. I will not translate it because confirmed Francophil though I am, I prefer to think this appalling brutality has never been said in English. ◇

Small waifs were not my only company. The anaesthetist, Ary, who was outstandingly honourable in this limbo of irresponsibility, had become devoted to me. We spent a great deal of time together in the frequent periods when the hospital had been emptied. Having once declared himself and been refused, he never plagued me with his desires but did everything he could think of to please and amuse. I was wooed at table with snails, frogs and blackbirds, which failed to please. He took me to Paris with him to stay with his parents and so gave me my only experience of French family life, for which I am ever grateful. His mother found me less dreadful than she had expected. She had feared a harpy. It was amusing to be so much liked because I was clearly not going to marry her son. His father was enchanting, an exquisitely courteous old man with a beautiful face. For the rest of my life I never went through Paris without visiting them. My friendship with Ary was of course noticed and avidly followed by the hospital and the village. It was so open that it was for that very reason intriguing.

As the spring advanced my roving habits increased. When not on duty I could not keep indoors. Apart from the early morning walks with the children, I would often go off alone at night and sleep in the woods or on a haystack up on the cliffs. None of the English nurses shared my fancies, nor my love of the sea. From the first of April to October I swam daily. It was easy to undress in an empty storeroom in the Casino and run across the terrace and down into the wide blue sea. For some reason this shore seemed not to make rough waves. The sea lapped eternally. If I swam far out I would meet white butterflies purposefully crossing over from distant Le Havre, flying in wavering but direct lines close to the surface of the water. Sometimes Ary joined me, but never anyone else. On warm nights of full moon the sea was irresistible. I would slip out alone, having the whole coastline to myself. Both sea and sky were the cloudy blue of skimmed milk, and the water at night seemed to be as full of small fish as soda water is of bubbles. They swam in under the neck of my bathing costume (ample and decent in those days) in swarms and felt most peculiar. I had to strip off my costume and turn it inside out to release them. I think they were whitebait. This delicious freedom and solitude was in France, in the Great War, and only just beyond the war zone.

In Rouen a little further up the Seine, Harold's elder sister, my particular friend, was nursing in a British hospital under great hardship, sleeping in a tent overrun by rats. We for our part had nothing worse than bugs and fleas. Bugs went to the laundry in our clothes, and after being well beaten on a stone by the brook, which was the method of laundry still practised, they came back hungry in the same garment. Fleas were easier to dispose of, but one day, knowing I had killed my fleas overnight, I was still plagued by itching. I admonished myself not to be neurotic and even persuaded myself the agony of itch was imagination. That night on undressing, I killed eight fleas on my person.

I decided to go and visit my friend in Rouen. From the easy-going anarchy of the French hospital nothing seemed simpler. I bought a ticket and took the train, arriving at Rouen late at night. At the station the exit was barred by a cordon of British soldiers. Where, they asked, was my permit? Permit? What for? Rouen was a British base and no one was allowed in without a permit. But I *am* British! Where's your *passeporte*? As I wasn't leaving France I didn't bring it. To my amazement I was arrested and taken before a very grim Colonel. The stony severity never left his face, it might have been a court martial leading to execution. However he sized up my silly innocence and ordered my guards to escort me to 'the convent' for the night and have me put on the first train in the morning. Could I not even see my cousin? Out of the question. I was marched off.

We arrived at the convent in the dark and I left before dawn, so I never saw it. I do not know where it was or what it was called. The Mother Superior received me with the greatest kindness. By a sudden change I found myself an honoured guest. I was given a charming guest room and supper was brought me by a nun. She left the door open while she arranged the tray, and in the passage outside a surge of nuns with wide-winged starched caps catching on each other like cows' horns gazed at me in fascinated curiosity and even delight. A novelty had come in. I've seldom had such a welcome, though wordless. However, before it was light I was woken and hurried off, being entrusted this time not to a posse of soldiers, but to a sinister figure like a stage Satan in a flapping black cloak and slouch hat. Without the convent's sanction I would not have dared to pass him in the street by daylight. I followed his beckoning as he strode off through narrow alleys across the unlit city back to the station, where he merely pointed, and left me.

The train was packed with French soldiers going on leave from the trenches. I was the only woman in the train. I squeezed myself into a compartment where they were already falling asleep as if they had not slept for weeks. They were a grievous sight, haggard wrecks of men hardly expecting to be alive. Many of them were having nightmares, shouting out or groaning. Before very long I had a heavy, unconscious head on each shoulder and another on my knees. I felt motherly and had an arm round the shoulders of one to keep him from slipping. My hand thus came into the keeping of an older man who could not get to sleep. He had a good face and why should he not hold my hand for comfort? I dozed, and when I woke he had put three rings on my fingers, made from bullets or the metal end of cartridge cases. 'Remember me,' he said like the ghost to Hamlet. Going on leave must have been almost worse than the trenches, if that was possible.

After this, the nearest I ever got to the real war, the indifference and incompetence of the hospital seemed worse than ever. It was as if nobody cared. Though we did not get the most ghastly casualties, what must have been in all these men's heads? The hospital had one good doctor whom all the English nurses loved. I never had the privilege of serving under him, but even he had an untroubled holiday attitude. Indeed there was a whole month in the summer when we had no patients at all. Perhaps during that month all the casualties were final.

When I revisited Houlgate after the war, it was packed with elegant and wealthy holiday makers. It was the family resort, highly decorous and stylish, like a Boudin painting. The more worldly Trouville-Deauville was a few miles away on one side, the demi-monde at Cabourg at a decent distance on the other. The whole coast hummed with activity and pleasure. Now it was deserted. A few villas were inhabited by the doctors and administrators, the rest shuttered up. During our enforced month's idleness the *Médecin-Chef* gave tea parties at his villa, the one admired doctor gave picnics on the Casino terrace, and Ary took me to his uncle's shooting lodge deep in the centre of Normandy, where in the woods there were wild boars. In the course of conversation he told me that when young men in the hospital asked him, *'Est-ce qu'il y a à faire avec Miss?'* he replied, *'Approchez-y, vous verrez.'* He had more faith in me than my mother.

Of course they approached. *'Si nous faisions une petite promenade ce soir?'*

One of my phobias, akin to uncompromising candour, was that words should be used for exactly what was meant, and that anybody approaching me must learn to do so. So when an evening walk was suggested it was with pleasure accepted. The unfortunate man found himself accompanying a brisk English stride for perhaps ten miles through the night and never even got to the point. Naturally no man ever confessed to this, but more probably boasted, so that I acquired a legendary bad name that nobody knew whether to believe or not. It is surprising that in spite of such idiocy I had some staunch female defenders. For the would-be amorous man I had a laughing but friendly contempt. There was no malice in my behaviour nor any aggressive ideas of Women's Lib. I thought I was proving my mother wrong again. Every girl must hold her own tiller.

In strong contrast to these wilful pranks I went to Paris for a weekend with Harold on leave from his chauffeuring. We stayed at the Crillon in the most elegant luxury. It still

Harold

preserved its pre-war standards. I have no recollection of what I wore, but certainly it was not what those doors usually admitted. I was living free at the hospital and so had no money problems and Harold had a lieutenant's pay to spend on leave. We ate at various superb restaurants with famous names, and idled about the town and the Bois de Boulogne. At night we shared a bedroom fit for Ninon de Valois. The curtains, hanging from ceiling to floor, were of heavy damask whose glorious colour I can only describe as gold, but rich and deep. Played over by the dim bedside light it was beautiful enough to caress one's eyes all night. The bed curtains were the same. Everything was perfect, nothing was too much. The room closed us with exquisite voluptuousness.

We laid our young bodies together in this ambience as passionate as we were separate, no sword between us but an age old principle not yet questioned, no gesture but of dear trembling friendship, and we did not sleep for pure joy. So great a trust engendered in me a love that was etched into my being, never to be erased. I was too ignorant to know that trust to this extent can be less perfect to the one trusted, could indeed cause love-hate. From now on I was from time to time subjected to slights and woundings that I could not understand. But I loved and had to take what was given. We met in Paris several times again, but found ourselves less ambassadorial lodging.

◇

The hospital was ordered to make room for more wounded and so the nurses were turned out to find accommodation elsewhere. I was taken in by the *pharmacien* and his wife, free of charge again, as a patriotic gesture. They were good to me. The young wife was charming and of that willing correctness that the French do so beautifully. The house was faultlessly kept. I blush now to think what a shock I must have been to them. I should obviously have cleaned my own room but I had never cleaned a room and did not even realise it was necessary. My hostess never chided me, but if she ever looked in while I was out she saw a horrific mess. My nightgown too was an old frayed woollen shirt of Harold's with sleeves longer than my fingertips. My outdoor coat was one of his cast off mackintoshes, tattered and oily. If my morals were out of date my habits were two generations ahead. I would have been 'with it' now. While I was there, the wife's sister came to stay, bringing her son, a hefty two-year-old. His mother told me with pride that he was still breast fed. The little man in a sailor suit and so-called sailor hat was led in. As he was lifted on to her lap his mother said, '*Ote ton chapeau à ta petite maman, cheri.*'

◇

The wards were busy again as summer drew towards autumn. I was glad to have work. Halcyon as my summer had been, the thought of the trenches was never absent. The one highlighted the other. The patients never talked about it. They were not a talkative lot. They probably knew there were no words for it, at least to us. Perhaps they talked among themselves at night, or in the bistro if they could get there. All the time I was there, as far as I know not one had a visitor. Perhaps it was about now that the fat sergeant in the office, of whom I spoke at the beginning, told me that there was a patient who had to be escorted to his home in Alsace Lorraine. He was not strong enough to travel alone, no man could be spared to take him and none of the nurses would like to travel alone with a man. What about me? Of course I said I would. It delighted me to agree. I was the youngest by far and the least imposing of the nurses. That only made it more of a snook to pull. The journey was totally uneventful. I remember of it only the strange Alsatian countryside out of the railway window, like an illustration to fairy tales. Also that I spent the night in a hotel on the main street where my bedroom was on the ground floor. Being English I never slept with my windows shut, so I opened them – the tall glass doors, a very conspicuous sight in a

French street, but not even a thief noticed. Men's voices loud in conversation passed on the pavement all night, but I was undisturbed.

The English nurse I saw most of had fallen in love with a classically featured young man from a farm in the Basses-Alpes. He had been badly wounded and could never do active service again. She was older than he, too individual to be called plain, with vivid blue eyes in a long red face, and awkward but expressive movements. However, her face had the capacity of showing the intense despairing, fighting-for-life quality of her love. She had a quick sense of humour, but he had none. He was tired from the war, would not be able to pull his weight again on the farm and had no will to contend with her obsession. I watched him slowly and it seemed to me apprehensively drawn in. He had nothing to pit against her. When he was released from the hospital he agreed to marry her and went home to prepare his family and get his demobilisation papers.

In the lovely early autumn the bride and I set off for the Basses-Alpes. At the end of the long railway journey from Paris across the width of France we still had to travel half a day's ride in a carrier's open cart along small country roads. The scenery was bewitching, with the real Alps just visible beyond the rolling hills. I was so serenely happy taking it all in that I must have been poor company for my wildly agitated friend. We arrived at last, to find a small isolated farm on the top of a hill, and were received by an elder brother and his wife, and the bridegroom.

The room downstairs was the kitchen, where hens, ducks and goats ran about, the open door being the main light. The sister-in-law showed us her baby. It lay on her lap, its arms and legs trussed up in a tight criss-cross bundle as stiff as a log, as in early pictures. My friend and I shared a bedroom over the cow-shed. The floor boards were loosely fitted to allow the warmth of the animals to rise, as also the warm cow smell. Rustlings, sighs and low moos sweetened my sleep, but I daresay the bride's wakefulness was consoled by thoughts of the Surrey comforts she was offering him, poor boy. But what nostalgia he must later have suffered.

The wedding next day was only half a ceremony, conducted with ill grace by the priest because the bride was not a Catholic. He insisted that she must promise to bring up all children in the faith if she was to be married at all. She said she would say it aloud if it was all right to say inwardly that she was sorry she did not mean it. The priest passed this over without comment — she was only a mad English woman — and married they were.

We then had the wedding feast at a long trestle table in a barn or village hall. The special dish in honour of the occasion was a broiled calf's head, whole, and of a ghastly whiteness like that of a dead human. The bride and bridegroom were given the eyes. She disgraced herself by refusing. I was let off lightly with the soft warm nostrils. The men all ate with the jack knives out of their pockets which they also used pertinaciously and openly for picking their teeth, but knives and forks were found for us. I enjoyed the Breughel atmosphere very much, and received an offer of marriage from one of the guests before the end.

After the meal we formed up in procession and walked from farm to farm over the hills for hours to show ourselves to the neighbours, with much singing along the way.

That night I went off alone, seen off at the train by my would-be husband who had driven me there in his float.

◇

The ensuing winter was very severe. In my bedroom the water in the ewer was frozen an inch deep every morning. It is not surprising that we had a trainload of bronchitics. The noise of coughing in the ward was like the hunt kennels before feeding time. The echoes of it came down from the Casino ceiling above the shrouded chandeliers. It was heard everywhere. The approved treatment — I guess originating from Louis XIV's time — was cupping. I was shown how this should be done. The patient lay with his

back bared. I had twelve small glass cups like very thick
sherry glasses, into which one at a time was put a tuft of
cotton wool soaked in methylated spirit and set on fire.
While it was still flaming it was clapped on to the flesh. If
it was hot enough when put on, the vacuum caused as it
cooled drew up a red balloon from the back inside it. If not
hot enough, it fell off. To get a back covered with these
horrors took at least a quarter of an hour while the patient
got cold. I cannot think it ever did any good. And how
could a man lie down after it?

On the other hand, experimental medicine was going on.
Someone had thought up that medicines swallowed
sometimes upset the stomach. So the order went out that
all medicines were to be given by hypodermic injections. I
had till now never had an injection myself, still less used
a hypodermic needle. I was nervous, having no idea how
hard one would have to push it.

Injections in France were given in the buttock. Morning
and evening all the men in my ward were drawn up facing
a wall, their trousers down to their knees. An elderly
Frenchwoman had drifted in to help. She had armed
herself with an instrument that perhaps was meant for
drawing fluid out of the lung, a huge thing. With this she
was stabbing the unfortunates. I managed to get a needle
of sorts, lamentably blunt, and set to work. The scene was
farcical, the old one with her prong, the young one with
her needle, and my irresistible mirth spread to the whole
row. It turned into a lark. When after two days the old
lady withdrew and I had a little more confidence we settled
down to a nearly professional routine, but solemn I could
never be.   ◇

In the early spring I went on leave to England to meet
Harold. I had the usual long day to pass in Le Havre by
myself before the boat and felt far too excited to endure it.
As I walked aimlessly about, I saw a group of four English
officers sitting at a table outside a building. Spontaneously
wrong, as usual, but moved by a feeling of our being all

English in a war together, I went to their table and said simply, 'I haven't seen an Englishman for six months. May I sit and talk to you for a while? I'm waiting for the boat.' At once the three nicest of the group rose and fled. The remaining man too got to his feet and said, 'Shall we go somewhere else? This is Headquarters.' I apologised. I didn't know the English were now established at Le Havre. He led me away, saying he knew a quiet place where we could go. It turned out to be a small hotel. The patronne greeted him as a valued client and said to my surprise, 'Your usual room, Monsieur'. We went upstairs, not to a salon but to a bedroom with a large double bed. No sooner were we inside than a maid came in and turned down the sheets at both sides. I began to laugh with real enjoyment of the ridiculousness, the ready speed of those turned down sheets. I explained that he had got it all wrong. I tried to convince him of the simplicity of my approach, but he could not believe it. I kept him off with the hot end of my cigarette and laughter without resentment. In the end he accepted defeat, saying as we parted at the hotel door, 'Well, you can't say I haven't behaved like a gentleman.' Rather touching, because he wasn't one at all.

So there was an afternoon passed with some interest and another lesson rubbed in. Alas, may one never behave naturally?

◇

I do not clearly remember much about London that time except that we saw a Zeppelin caught in the searchlights over Wimbledon Common. We were visiting an aunt who was hysterical about the danger, clinging to her husband. Had it been the Second World War she would not have been so ridiculous, might perhaps even have been brave. The Zeppelin was brought down harmlessly except to the pilot.

The really sharp memory of this leave is the Alhambra, its galleries packed from first floor to ceiling with young officers in uniform, a sight to blink at, to try to take in and never forget. At the point the war had reached it was written as if on the wall that they must all be killed. The face of any young man who is fit and going arm in arm with death has a glory with its tragedy, and in the romantic light and excitement of the Alhambra there they all were, some remembering what they came from too vividly to laugh, some even more tense in the effort to forget. Enough to choke a girl's heart. These were my real English.

In the stalls where I sat in full view of this reredos of those ready to die, I was abandoned by Harold who left me for the Promenade, improper for 'ladies', where he said he would meet other old friends. So there I sat throughout the show, alone in a non-world of my own making with an empty stall beside me, and took in the totality. Meanwhile Robey was singing 'If you were the only girl in the world', a song of bitter-sweet truth for us all.

◇

Back once more in Houlgate I found the hotel where the nurses had once lodged was now given over to tubercular patients. My ward in the Casino had only a few wounded who had lingered on, so I had little to do. A large room opening out of it had eight or ten men said to be tubercular. They were being subjected to an experimental treatment. They were encased in plaster from neck to ankles, leaving only their arms free, and their feet sticking out at the end. Each man, as he could not move his head, had a small tilted looking glass above his face so that he could see something besides the ceiling. I was asked, as I had time on my hands, to massage their feet. Of course I had no training in massage but was not likely to do any harm, so I made it as long and pleasant as I could while talking to these medical martyrs via their mirror. It was a room that horrified me, but I never heard a grumble from them. The way they took whatever was ordained was astounding, for it must have occurred to them that this treatment was medical lunacy. They died one by one, not of their disease but of dreadful bedsores, which might have been foreseen. My Scottish Nanny was shocked beyond comment.

◇

About this time my brother Phil was reported missing. His plane had been shot down. This may very well have shocked Harold into further action for I learned from his letters that he had offered himself for the Flying Corps, where in the growing shortage of men, his lameness was not considered a serious handicap, and he was taken on. He had been sent to a training centre outside Tours, whence I received enthusiastic accounts of his new made friends. His men friends were always for life. Needless to say, in midsummer I went to visit him, in a part of France new to me, but of which I actually saw very little. I put up in a small hotel, which had a pleasant balcony overlooking open spaces and trees, where meals were served. But it was not Harold who shared it. He could only get away for a couple of hours in the evening, after which he returned to camp. We sat on a bench at the edge of a wood overlooking the town and he talked to me about the new and wonderful Bristol Moth, and about his friends, but was always careful to keep them away from me. But my constant companion, arriving even at breakfast time, was a young Canadian flyer who managed to get away from camp more enthusiastically than Harold and was deluded enough to think I would make the ideal wife for a trapper, which was his peacetime occupation. He saw me going round with him to get the fur – not the poor creature – out of his nightly traps. Otherwise he was a nice boy and had got it badly, for the moment. Marriage was in the air. At Houlgate there was a little village baker, as good as gold, who was now the hospital ambulance driver. He offered to teach me to drive. He took his engine to pieces to show me how it worked and explained very clearly, while he and I put it together again. The ambulance was kept in a small yard behind a restaurant. The yard was lined with cages of rabbits stacked one above the other all

round. In this very cramped space he made me use all the
gears and turn the car completely round in short zig-zags.
Under his placid common-sense tuition it seemed easy. I
did it without startling a rabbit. After that he arranged that
I should walk a good way out of possible observation from
the hospital where he would pick me up in his cab and I
should drive the wounded into Trouville. I do not think I
shook a patient, but of course we were the only car on the
road. In return for these lessons I began to teach him
English, sitting at a table in my bedroom. He had very
formal manners. Alas, one day he arrived in his best
clothes with a neat little posy of flowers, to offer me his
heart. There were no more lessons. Much later when I first
drove Harold's car with himself beside me, at a bad change
of gear up a very steep hill he so hissed through his teeth
that I lost my nerve and took him straight into a fruit shop
among flying oranges and apples. For him driving was a
religious exercise. The engine was the divinity.

To come back to Tours, Harold had the weekend off and
arranged to meet me at a tiny place called Gué de Loire,
where there was a riverside inn. He borrowed a bicycle for
me and promised to meet me at midday. I rode off happily
for what seemed a very great way, through vineyard
country most strange to me as the vines were painted
brilliant blue. I do not think I met anyone all the way
there. I arrived at last at an idyllic place and took a room
at the inn, then sat down to wait for Harold. Hour after
hour passed and he did not come. I had a lonely lunch,
and finally in tears a lonely supper under the suspicious
eye of the landlady who obviously thought that if my man
was dropping me I should not be able to pay the bill and
so must not be allowed out of sight. I suffered great
humiliation but at last as it was growing dark he arrived,
with a believable excuse. I chose to believe it, and
friendship was restored. Next day the weather was
brilliant. We spent the morning lying on a hillside in the
sun in great content to be in such a country, and the
afternoon bathing in a little river that ran beneath

over-arching trees. Above the water hung a loose bluish haze, made of dragonflies' wings that flashed in the sun-specks as they hovered and darted in great numbers.

Though it had its charming moments this brief visit did not advance our affair at all. Harold's conversation had been largely about his new friends, one in particular who was having a love affair with a local girl. Harold found it very entertaining to see his friend hampered and guilty because he had a wife in England who 'absolutely idolised him'. I saw nothing funny in it and said I would rather be a mistress treated with frankness than a wife treated with deceit. It did not occur to me that a ladylove could be treated with as much or more deceit than a wife, only a man would not be bothered by it.

◇

When I got back to Houlgate, I was told that Ary was leaving. He had been posted to Paris. He came to say goodbye to me, looking very white. He had looked ill for some time. I thought it was with breathing too much chloroform. His clothes always smelled of it. I was sorry to lose him. 'Ary, do you really have to go?'

'*Je l'ai demandé moi-meme. Ah, Miss, c'est que je vous aime mieux que Dieu. Ainsi il faut que je m'en aille.*'

Such a confession commands entire respect. I have never made light of Ary.

The hospital was growing dreary. My two best friends had gone, as also my Scottish Nanny. The surgical side was closing down. The hotels were full of the tubercular. No treatment was then known for tuberculosis but the amelioration of fresh air and good food. I doubt if their diet was enlarged. Certainly they had no fresh air. I once had to go through the hotel looking for one of the nurses. Each room all along the corridors had four men in it with the windows tightly closed. They just sat there with nothing to do or think about till they died, which they did each in his turn, and were taken to the dying cupboard. The hospital had become a dying-house, quite as a matter of course. In the trenches or here, what did it matter? I admit I was not nursing them so can only give my impression. Of course at any moment it might be changed. They might send us a trainload of typhoid. We hadn't had that yet.

My thoughts must at this time have been elsewhere, for I remember very little of what I did. I had at least one serious case to look after and was beginning to feel a little more confidence in myself as a nurse. I went now for company to the office in the Casino, where the old sergeant and the gentleman seemed equally short of occupation. The sergeant amused himself, as the men had so often done, in trying to shock me, but he went much further. He went a very long way, with the most outrageous Rabelaisian grossness that must have pained his reserved and proper colleague. All ran off me like water off a duck's back. I understood it, and I understood him, I was simply interested in what could be said. It fascinated the old man, but had he succeeded in offending me, he would have been miserable.

In September Harold wrote that he was back in England, at Portmeadow in Oxford, finishing his very brief training before going to the front. If I wanted to see him I must come soon. Off I went, and he met me in London. We went to the current reviews, Violette Lorraine and George Robey still our favourites. The songs of the time were woven into the fabric of our being as I think the current songs always are for each generation of the young, but then they were ennobled by the omnipresence of death. It puts a size and an edge on everything.

The imminence of the front rocked our established if abnormal relationship. The last night I found my face being covered with kisses the whole night through, hour after hour till it was perforated and smarting from the morning's bristles. When it was time to leave me he sighed, 'Aren't you *ever* going to marry me?'

I think I may have said something like Perhaps; but marriage had never before been mentioned. I did not know if his question was rhetorical or the *sincerité du moment*, or real. He got up then, put on his Flying Corps uniform on which I had sewn the wings, and we parted.

I went back to Houlgate in a daze, but once there my mind was clear. For God's sake, instead of all this death, let us have some life. If a man only wanted to have an heir to his name, would I refuse? I ardently wanted to be given this to do for him. I sent a telegram saying Yes, and proceeded to pack up and close my connection with the hospital. In a very short time I was back.

◇

Portmeadow was a romantic setting near the tiny village of Wolvercote, which consisted of a few cottages, a church and the Trout Inn. The inn stood beside the river at the foot of a bridge. A narrow stream divided it from an island which now was covered with white bell tents, looking, especially by moonlight, like a medieval picture of a battle confrontation. This was where the pilots slept. The Trout too was like something out of Chaucer, so remote and simple, but the landlady could cook. Before the war it may have been a place where parties from Oxford came for supper, taking the long walk across Portmeadow. If it had a bar, it must have been somewhere at the back. I never noticed it. No crowds of officers came to drink there, no local merriment was heard at night. I seemed to be quite alone. The strip of riverbank outside the inn door was so neglected it had turned into a series of ivy grottos, one of which had a bench where I could sit and listen to the roar of water under the bridge. The omnipresent noise isolated me from the sounds of the camp, though so near. A narrow plank bridge crossed from the island to the inn, but no one crossed it except Harold. Inside the inn there was a good deal of noise at night. The innkeeper was a drunkard and perhaps bedridden. From his bedroom he bombarded his wife with bottles thrown at random down the stairs accompanied by ravings. But this forsaken and down-going place was my love and sanctuary. I could imagine nowhere I would sooner be.

We had decided to get married by special licence at once, and as privately as possible. I sent a telegram to Mother to tell her.

Two pieces of advice were offered me at this turning point. The old landlady hung over me watchfully.

'Don't you give him what he wants before you're married, dearie. Take my advice. *Don't do it.* It's always a mistake.' She couldn't keep it in, it seemed to touch her closely.

Mother sent Mary post haste down to Oxford to bring me a message. I met her in the Mitre and she stayed only long enough to deliver it. She was embarrassed and could not find words that she could bring herself to say. She grew red and scratched herself, but finally brought out,

'Mother says, if it's for *that*, don't.'

But, as usual, I did.

Interlude

by Peter Boston

Lucy and Harold were duly married, and in September 1918 I was born in an isolated rented cottage on the coast, about two miles east of Looe.

Within a year or so, Harold having returned to work at the family tannery in Liverpool, we were settled in the hamlet of Norton, in Cheshire. Although now being rapidly engulfed in Runcorn New Town, Norton was then a loose collection of about fifteen houses and two farms, without shop or post office. It had a railway station where a hand bell rung by the station-master was, in those peaceful days, a perfectly adequate notification to all within a radius of half a mile that a stopping train was due in ten minutes time.

Norton Lodge was a plain, and completely square eighteenth-century house, unpretentious but symmetrical and well proportioned, and commanded an extensive view to the south across a shallow valley of farm land. Only a few houses were visible, a mile and a half away on the far skyline, but the valley contained two canals and two railways so that the view was always animated by scurrying trains and, if one looked more patiently, the slow progress of horse-drawn barges.

The interior was generous, elegant and sunny. For about ten years we were without electricity and our evenings were lit by candles and paraffin lamps. Being sent up to bed with one flickering candle along the large bare landing was good training for the nerves since, if one panicked and ran, the candle went out.

Luckily the gramophone relied on muscle and clockwork rather than electricity, and, both my parents being passionate lovers of classical music, once I was safely in bed I would go to sleep to the accompaniment of Bach, Mozart, or Beethoven flooding up in slightly muted condition through the ceiling below.

Lucy lost no time in grappling ambitiously with the three acres of garden, and two of my earliest memories are of being introduced to the smell of a white rose and of being lost in wonder at a picture of an immaculate lawn and flower borders on the cover of a gardening magazine.

I have a vague memory of a visit to Lucy in a nursing home at the age of three or four, and believe that this was on the occasion of a miscarriage although I can recall no specific mention of the matter subsequently. At any rate, I remained an only child. Many years later Lucy told me that things might have ended differently if she had had a daughter.

The quality of the house itself, coupled with the love and effort expended on the garden, decoration and furnishings (many items made by Lucy's own hands) provided all the potential for a supremely happy family home. I was too young to suspect that the halcyon days might not be everlasting. In later years Lucy once told me that Harold never tried to make the marriage work. Her wistful memories of those Norton days were almost unbearably evoked by the Largo in Beethoven's third Piano Concerto.

Harold was, as he frequently quoted, 'a man of few words', but his words were usually surprising and passionate. He was intensely moved by music, painting and architecture, and ruthlessly intolerant of anything which he considered meretricious. The paintings of Alfred Munnings or Fortunino Matania would send him into apoplectic rage; so did our loyal and devoted gardener when he was once rash enough to state that 'no power on earth would shift' a certain stone which needed removal. He also caused a tearful riot one day in the kitchen after one of our maids had confessed that she was uneasy coming to the house at night, because she was frightened of the dark lanes. Harold got to hear of this, and marched into the kitchen with his army sword, telling the poor girl that if she was such a baby she had better wear that for self-protection. Lucy's diplomacy was taxed to the limit in preventing a mass walk-out. I may add that all our domestic staff were absolutely devoted to Lucy and continued to correspond with her to the ends of their lives.

With his intemperate tongue, Harold combined an acute and totally irreverent sense of humour. Self-important, pompous or solemn utterances by politicians, churchmen, royalty etc. would be greeted with shouts of side-splitting delight.

He took an intense pride in the manufacture of top quality leather, and frequently brought small pieces of leather home to be proudly displayed to visitors and myself. From my occasional visits with him to the tannery I was aware that the staff in the tan yards and warehouses regarded him with both affection and awe.

He was also an enthusiastic naturalist; the house was full of stuffed foxes, cats, moles and all manner of birds. Being a very keen ornithologist, he was always emotionally involved in monitoring the fortunes of every nest in the garden.

They were both early campaigners on behalf of the environment, and for many years Harold was engaged in a constant baiting of ICI at Runcorn, whose chimneys discharged smelly smoke over the area, leading to an ever increasing number of dead trees. He had special postcards printed addressed to the chairman of ICI stating, 'Further to my communication of. . . I have ONCE AGAIN to report that on . . . the air was polluted by filthy stinks from your Runcorn factory . . .' (I forget the exact wording of the text, but that was the gist of it.)

About 1930 Lucy embarked enthusiastically on the reading of hands. She would take a sheet of paper, blacken it with soot in the flame of a candle and then place the subject's palm on the paper and draw the outline of the fingers with a pencil. On removing the palm, a beautiful black-on-white print was seen on the paper, showing every line and wrinkle. Both left and right palms were done in this manner and a spray fixative then applied through a mouth tube. By careful comparison of these two palms, she would then propound the character and likely fate of the subject. The prints, which were highly decorative and remarkably varied, were festooned around the house, hanging from mantelpieces and cupboards by means of strips of sticky tape. This craze lasted for about three years but she then gave it up, saying that she had become too expert and could no longer bear to see the fate awaiting her friends.

We began to keep horses when I was about seven. Lucy went through the motions for a time, and even bought some very expensive riding boots, but her outings occurred with diminishing frequency. I suspect that Harold probably made some wounding remarks about her lack of prowess and bravery on temperamental horses. I exercised every day in the holidays and, from the age of twelve or so, accompanied Harold out hunting on Saturdays. Thus we spent countless hours together in the saddle. We never spoke much but forged a quiet telepathic intimacy.

I was about fourteen when a young newly-married couple appeared one day to play tennis and rapidly became our most frequent visitors. They were full of the sparkle of fresh conjugal bliss, and I thought that I had never seen a man so besotted with love as the husband. She was a keen horsewoman, and before long she was turning up in the morning to exercise the horses with Harold, who would come back full of spoken enthusiasm for her determined schooling of the horses and fearlessness over fences. I observed occasional unnecessary touching of hands. I was also surprised, a little later, to see the same phenomenon occur between the husband and Lucy.

I noticed these things without any deep thought about the implications. In so far as I thought at all about the direction of events, to me our two visitors were the most perfect company imaginable; therefore their continued presence, on any terms, was to be welcomed as a sort of extension of the family.

I was away at school when Lucy informed me that she was going abroad to Italy and might be away for a long time. I do not remember feeling dismay at this, since I was excited at the prospect of spending the Easter holiday in Florence. The three weeks we had there, opening my mind to the music, architecture and literature of the Renaissance, changed my life; and leaving the place to return to school was heartbreaking.

From Florence she moved to Salzburg, where I joined her for the summer holiday and a daily round of concerts and Mozartiana. At Christmas she was in Vienna, where I joined her again and at Salzburg the following summer. I was, by this time, becoming a connoisseur of continental railway stations and trains. While at Salzburg, she informed me that Harold had announced that he wished to marry Barbara. In my thoughtless way I said, 'Well, he can't, can he, because he's married to you.' She laughed loudly at this unexpectedly simplistic view of the world.

While in Vienna, she enrolled in the studio of Robin Andersen to study drawing and painting in oils, and this, with music, became the focus of all her enthusiasm. During my holidays we would go out into the mountains round Salzburg, and while she painted, I would do drawings in charcoal.

As I was quite as enthusiastic about my future step-mother as my father was, I tried to divide my holiday time fifty/fifty between the two ménages. This was, at times, a little hurtful to Lucy, although she never complained.

With the threat of war in the offing, Lucy decided to return to England, and in 1937 rented a flat in King's Parade, Cambridge, at about the same time as I went up to King's.

The Georgian north front of the Manor. Above the second-storey windows are the old arches left in the brickwork when the windows were lowered

Memory in a House

His memory he had about him like a scarf;
his thoughts a flight of starlings.
(Rabelais)

Acknowledgement

The extract from the article *Rageries de grosses pelotes* by Jerry Weinstein is reprinted by permission of the editor of the *Cambridge Review,* in which it first appeared on 2 May 1953

To my Son

The author in Vienna, 1936

Prologue

I first visited Hemingford Grey in 1915, when it seemed to my eyes the most forgotten bit of rural England, wonderfully left behind. The Cambridge to Huntingdon road had then hardly outgrown the pony trap. It was bordered by hawthorn hedges and wild flowers and just wide enough for two carts to pass with care, taking perhaps to the grass verges. The motor age was in its innocent infancy, cars were rare and mostly small.

A home-made signpost on a corner said merely TO THE BOATS ☞, and there one turned off into a lane avenued with immense elms, leading obviously to some total retreat. The tiny village (Front Street, Back Street) turned away from the river and in those early visits did not enter my consciousness. Some inhabitants were to be presumed. There was Mr Giddins who hired boats. The boat house (which as I write in 1971 still stands, though doomed according to village rumour) provided punts and skiffs.

As soon as one had pushed off onto the river, time was obliterated. These dreamy lethargic meadows and old trees had cast off from the stream of life, as we had in our punt, so that moving over the surface to the lovely sound of the punt pole striking pebbles on the bottom, we were doubly liberated. In many days on that stretch of river I do not remember seeing another soul boating, fishing or working. The only eyes were cows'. I bathed freely without a costume — a daring act in those days. The swim-suit of the time was a heavy, floppy, skirted thing, a real wet blanket. To sit naked under a small weir with the current rushing over one's back, or to swim like a fish among the waving water weeds — not in this condition so dangerous as one had heard — was real delight. The river then was crystal clear, one saw the weeds down to their roots and there were colonies of yellow water lilies with snake-like undulating stalks. The splash of the water expanded and wandered and faded away into the huge surrounding silence, in which every tiny sound of dipping swallow or busy fly or the high distant lark was separately enjoyed.

More and more now as the hum and roar and scream of engines grows and closes in, I remember the silence of my childhood and youth. As I lie in bed wakened by the flight of aeroplanes or kept from sleeping by the drone of dynamos from the poultry houses, I recall my night nursery bed in a town house. I re-hear the lamplighter's steps pausing, moving on and pausing, the clip-clop of a late horse and the following purr of wheels; then no sound until long before it was light, the chorus of cocks from the back-gardens. If we except the noise of the steam engine, which of course was pure drama, emitted by a loved and revered object which in the day-time one would go a long way to see and hear, the loudest noise of my childhood was the passage of the early milk cart rattling over the sets, and that only once a day. How it rang!

Pockets of divine silence still exist in blissful distant places. Their fascination is in the maintenance of what was a condition from the beginning of life, a natural beauty so taken for granted as to be unrecognised until it had gone. The present generation has no conception of silence. If it could be imagined it would be the silence of death, not of abounding life. Formerly it enfolded everything. We broke into it and it closed round us again. This gave great interest to sounds when they occurred, lost now since noise is the continuum.

In 1915 Hemingford Grey was wrapped in this primeval

A postcard of the house as Lucy Boston first saw it

quietness, which in fact remained unbroken for another generation. Every time I took a punt out, I passed the north front of the old Manor, of which I knew neither the name nor the history. It appeared a semi-derelict Georgian farm house, lived in joylessly if at all. Yet it held its position in space with dignity. It faced into a paddock of scythed grass, and was surrounded by pastureland, outbuildings and trees, its only garden feature a flag pole. Had it flown a Union Jack for Trafalgar? Some retired naval man perhaps had once lived in this sad, waiting house. I was not to know it was waiting for me, but as I punted past I gave it a friendly thought. If I lived there I would at least give it sweet briar.

At this time I was waiting to work as a V.A.D. in Addenbrookes' Hospital. All the males of my family had always gone up to Cambridge and I had three brothers and two cousins there, divided between school, university, the Suffolk Regiment and the Flying Corps. They all tended to meet in my lodging in King's Parade. Those in the services had motorbikes, on the carriers of which I travelled round and was sometimes permitted to career off alone. Later when I moved into lodgings chosen by the hospital for the better control of their nurses, the number of times the front door bell was rung in the evening was too much for my sour landlady. No doubt I looked bold and wild and hostile as the young often do, and the plea that it was my family was not believed. Gentlemen were not allowed in the nurses' rooms, so we sat and laughed on the stairs. For this I was dismissed by the Matron. I continued to skirmish (how else can one describe the sudden passionate, undeveloped doings of the young) in Cambridge, on the Cam and the Ouse, making it all part of myself, until I found a place in a French hospital in Normandy. After that I saw no more of Hemingford Grey for fifteen years.

By the middle thirties a slight ripple was discernible, but instantly discounted, of the coming invasion of beauty spots. We were indignant to find that one could no longer be sure of a boat at Hemingford Grey without booking beforehand, but still it was only punts and skiffs, and there was ample room for them to disperse. The river could no longer be thought of as my personal secret sanctuary, but it had the tranquillity appropriate to a long unchallenged way of life, a valid half though not the whole. Happily one had no foreboding of what was to be lost. The golden spread of buttercups, the song of warblers, the flash of the kingfisher seemed quite naturally immortal. My married home was in the industrial North, in a pocket of country depreciating rapidly under air pollution from Widnes. Its former hilly beauty showed ghostlike through, enough to feed imagination and melancholy in equal proportion. The distant Ouse was woven into my thoughts like a thread of faith. Such a place was beyond the reach of industry.

The break-up of my marriage caused me to move to Italy and Austria to learn to paint. Mussolini pushed me out of Italy and Hitler out of Austria, but by that time I was launched on a new career and did not contemplate ever doing anything but paint, all day and every day, with passion. I had become a solitary. I came back to Cambridge because my son Peter was at King's. I took a flat in King's Parade next door to my original lodgings and settled down to paint still life and to celebrate King's College Chapel by day and by night, outside and inside, in picture after picture. It was for me at that time the most important symbol in the world. I wished to record it stone by stone. I half lived in it, as the inside had to be painted from memory. I might have gone on for years pursuing this ambition, had not someone chanced to say, 'I hear there is a house for sale in Hemingford Grey.' I had not revisited it since my return to England, but such was the force of the latent past, or the magnet of what was to be, one hardly knows which, that without further question or thought I took a taxi out to that sombre house standing in a perfect position.

'I hear this house is for sale,' I said at the door. They asked how I knew. It was their intention but they had not yet begun to advertise it. (The house I had been told of was another which I had never noticed.)

1

First Acquaintance

All that I had seen of the house from the river was the Georgian gable end. The longer sides east and west were cluttered with lean-tos and outbuildings hiding the original features and compromising the barn-like shape.

Now for the first time I saw the unexpected south front. Here the walls were whitewashed over old plaster with bulges and facets to catch the light. On the first floor there was a Norman stone window with double lights and an arch with chevron decoration. It was beautiful and right, and that was its place where it had always been. It quietly dominated and enchanted one's thoughts. The stone outline of a second arch could be seen, bricked up but with a sash window inserted. On the ground floor a french window with elegant Regency panes had been set in the massive original walls. There was a lean-to covering the west wall which widened the house on this side to a squat, comfortable dowager shape, and from it a fantastic chimney in the form of a flying buttress sprang up over the roof. It can be seen in the photograph on page 196, laden with ivy. Huge yew trees hugged the building, which showed on this side a character the very opposite of the northern aspect. It seemed long settled, more or less adapted, highly romantic in a Gothicky way and yet endearingly villagey. It opened onto a big lawn surrounded by the rushy moat, another surprise. I had not known of its existence. Beyond the moat were meadows and a small orchard. It was all instantly lovable and possessed at sight.

I was shown round, and learnt for the first time that it is a Norman Manor house. The owners — Joseph Macleod of the Cambridge Festival Theatre and later of the BBC, and his wife — were proud of it, talking of the historians and antiquarians who visited it, and the research done on its history. They gave me the date of the building, 1120, as an established fact, which I received with willing credulity. I did not at once ask for proof and have found none since, but the builder, Payne Osmundsen, died in 1154. There was a Saxon building before this, and possibly a Roman villa before that.

It is clear nowadays why the house has so much atmosphere, because you can see the vessel that holds it. As I went into it first it was the atmosphere that took me by the throat and filled me with a welcoming and headlong excitement.

I needed to take the pre-possession in with me to survive the first discouragement of the interior. Only the two large rooms facing north with high Georgian windows had been considered suitable for living in. This façade is all that is left of a larger, higher house that had been built round the old one. It was in that now vanished larger house that the famous beauties, the Gunning sisters, were born. It was burnt down, probably in 1798-9. The Georgian façade had not been built square with the Norman hall, but at a fairly wide angle to it, which gives the interior an interesting expanding shape. It also accounts for the rather baffling impression the outside of the whole building makes, of being more firmly settled into the ground than is usual. The older southern half had been subdivided into pokey low-ceilinged ill-shaped rooms on different levels, served by a corkscrew wooden staircase on each side. Only at the head of one staircase on a cell-like landing the double light of a Norman window shone in the depth of its three-foot wall, making so powerful a statement of the reality that belonged to it, that already I began in imagination to evoke its corollaries and give it space. But if this should prove to be all there was, I would yet live in a house that had a window into the twelfth century. Opening out of this pausing-place at the stair head, there was another cell-like room of odd charm. Three sides contained doors and the fourth a sash window. There was just room for a small bed, the foot of which overlapped the recess in which the window was set. This had been the Norman entrance door. Opposite the window a panelled Jacobean door opened onto a closet fitted with shelves, but by lying down to look under the lowest of these with a torch the base of a small pillar could be seen — one side of the Norman fireplace. The other side was in a twin cupboard in the northern room. The third door led into the Brown Guest Room, a room shaped like a pencil box, long, low and narrow, into which one descended as into a tomb by stairs cut through the three-foot wall. It was painted chocolate all over, with one small casement window, as dispiriting a room as I ever saw.

I was offered tea in the dining room, out of which the french window gave onto the garden. The walls were dark brown wallpaper, the low ceiling Prussian blue, one wall was curtained with black velveteen. Behind this an opening gave into the blank wall of the narrow lean-to. The dining room had a small Regency hob grate containing two or three flickering pieces of coal, and at each side of the fireplace a corner of the room was boarded off asymmetrically to form lobbies, one to the kitchen, one to the stairs. It was so dark that I could not see what was on the plate proffered by my hostess. In my mind I threw this room away as impossible to make anything of. It could be useful for storing deck-chairs, gumboots, trugs and umbrellas, but nothing more. I would pass through it into the garden. Surprisingly it has become my life's centre. Everything goes on there, the garden and the house meet on its threshold and offer every pleasure. It is a room with panache. But that was in the future.

Looking back now, it is hard to know why I acted with

such certainty and passion. It was like falling in love. Faults were brushed away as having no valid reality, common sense or waiting-till-you-are-sure were not to be considered. I was going where it took me. I was in my late forties, I knew not a soul in the district and was going to live alone in this overwhelming atmosphere. Furthermore, to a practical mind the house was simply not fit for rational habitation. It had no adequate drains and all water was drawn from the well by hand pump; but this was real country living, almost romantic. Worse than that, it was ramshackle madness from top to bottom. For example, the servant's attic bedroom under the south gable was reached off a corkscrew staircase through a two-foot square hole at floor level, underneath a tie-beam, and could only be entered on one's knees. The beam had been cut into for half its depth to facilitate the passage of the rump. There was no way of closing the opening, so that the unfortunate woman sleeping there would know that anything coming into her room during the night must drag itself in on all fours. The little window in the apex was out of reach above the great tie-beam that spanned the room. I know now how that window lets in the moonlight, particular and searching. The room contained two beds and sentinel-box wardrobes which, owing to the droop in the floor, both leant forward as if about to topple. I was told later that the last maid had 'gone queer'.

Another curious feature was that the large Georgian windows of the 'best' rooms did not match the floors, so that the upper rooms had the top of the downstairs windows sticking up through the floor to light one's feet, while the legitimate windows were skied and disappeared through the ceiling. Nevertheless, in this hotch-potch, on one small landing one shared the light of the twelfth century, and in the darkest corner of the tumbledown draughty kitchen was a low Norman door into the main building. To these two magnets must be added the superb situation. I bought it then and there, with so little bargaining that I could read surprise mixed with contempt on the sellers' faces. Suggestively, their last words to me were, 'Are you psychic?' When I replied, 'Why, have you a ghost?' they laughed it off. No, no, they were just wondering. I returned to King's Parade till it should become vacant.

Towards the end of the waiting period I went alone to Hemingford Grey to gaze on the outside of what I now possessed. It was Whit Saturday again and only four years since I had last spent the holiday there. What had happened in England during my short absence abroad? The crowds on the river path were so dense I could only crawl along as slowly as in a queue to get within sight of my house, and the meadows had disappeared under the multitude of picnickers. I was incredulous and appalled, and suffered my only moment of real doubt. But the die was cast, as in marriage.

2

Exploration

I had by this time a small car, so that as soon as the Manor was vacant I could go over daily, taking my son or nephew or friends. I installed two beds and a table and frequently camped in the lower room. The previous owners had told me that they had explored thoroughly and that there was nothing more to find. I was unable to believe it, the whole house insisted that it was there. Finally we jettisoned doubt and bought pickaxes.

It surprises me that I cannot now remember the exact point at which we first breached the stuffing and uncovered stone. The whole interior was wallpapered – in places the layers of paper were a foot thick – backed by canvas stretched over studding. For a long time I kept a wad of wallpaper, meaning to steam layers off one by one back to the first to make an album of them, but this long and difficult job never got done. The house, practically unheated, had been desperately interlined. To make a hole in this was a commitment.

In one day Peter uncovered in the maid's bedroom the heads of three Norman arches belonging to the windows of the rooms below. He said that while he was working there the room filled him with terror and he had continually to look behind him. (We all experienced considerable unease in the house at first, and inexplicable happenings continued for a good many years.) As Peter up

Above: the north front and west wall with its two Norman windows, of which the right-hand one was restored as a door opening on to a balcony (hidden.) *Below:* the west wall, showing the door which replaced the Georgian entrance destroyed by fire. It has now been replaced in turn by a window.

at the top was discovering the arches, working underneath him I uncovered on the east wall the window belonging to one of them, and more of the Norman fireplace. This meant that we must pull out all the sub-divisions and also the floor of the maid's bedroom in order that the Norman arches and fireplace could be seen complete.

A chimney-stack like a steeple rose through the centre of the house, serving only two small Regency fireplaces on the ground floor. We felt sure the Elizabethan fireplace must still be there, bricked up. All over the house quoins of trimmed stone were now showing through gashes in the wallpaper, but we had not yet explored the less engaging dining room. Should it happen to have an Elizabethan fireplace, that would be one redeeming feature. An expert on Norman houses who knew the previous owners had asked if she might come and look at our discoveries. She assured us that if the fireplace beam was still there, it would be at four feet six inches from the ground. They 'always were'. This is a phrase I have come to expect from experts, who tend to think that anything that the very small number of remaining Norman houses happen to have in common must have been an unbreakable rule for the great majority that have disappeared. They try doggedly to fit this rugged and individual building into their fixed pattern, but it will not go. Under the expert's eye Peter gingerly tapped away a small hole at the height she suggested. (Economy in repairs was still a factor borne in mind. Holes were made where pictures could be hung over them if they proved negative. Later on all such thoughts were discarded. What must be must be.) The chisel met only brick, and again six inches higher, brick. 'Don't waste your money,' said the authority. 'There's nothing there.'

When she had gone I said to Peter that I was not convinced. In immediate agreement he picked up the hammer and chisel and began again. A foot higher than was to be expected we found the beam. It proved a fine thing, a seven-feet-four-inches span over a fireplace three and a half feet deep. The supporting sides are of chamfered stone. The ingle-nooks were complete with oak seats, and a vaulted brick oven was in the back wall. Over the hearth is a massive hook. All this had been left complete behind the brick partition. The little Regency fireplace projecting into the room had a vent for its smoke into a space big enough for a modern bathroom, over which towered the wide Elizabethan chimney. Perhaps its incurable smoking was the reason for the room's dark coffee wallpaper. It takes more than three or four coals to lift that volume of air three storeys high.

3

Restoration

The restoration of the house took two years, which were by far the happiest in my life, even in spite of the war which broke out as soon as the builders began. I propose to describe as accurately as I can what was done, because I think it should be put on record. The antiquarian societies that visited my predecessors continue to visit me, no doubt writing articles on the house and adding particulars to their lectures. The standard approach is for one leading member to say to another 'What do you make of that?' pointing to some restored feature. An argument then begins, exploring possibilities, drawing false conclusions. If I then interrupt, explaining that the restoration was done under my orders, that I know and can tell them, they do not want to know. I am spoiling their game.

Quite apart from what I know has been done, I have lived in the house throughout and it has seemed as if in a sense walls did speak. I lived in it when it was so stripped down that it had neither roof, windows nor doors, and the walls gaped in section from rafter to ground. It has a very strong personality, to which I submitted once and for all. I forced nothing, and faked nothing. I explored lovingly and yet seemed to know what would eventually come of it. Now after thirty-three years of living in it, it begins to be taken for my work of art, and in the sense that it lives in this century there must be some truth in that. Shamefacedly I remember Michelangelo who said his statues were already in the stone and he only had to uncover them. Did I then only find what I had invented in imagination rebuilding it to my dreams without realising I was doing so? The answer is No, and with all my conviction No. But it is a love affair, and like all old lovers the house and I have grown alike.

Beneath the wallpaper and the wooden framework, the subdivisions and the lean-to, the original building was revealing itself as a simple rectangle two storeys high with a steeply pitched gable roof. Its walls are of Barnack stone, three feet thick, except for the north end which is now Georgian brick. On the ground floor were arrow slit windows only. This was the undercroft or storage room. If it ever was vaulted no vestige of that remains. Its ceiling is heavily timbered with crooked and unsafe beams mixed with and overlaid by newer ones. It was covered when I came, and one look was enough to decide it had better remain so. The architect did not interest himself in the date of the timbers and I had not yet understood the importance of the historical evidence that was my responsibility. A lot of points could be cleared up now if one were to take the house to pieces again, but that must be for my successors.

The upper storey was originally the living quarters, extending from end to end, with two windows and a fireplace on the east, one window and the entrance door on the south, and two windows on the west. There is also a small window under the south gable suggesting a loft. [This window has been much altered.] Four windows have the remains of Norman iron hooks for hanging the shutters, and the two best preserved windows — south and east — have very curious decorative cusps in the twin lights, for which no antiquarian has yet had an adequate explanation.

The question most disputed (and how hotly, how positively!) is whether the building is an unusually small hall of which the little solar has disappeared, or whether it is a uniquely large solar of which the important hall has disappeared. If that were the only choice I would in common sense decide that the solar (for which there is an apt position on the east side) would the more easily be removed. Big ruins tend to leave traces. Also the big room as one lives in it has so much the feeling of a hall, a room for busy coming and going, not for retirement. Nothing less than a duke would have retired into this. Payne Osmundsen, who built it, was not even a knight.

But my business is merely to live here. I hope I have made clear the stark simplicity of the Norman remains — one rectangle lacking its north wall. Through the middle of the hall an Elizabethan or Jacobean chimney goes up tapering like a steeple. It stops now at the roof ridge and is shoddily topped with old yellow brick.

My architect was Hugh Hughes of Cambridge. He is an authority on Norman buildings and no doubt this interesting job was one on which he would have strong feelings. Owing to the war, petrol was scarce, so that he only came at intervals. On these occasions there was a ritual constantly disrupted by my failure to conform. Those who for the first time employ an architect often have the shock of discovering that their wishes are of no interest to anyone but themselves. On the other hand, I know one architect who left the profession because he foresaw he might come before long to murder some female client. I had found a house that, from that moment and for the rest of my life, was opening up for me emotions and interests of a range and depth I had never imagined. I knew what I wanted and I was going to have it.

The architect brought his assistant and the builder brought his son, and below him came the foreman. This was the hierarchy of the procession that went round the house. The architect would courteously request his assistant to draw in detail some plan he had outlined. The assistant would ask the builder if he understood. The builder would ask his son if he felt able to carry it out. The son asked the old foreman simply 'Can you do it?'

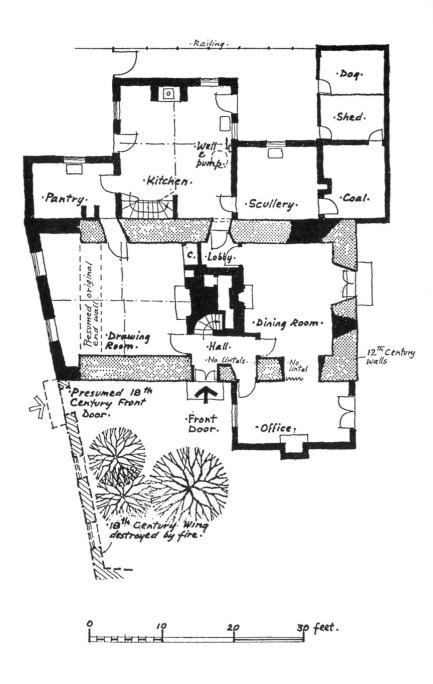

Plan of the ground floor of the Manor as it was in 1938: the north front, facing the river, is on the left

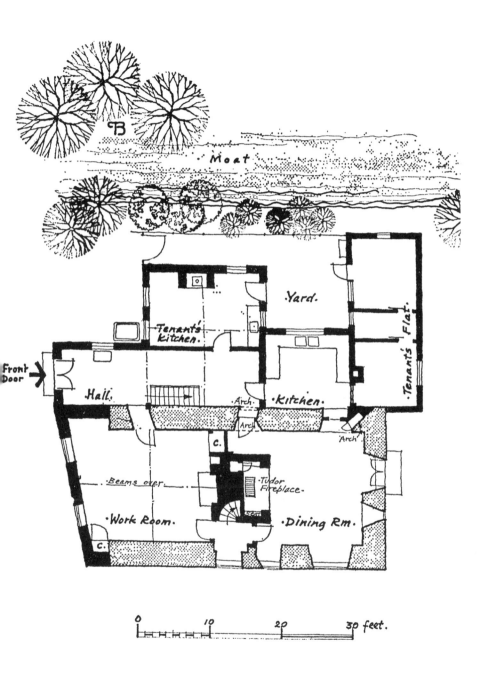

The ground floor in 1940, after the restoration of the house

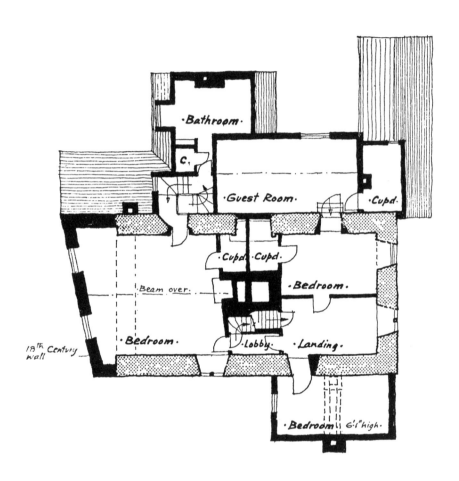

· Bathroom ·

C,

· Guest Room ·

· Cupd ·

· Cupd · Cupd ·

· Bedroom ·

18ᵗʰ Century
Wall

· Beam over ·

· Bedroom ·

· Lobby ·

· Landing ·

· Bedroom · 6'1" high ·

0   10   20   30 feet ·

The first floor as it was in 1938

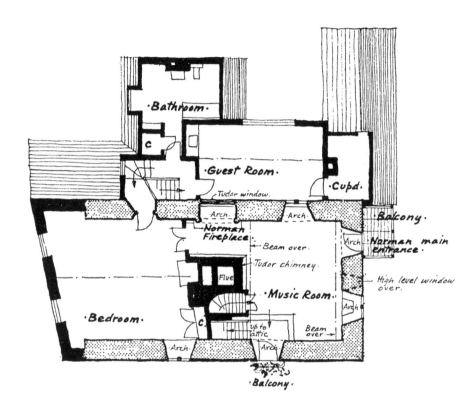

·Bathroom·

c

·Guest Room·

Tudor window.

Arch.   Arch

·Cupd·

·Balcony·

Norman Fireplace

Arch

Beam over.

Norman main entrance.

Tudor chimney.

High level window over.

Flue

·Music Room·

Arch

·Bedroom·

C.

up to attic.

Beam over →

Arch.   Arch.

·Balcony·

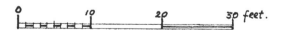

0   10   20   30 feet.

The first floor in 1940, after the restoration of the house.
Drawings by Peter Boston

The foreman said 'Yes' to the son, the son said 'Yes' to his father, etc., as in a nursery rhyme, back to the architect. At this point from the bottom of the social scale, too low even to have been credited with presence, let alone an opinion, I was usually obliged to say 'No'. It seemed to cause as much shock as if I had said it in church instead of now and forever after holding my peace. For the very reason that the house meant so much to me, the fight to preserve it left me shaking and exhausted.

Mr Hughes was responsible for the safety of the building, and all the panelling, staircases, windows, doors, etc., that he designed are charming. I greatly appreciated his readiness to let anything alone that it was possible to leave, but on questions of restoration we differed strongly.

These dreaded battles were rare, but every day some difficulty or new possibility cropped up which I on the spot had to settle. The builders were M. & J. Allen of Brampton, a firm whom I cannot love enough for what they did then. Young Mr John was always a friend and supporter, with an entirely individual smile which, while promising aid, was yet made impish by an appreciation of the slipperiness of all mortal plans. The foreman was 'Old Childs'. He was a small wizened man, soured with too much bitter cold in exposed places, very deaf and grim-looking. Nevertheless I recognised him as my real collaborator. For two years I spent most of my days with him in great amity and mutual respect. He revered the house and took pride in all that he did, and from the start showed that his first loyalty was to me. Between us everything that I wanted got done, often against the architect's orders. He made me follow him up onto the precipitous roof, though I have no head for heights. He showed me Roman tiles mixed with the others that were being replaced. (The roof had been stripped and re-slatted, retaining the old crooked rafters that were judged good enough. Again, I don't know their age, but the south end must be very much older than the north.) He showed me how, in building with stone, each piece must be laid with its grain in the right direction, otherwise it will crack. He only made one mistake, by taking out and re-setting some of the Roman tiles of which the flue of the Norman fireplace was made. He was upset that I didn't like it, for he was exceedingly sensitive. Once I had to give in to his feelings. I wanted the Georgian windows on the north side, which were seen from the river path, dropped to the appropriate position for the rooms they served, and I wanted the old brick lintels left in position and new ones put lower down. My reason was a good one. I wanted to keep a memento of the proportions of the larger Georgian house that had been built round the Norman one, a storey higher and extending to the west, giving a wide façade. This had been burnt down leaving only the present fragment. (It seems reasonable to suppose that the date 1799 on the plaster under the south apex, marks the restoration after the fire.) However, my plan would have meant that on the ground floor one curved brick lintel would have lain exactly on top of the other. Old Childs implored me, not far from tears, to spare him this, for, he said, his friends going along the river path would see it and say, 'Old Childs is past his job. Just look what he has done there!' Who could resist such a plea?

The lowering of these windows gave room under the gable for an extra window in the attic. I felt at the time guilty for putting in something at variance with the Georgian remains, but the view from up there is the last wonder of the house, as well as taking away the blind, sad look of the front as seen from the river.

The first work for the builders was to take out the sub-divisions so that we could estimate what we had to deal with, and also to demolish the lean-to which covered the west wall. This was only eight feet wide, two storeys high, and had that extraordinary flying buttress of a chimney to serve a minuscule fire. I was sorry to lose the extravaganza, but gained in doing so not only the clean outline of the house but a Norman window upstairs and two apparently Norman openings downstairs in the dismal dining room.

For simplicity, I will describe our findings room by room. If I deal with them at once they can be more easily skipped by readers with no special interest in Norman houses.

To begin with the dining room. I suggest that the smaller of the two western window openings might be a seventeenth-century adaptation of twin arrow slits, by knocking out the central division to make room for a mullioned window. The measurements are right for this and the stone quoins, lightly splayed, start at window height. (The larger opening has been too much disturbed to hazard a guess.) There is a corresponding opening on the east side. There is no sign now that these large openings were ever arched, though the arrow slits were. The eastern opening was entirely bricked up inside and out and when uncovered revealed two oddities. Firstly between the two brick facings was a middle wall containing a door which was painted with a sinister moonlight scene, much blackened and so obscure that one guessed what was going on more by the *frisson* it gave than by anything actually discerned. Whatever it once led to was now a scullery. I was making use of displaced doors and windows wherever possible in more convenient positions and this one was stored in a shed with many others. I would have kept it, but would never have used it. Anyway it has disappeared, though others still remain and are brought out as temporary wind breaks for delicate plants. The removal of this door and its surrounding framework showed that the solid stone of the right hand splay (the south-east corner of the house) had been chiselled away at a receding angle right through the wall, with a section of an arch remaining, and had been fitted at the outside end with a rough wooden-barred window, unglazed, which gave a view of the coal hole. Its purpose is beyond any imagining. The coal hole may originally have been part of the undercroft of the chapel known to have existed in the fourteenth century, but a cowshed window hardly fits with that. The whole of this opening, including the peep hole, is now panelled with cedarwood linenfold, and opens as a hatch into my kitchen. I am reminded of the late Mrs Butler of the Manor, Papworth St Agnes, whose kitchen hatch passed through the shaft of a twelfth-century privy. Old houses are eccentric.

Still exploring the dining room, I considered a pleasant carpenter-made Regency cupboard. It was recessed into the south wall and had a semi-circular back. Would anybody hack a deep recess out of a stone wall specially to put a cupboard in? Was it not more likely that a recess existed and gave the idea of a cupboard? We took it out, and so acquired our first arrow slit window, plastered over without trace outside. Inside, the arch had been replaced by a beam. We found a second arrow slit on the east side, of which one splay had been removed to let in a door — on the outside a late Norman arched doorway, on the inside the filled-in head of an arched arrow slit. Among the stones used for filling in was one showing the base of a window with slender side columns, possibly from the vanished chapel. To restore the window and keep the door was the most troublesome problem we ran into. But it now looks quite obvious.

The two big openings on the west of the dining room had been cased, and when the casing was taken away to reveal the stone quoins, we made the dreadful discovery that over them — the smallest span is six feet — there were no beams. The whole weight of the loose stone wall and the heavy timbers of the upper floor rested on half-inch planks which sagged like hammocks. Beams had to be found quickly before it all dropped, and at the thought of the risks of insertion the builders looked strained. Old oak was promised for the morrow. It was wonderful that it could be supplied so promptly, but it is the only wood they put in for me that was not hand adzed. Here again I must pay a tribute to my architect, because until he used it the word adze was not in my vocabulary.

That evening when the builders had all gone, a strong gale blew up. I was afraid to sleep alone in a building in such a precarious state, so I returned to Cambridge.

The south front, c. 1925. On the left the lean-to covering the west wall, with 'that extraordinary flying buttress of a chimney'. Round the sash window are signs of the Norman entrance door. Behind the tiny window above was the maid's bedroom

The south front, 1973. On the left of the french windows the first arrow-slit
window to be uncovered in the dining room; above, the Norman entrance door,
opening into the Norman hall, now the music room

At some moment in that wild night the three-foot wall split from top to bottom, but it did not avalanche. I have often wondered what I would have heard if I had stayed. A creak as of an old woman sighing in corsets, a pistol shot and a rattle of sand or the shuddering hoosh of a withdrawing wave? I am ashamed to have missed it. Next day with sweat and anxiety the new beams were put into place.

The former undercroft was now full of light. When the lobbies that had been cut out of it at each side of the fireplace had been removed, the room had a beautiful shape with wide deep window recesses succeeding one another along three outer walls and a corresponding projection into the room of the stone fireplace. The house is much smaller inside than it looks from outside, because of the thickness of the walls, but its shapes are so generous and simple that the impression is one of greatness. In spite too of the stern rectangular exterior, each room inside is a quite different shape from any other, they open out in a continual surprise, unlike the modern box where the very monotony is cramping.

Meanwhile, overhead, what is now called the music room stood like a fortress that had been sacked, light pouring in through all its gaps, its pale golden arches showing wounds, dripping pebbles and sand. Only one south window was complete. There were indications that it might have had the expected knee-hole seat, but these were not confirmed, so this pretty feature is guesswork, and our date is carved on it. In the plaster at the side of the window is lightly scratched EN 1639 (or possibly 89). I would like to meet EN. I like his hand. We stripped off all that layer of plaster except the bit bearing the initials, to expose the earlier, which is sandier, and warmer for being less smooth; but of course it is very patched.

Next to this window on the same side, at the eastern corner is the Norman entrance. The flat arch of the door had widened and the key stone fallen. The whole east wall of the house has an alarming outward lean. It is near the edge of the moat which tends to suck at the under soil. After the big flood of 1947, the newly mended arch loosened again. The process is very slow, but continuous. In thirty-two years it has widened from a hair crack to a millimetre.

In the east wall the doorway down to the deplorable Brown Guest Room had passed underneath a window head leaving that hidden but undisturbed. We only had to give it a centre shaft and fill up below the window level. (Later its outer arch was found above the ceiling of the Guest Room and was exposed by taking the ceiling out and letting the room go up to the roof.)

Beside it on the east wall the two pillars of the Norman fireplace stood freed of their cupboards and shelves. They have dog-tooth capitals, but the arch between them had gone, as had the upper flue. A seventeenth-century wooden window frame had been let into the back of the chimney. It would have received light from the Guest Room. This window frame was set in against trimmed stones, which proved to be the missing arch. We put that back in position, but above it the front of the chimney, probably a hood, was gone. We could only close up the space as neatly as possible. It was above the arch that Old Childs interfered with the Roman tiles of which the flue was built. Below the arch they are undisturbed. (Small pieces of Roman flooring have been found in the garden, but they could have come in any load of gravel or soil. Roman remains are fairly common in the district.)

Throughout the house every eighteenth-century doorway connecting with the new wing passed through what had previously been a Norman window, as the walls there were already partially breached. One such door was on the west wall of the upper room and had been widened to admit portly Georgian figures. One half of the window was destroyed inside and all of it outside. The half that remained was perfect to within a few inches of the exterior. It even has the Norman shutter hook still in it. The stones also have graffiti of consecration marks,

The Norman hall, the music room. The south wall with the window containing E.N.'s initials, the Norman entrance, and, above, the window formerly in the servant's bedroom

The music room. The Norman fireplace in the east wall, formerly hidden by shelves built into a Jacobean cupboard

showing that they must have come from the inside of a Saxon church, destroyed before this house was built. We felt justified in rebuilding the other inner half of the arch since we had proof and all the proportions for it. It did however present a problem — what to do on the outside. The window had once had a round stone head with the tops of twin lights cut in it, and that had gone, with its moulding. We decided to keep the opening as a door, giving it a balcony, but this involved building on the outer surface a stone doorway that was not original though built with Barnack stone found around the place in rockeries. This was the nearest we came to faking.

It was over the interior arches of these four openings in the Norman hall that I had my hardest battle with my architect. He was on certain points a die-hard purist. He wished to repair the arches with red brick so that future visiting antiquarians could identify at once what was old and what new. I insisted on using Barnack stone and having it hand cut. I think the beauty and truthfulness of the room fully justifies me. Besides treading on my architect's principles, the hand cutting of the stone introduced an element of discord among the workmen. The two masons considered themselves superior. They were fat well-favoured men who put on aprons over decent clothes. They came in their own car and ate their dinner inside it instead of joining Old Childs and his company in our glorious ruin. The masons — who must have been the last of their kind — were fascinating to me. They were father and son, and claimed to be descended from Huntingdon masons back to the Middle Ages. They said there was no church or old stone building in the county not built by their forefathers, and that this was proved by the family mark, which they showed me. It had a kind of comet's tail to which each generation added a tick. It was always placed underneath the stone, so that it did not show until something fell, when the culprit was identified and had to answer for it 'in this world or the next'. I asked them to mark the stones they put in for me, but I never saw them

do so. They condescended to me as to a child. I liked
talking to them, I liked their tools and being allowed to try
my hand. I even liked their grandeur. It was only when
they had finished and gone that I realised the jealous
contempt they had earned from Old Childs and his men.

The masons repaired the inner arches of the two upper
west windows for me. The outside of the second of these
in the northern half of the hall was done before my time,
probably by my predecessor. It is a copy of the original
south window but without chevron moulding or cusps.
The right-hand side is original (inside and out) and
possibly the sill, though this is of different stone. On the
eastern side of the north end is another window turned
into a door. This has lost its arch, now replaced by a very
old beam.

It opened when I first saw it, straight into the corkscrew
staircase from the kitchen, up which the maid had hurried
with the morning tea. Now my new stairs serve it and the
Guest Room. The latter, once overlooked by two windows
from the Norman hall, may well have been an Elizabethan
'gallery'. It has been suggested to me that it would have
been over an open arched passage way, later bricked in.
From first floor level the wall is very infirm half-timbering.
I doubled the window and shortened the room to
accommodate the stairs.

The northern end of the ground floor revealed nothing
when stripped except that the west wall had been much
altered. There is a flue in the thickness of the wall to serve
the fireplace of a vanished room. No trace of arrow slits
survive, nor of the old fireplace which shared the
Elizabethan chimney. The door is of the same odd shape as
all the others that have gone through window openings,
but none of the stone quoins are left.

The last alterations before mine, with the exception of
the makeshift plumbing, must have been done after the
fire that destroyed the Georgian wing. The owners appear
to have been hard hit, for the repairs done then were
inadequate, stingy and lunatic. A front door was put in the

west side, presumably to replace the Georgian entrance that, with its staircase, must have vanished in the fire. This door recently blew out in a gale, showing timbers affected by deathwatch. It has been replaced by a window. I have mentioned the omission of essential beams. Here the great central chimney had had one wall cut away at the base in order to wind a staircase through and over the Elizabethan fireplace. The old hearth was not then being used so there was little risk of fire, but the weight of the chimney was left unsupported. Putting in a girder to carry it was one of the trickier jobs. I now use the fireplace with the underneath of the stairs, thickly coated in asbestos, jutting over one side. This also is less than common sense by text book standards. I promised Mr Hughes that I would put a metal plaque saying 'Only fools light fires under their own staircase' to remind me and future owners to be careful. This has not yet been done.

Another shock was the discovery that the floor of the servant's attic bedroom, which spanned the width of the house, was only supported by the ceiling paper underneath and long habit. The beams no longer met the wall. An owner might well be ignorant of this, as the rot was hidden, and one does not keep on taking up floors to look. But downstairs in the big kitchen there was a grand old beam a foot through and eighteen feet long which, in full view and good daylight, stopped six inches short of its wall. The gap had been filled up with plaster and painted black to match the beam. This is evidence of an ingrained belief that if only appearances are kept up nothing too dreadful will happen.

The kitchen which I have now reached in my account, judging by this beam, might have been any age back to the fourteenth century. It was too large and too cold. I cut off it enough space to form an entrance hall and the new stairs. (The old had been unvarnished worm-eaten corkscrew.) The dividing wall now supports the previously floating beam. I put in two extra windows. There is a brick floor under which lies one of our two wells. I continued

Above: The music room, south and east walls. Formerly a doorway under one of the window heads in the east wall led down through the three-foot wall into the Brown Guest Room

Below: the music room, east wall, with window and Norman fireplace. On the left the great central chimney of the Elizabethan fireplace in the dining-room below

for several years to pump the water by hand, two hundred swings on the handle to get a bath, and visitors expected to pump their own.

The kitchen is outside the original walls towards the moat. There is another outhouse parallel with it, thus enclosing a small yard. This second building was terribly dilapidated and contained a dog house, a disused power house and the coal hole into which the mysterious window looked from my dining room. My theory, unsupported by evidence so far, is that the foundations may be those of the chapel. One of the de Greys left money in perpetuity for masses to be said 'for the soul of my mother in my chapel at Hemingford Grey'. These assorted sheds were converted, without digging to examine the foundations, into a minute flat for my presumed staff of two servants. The reason for what now seems a disgracefully casual lack of investigation was that if we used what standing fragments of the existing wall we could, it counted as repairs and planning permission would not be needed. I had not taken in that there would never be resident servants again. Every room in the house, including the bathroom, had a bell you could ring if you wanted attention. Not one of them has ever been used in my time here, and now all have been cleared away. Alone is alone, and 'Every butt must stand on its own bottom,' as John Bunyan said. With what reluctance and indignation I have had to learn to cook! I have acquired a limited ability — skill would be too much to say — but the indignation never leaves me. In fact as I get older I get angrier at the burdensomeness of it.

4

Living in the Ruins

I came and went between Cambridge and Hemingford Grey, sometimes alone, sometimes with friends, chief among whom was Elisabeth Vellacott, whom I had recently met. She had an entirely original type of face, as far from the accepted design as can be, yet so integrated as to be beautiful. Her expression was raffish, despairing and utterly charming, her voice and laugh delicious. Having met once we met often. Her face, I have said, was something new in human possibilities – or perhaps very old. Perhaps Isis resurrected. I have done at times many portrait drawings, and do not know how to describe it except in studio terms. It is quite easy to remember most faces without the head that backs them, as in beauty queens. To see Elisabeth as in her special way beautiful it is essential to see the delicately balanced shape of her head. Her face is extremely narrow and her features large in it, but the subtly merging planes of brow, temple, cheeks and jaw are all receding, as if retreating in close formation out of reserve, and all their lines are completed in the circuit of her head like the veins round an egg-shaped stone. Her long curving eyebrows run over her temples almost to the ear, but her wide mouth very oddly shortens in smiling. It is as though her face showed only as much of herself as the active contents of that skull wished to be known or could not hide. Not everything can be hidden, the resident needs a look-out.

Elisabeth's eyes are formidable. The line of her underlids is as straight as if drawn with a ruler across her face, not the faintest curve, serious or smiling, so that her eyes are like the sun rising over the horizon, fierce and very bright, but in happy moods less challenging and more star-like. Now that she is older the taut lines are loosening. Her expression is often quietly profound, but at any moment of excitement she can slip back and dazzle me with the presence of Isis. In those early days she was as nervous as a thoroughbred filly. She was not one for sleeping in my ruins with me. She expressed a fear of big trees, especially at night.

I would not call myself psychic but I have an awareness, and very odd things were registered by my senses in both my previous houses. In this house, my great trouble and self-contempt is due to my failure to perceive what is so inescapably there. Queer happenings there certainly have been, but they do not add up to any knowledge of the house's history or inhabitants.

There was a period when the demolition had reached its furthest point. The roof tiles were off, the floor boards up, the windows were gaping holes, there were no doors in the frames. It was what one might call the dead low tide of the house. The one room downstairs where nothing of interest has been found was left for me to camp in. It had a fireplace and windows, and a door that would not lock.

I cannot adequately describe the pleasure of living in a vital ruin. Melancholy could never be ascribed to it. The old house warmed its bones in a long balmy autumn. Butterflies fanned themselves on quarry-like sections of wall, birds and bees flew in at one side and out at the other, crossing between the two guardian yews whose branches almost touched the walls. From the time the workmen left until eight the next morning, ease and liberation and quiet captured me, with a sense of time both telescoped and expanding that was like the buoyancy of the sea. I was riding high on the pride that this actually belonged to me, and yet was aware that nothing ultimately belongs to anyone.

'They say the Lion and the Lizard keep The Courts . . .' I was living like a rabbit in its hole under the rubble, and I was absolutely happy. There was blackbird song and tumbling water, rising mists over the river bed and the call of owls. The smell of old dust and builders was an essential detail with its own invigorating promise. There is a future as well as a past. Or so I thought then. Now it is more questionable.

It was not that I was living in an escapist dream. The house was *there*. It was dominating. It was, and I hope still is, haunted and itself a haunter. It has a power felt by almost everybody who comes here. But what, and how? My psychic antennae are useless. Perhaps it is the unusual density of lives lived in it, superimposed and at length forming a sort of discernible sediment. There are different layers. The period of the Regency post-fire patching-up seems to have been evil. It is not fanciful to read that from the 'Tush tush, God shall not see it' attitude of the repairer. Nothing could be more different from the original building, so grandly optimistic in its intention to stand. I have mentioned the terrors of the maid's bedroom. They spread to the opposite attic (now so beloved of children) and afflicted the enclosed corkscrew staircase out of which that animal opening led. It was a relief when it was all cleared away and stripped down, but a considerable disturbance was left behind. It showed the character of a not very violent poltergeist, mostly in noise. I was only once frightened in the way one is supposed to be. One Sunday a young friend and I were weeding outside the front door of the supposedly empty house. This was the very first move that I made towards the future garden. We were bent, diligent and silent. After a while I said, 'There seems to be too much going on in the house. I don't like it.' Yes, she answered, she had been hearing it for some time.

We took weapons before entering, I a hammer and she

an iron bar — a measure of the unreasonable fear we felt in investigating a noise. I live alone and do not go armed. I do not take a poker when going to answer the front door bell at night. I think we knew this was not a snooper or a tramp, or an invasion of rats. We reacted to an instinctive need for some gesture of protection. We went in together. There was nobody on the ground floor, but as we went upstairs a little hand bell rang in the Norman room. It was of course a bell I hadn't got. The place was unfit for furniture. We grimaced at each other and continued up. There was nobody on the upper floor.

'Well, that's all right isn't it? I think I'll go back into the garden,' she said hastily. I would have gone with her, but the hand bell rang in the attic a short flight higher up. I went on into the expected but significant emptiness. This hand bell was to my hearing one of those genteel early Victorian things that stand on a table and are rung by twiddling the knob, in principle not unlike a bicycle bell. Could I have heard a distant bicycle through the unglazed windows? If so, why such a rush of panic? I have heard bicycle bells before.

As I reached the first floor on my way down, I heard a broomstick deliberately rattled down across the bannisters of my new staircase. This is a sound that could not be made any other way, it is positive and unmistakable. I yelled my friend's name — 'Anne Rose! Don't play jokes on me.' There was no answering laugh.

'Anne Rose! Anne Rose!'

She was far away in the orchard and came running in answer to my shouts.

This incident is told for what it is worth, which is perhaps merely that my hair had stood on end in the proper manner. If something occurs outside what we call the natural order, its very smallness may be more immediately unnerving than for instance, the eclipse of the sun to a tribe without astronomy, where holy awe must over-ride any other feeling. Very small cracks in our outer shell of reason let in very cold air.

Not long afterwards I was again sleeping alone in the house. I had dismissed my panic at the mild malice of that broomstick handle. It was the thought of tramps that was unsettling to someone living in an isolated house without doors. With the start of the war they had begun to leave London and the cities. I frequently passed them on the Cambridge road. What more likely than that one of them should choose an apparently empty building to sleep in? My room on the ground floor, being the only one glazed, was the obvious one to choose. It had outside shutters put in by previous owners, which proved useful for the blackout, but they were fastened by a slotted bar outside the house. In peace their only possible function would be to break the force of the north wind. They offered intruders every advantage. I did not think of this until later that night, after I had − infected perhaps by the general lunacy of the Regency inhabitant whose doings I was busy undoing − persuaded one of the men who lived in the village to come back at 10 p.m. and nail up from the outside the lockless door of my room. I had time in the night to reflect on my position. The invisible life of the house, whatever one imagined it to be, was whispering and shuffling about upstairs and passing through like the owls and the bats and the moving air, and if a sinister figure outside in the utterly silent dark, should begin to fumble at the shutter, I was trapped. I spent an anxious but entirely uneventful night, and opted in future for an open house.

I bought a flashlight as big as a shillelagh, with a hexagonal metal head that was nicely balanced for hitting someone if necessary. It gave me confidence of one sort, but on the other hand the weapon felt as if it could hardly do less than split open a skull. Without desiring their company for the night, I have a soft spot for tramps. W. H. Davies has given them a special claim for respect.

The beautiful autumn continued. During the day I was much in the grounds, which covered four acres of grass, with many trees, including an orchard and also a vegetable plot. Of garden as I should use the word there was very little. The time for planning it had not yet come. It will be described in due course.

I am not a worrying type, neither inventing nor dwelling on anxieties, and I loved the house beyond all nervousness. I lay down to sleep with it open all round me. The night was as still as a bird on the nest, and moonless. In the small hours I was startled by a very loud noise indeed. I have read since of a poltergeist that made a noise like a grand piano being dropped from a height. The sound I heard from above in the Norman room was in this class, crashing and reverberant, but I interpreted it as the sideways fall of a big step ladder with a bucket full of nails on the top step. The builders left such things about. The clatter as of rolling nails continued for quite a time, spinning and dropping into chinks. Many of the floorboards were up, so that a tramp feeling his way in the dark could easily have stumbled and upset the ladder. Ownership, like noblesse, obliges. I got out of bed, took my shillelagh and went up to investigate, playing the spotlight about as I walked. An incredible empty stillness had closed over everything. Nobody was there, nothing showed any sign of disturbance. The room had that feeling of nothing and nobody which is recognisable. It would feel different if anyone had even recently been there. What I had heard was totally unaccountable. On this occasion I was not frightened, only deeply puzzled. It had sounded like an accident, whereas the broomstick down the bannisters had suggested malice.

Peter often camped with me while he was waiting to be called up, and brought friends. I also enjoyed the company of a brilliant ten-year-old boy, Jimmy Johnstone, with whom I could share on an equality both music and painting. He dug in the banks of the moat looking for treasure. (I long to wear a Saxon ring.) He found what appeared to be a beaver's tooth, though he preferred the idea of a sabre-toothed tiger. The thought of beavers has pleased me ever since, suggesting a much older history for the moat than for the house, though some researchers

The author's son, Peter Boston, in 1938

now say there were beavers and bears in Saxon times. The whole valley is a maze of islands and waterways. The moat could have been a natural feature that only needed adapting to the defence of a house. There was a Saxon house here before the present one, inhabited by Bogo of Hemingford 1008-15. The river now flows within twenty yards of the obliterated northern side of the moat, but in the twelfth century the main stream of the Ouse was at some distance. It was artificially deflected by the de Greys in the fourteenth century to serve their mill, which stood till very recently. Originally it seems likely that between the moat and the river lay a discouraging bog. Huntingdon and St Ives received sea-going ships, so the river would have been a danger rather than a defence. Hereward the Wake rowed up it in his painted war boats to attack Huntingdon and Peterborough.

Elisabeth came when the restoration was a little advanced and we had at least windows. She painted a decorative panel for the old kitchen, and also frescoes on the new stairs and in my bedroom. She printed in her own studio linen for my curtains and chair covers. She has an infallible sense of design but no interest in practicality. At that time she sewed coloured sequins over her materials which though pretty were impossible to wash. Some of her sequined curtains are still hanging here with the dirt of thirty-two years upon them. She gave me lessons in block-printing, but found that I was incapable of an abstract thought. She has long since given up printing and returned to painting, but I still do it when curtains are needed.

As soon as the ground floor was usable, though practically unfurnished, one began to feel in possession, and therefore a dog was needed to celebrate the house-warming. I chose an Alsatian puppy, at the time of purchase the colour of a blue Persian cat, though they called him a sable. He grew into a black and tan but remained the most beautiful and intelligent animal I have ever had, with a faultless temper. I called him Arno after the satirist. When I first had him he was not reliably house-trained and excessively nervous. A ball that seemed to move of itself, frightened him as much as the broomstick handle had me. When I was in Cambridge with him in the flat, there was no place to take him in haste for his hygienic training but the green of King's College over the road. I could frequently have been seen at three o'clock in the morning standing in my dressing-gown on the green while Arno availed himself of the east end of the revered Chapel. I presume there must have been established precedents for this dishonouring, since I could not turn him from it.

At the Manor, life was more spacious and less difficult for him. His big floppy feet padded round everywhere after me. He was to have as a companion a rough-haired fox terrier pup. This was a combination of dogs I had always found brought out the most amusing qualities in both. An unknown little creature was sent off from the kennels in the west country and was somehow lost on the railway. He spent two whole days nailed up in a small wooden box with no food or drink and a hot bottle long since gone cold. Peter collected him at Huntingdon station and brought him home. We opened the box, and out leapt like a jack-in-the-box the thinnest scruffiest runt and failure of a pedigree litter, and flew straight into an attack on Arno. He had not lost a split second in claiming the Manor as his territory. He was fed and cleaned and made much of, and laughed at. He had been plucked of an obviously wretched coat and was practically naked except for his mustachios. His ears were awry like the points of a jester's cap, but his eyes were blazingly intrepid. As he grew up the cockiness of his ears left nothing to be desired. He is the Orlando of the Green Knowe books and the Cobweb of *Nothing Said*, tenderly loved throughout his long life and a constant component of my dreams.

The winter of 1939-40, the first of the war, was very hard. The Great Ouse was completely frozen so that one could skate from Huntingdon to St Ives. The ice became a thronged parade for families and dogs, and lasted so long that when at last it began to thaw several puppies were drowned who had never known it as other than solid. Icebergs then came down stream, big enough to slice away one side of my boat-house. My first flood followed. All the garden on the river side was under water and a chattering brook ran down the drive. It was clear now why there had never been a garden on the river side of the house. There had never been a gardener fanatical enough to disregard the frequent floods.

The war had not yet seriously disrupted life in the country. Work continued on the house until the autumn of 1940. My old furniture was released from storage, last seen by me in another life. No painful associations can detach one from furniture one has once lived with. I had been bereaved also of my Staffordshire plates and Trafalgar chairs, all the things I had handled and polished. Now they were here again. Everything was brought in or hauled up through the Georgian windows, and took its new place far more appropriately than before. I bought almost nothing new except some cottage industry rugs from the Shetland Isles and three old patchwork quilts. Rugs and quilts came from Muriel Rose's wonderful shop in Sloane Street, closed when she moved to the British Council. Every single thing in that shop was hand-made and violently desirable.

It was at this stage, when the workmen had gone and the house had become ours to live in, that one of the qualities of the Norman hall became its strangest and most inescapable feature. It has a profound, contained and powerful silence that is a continuing challenge. Nobody ever says 'How quiet it is just now', but 'How quiet it is!' Of course at first we were entirely surrounded by meadows, and during the war there was practically no motor traffic on by-roads. Most flying was at night and by modern standards a gentle sound. Yet even now the room imposes that intense stillness that suggests an awaited revelation.

5

War Yet Again

I now had to decide what part I was going to play in the war, whose future horrors nobody had yet imagined.

I had persuaded Elisabeth to leave Cambridge and live with me for the time being. She went to work on a farm, where she found carthorses and ancient rustics equally endearing. She looked like Harpo Marx, having much the same mad poetic face and straw in her hair and boots.

Meanwhile I considered what I was prepared to do. All the organised channels of work for middle-aged ladies looked grim and, what was worse, boring. What I had to offer that was of absolute value, not solely relevant to the madness of war, was my house. I remembered that in the First World War when I was nursing in a French hospital, I used to play my gramophone in the evening for the patients. There was an empty unused room where they sat on the floor leaning against the wall, and though I had only a dozen or so classical records they would always come to hear them again. I had in the last five years got together a large collection of records, and it occurred to me that I could now do the same thing on a grander scale. I wrote a letter addressed to the Welfare Officer at Wyton aerodrome, offering my house for hospitality, convalescence and particularly music.

The Padre was sent down to look me over. At first sight he was the standard stage parson, tall and young with starry eyes. They shone with the almost idiotic enthusiasm of a ten-year-old 'sold' on a plan, but his permanent wolfish grin was somewhat older. He was both brash and infiltrating, but quick off the mark, and a total candour now and then broke through from beneath the cloth. We came to know him very well. His curious character was unforgettable and indomitable, innocent and wolfish right through, quite a formidable combination.

At our first meeting he saw the possibilities in my offer and made none of the ridiculous mistakes about Elisabeth and myself that other more experienced officers made later on. Also he gave me credit for meaning what I said. As long as he was on the Station he used us and the house to the full, mercilessly, which was splendid. My suggestion of weekly concerts inspired him less, and he had to report to the Group Captain before anything could be agreed.

He began by sending down two charming boys, Eric and Vincent, both bomber pilots flying Blenheims. It was a good choice. It must have been just what they needed for they almost lived with us that summer. The war at that time was amateurish to a degree difficult to believe now. These two boys had a bedroom in my house and slept there whenever they liked. The Station had my number, and should they be required to go on a night sortie I was rung up. I woke them with cups of tea. They stretched and groaned like young dogs, and went briskly off with grins. Shortly after, a squadron would roar over the house from which one plane swooped down to shoot us up. The night might end with their return in the small hours to a sort of school dormitory supper, during which they told me their adventures, then they returned to their beds. Breakfast later in the garden. Or, they might be detained on their return to the aerodrome, in which case they rang up to report.

'Have you picked up our message?' Vincent once asked. 'We dropped it over your garden on the way out.'

I had not of course been out to look for something so unexpected. They came back themselves, determined that this note should be delivered. They found it dangling in a tree. It was the sort of clue that small boys playing Indians might design and had to be explained to me. It meant simply 'Here we go.'

As the number of pilots coming to the house increased, it became my regular practice to ring up Wyton in the morning to ask if my friends were safely back. It was all perfectly frank and information was freely given. It was quite a time before Security became a word in use. When it did, it became a mania.

This is perhaps the moment to mention a detail that still seems to me of no relevance. While living in Austria I had adopted their irresistible national dress. The dirndl is both practical and becoming. I had been wearing it for three years in Cambridge without comment and continued quite naturally to do so. I never thought of it as other than my clothes. But Hemingford Grey, as will be seen later, was narrower-minded than Cambridge.

In Austria I had received great kindness when I most needed it. This warm-heartedness went right through the population from the Von Arnims to Mitzi of the St Anton Gasthof. I do not know her other name. She can have no idea of the gratitude I have felt all my subsequent life. Her boundless humanity must have got her into serious trouble with the Nazis — unless she outwitted them. She was very quick.

I met almost no one in Vienna who had not some Jewish connection, and any of those who were lucky enough to get out I most gladly received. I was not even aware that some were leading nuclear physicists. The atom bomb was a wild but still avoidable idea. To me, an exile was the opposite of a spy. Who should hate a regime more than its victim? I loved all exiles because I had, though for a different reason, been one. Much later on, after the war, I learnt that most of my particular friends had been engaged on very secret (but not treacherous) work. This continuous pattern must be due to an innate preference on my part for people to whom reserve is natural.

Quelque chose derrière
Convient toujours garder

I had a loyal woman who cooked for me in Cambridge and when I was in Hemingford Grey came out daily in the train to St Ives bringing her bicycle to complete the journey. The spring floods finally defeated her, or it may have been because I then took on a second woman to clean — my fighting bantam Ivy Violet, a diminutive self-willed cockney comedian who ruled the roost for thirty-three years with arbitrary devotion. She had unanswerable repartee for every occasion. Like Birkie the terrier, she no sooner entered the house than she took it as her own.

Mrs Merryweather was house-proud, and her husband had bought her a new carpet that was the great joy of her life. Constant reference to this caused sniggers between Ivy Violet and a temporary gardener (now my prop and stay). Mrs Merryweather could never have forgiven that. Later she was one of the unlucky ones. She was allotted slum evacuees who so defaced and defiled her house that she was reduced to sitting on the pavement outside it in tears. She couldn't bear to go in. I forget how this injustice was resolved.

Evacuees arrived in Hemingford Grey, wrecking many lives. Elisabeth and I came in one evening to find a woman and toddler sitting on the back door step. They came from the East End and had already been sitting outside an empty house for some time, having spent the previous night lying like sardines on the floor of some church hall in St Ives. No one had told us to expect them or I would have had some welcome ready for them, however great my reluctance and fear.

Elisabeth and I had been sleeping in the annexe in order to leave the main house empty for 'the boys'. We had to turn out our things there and then and establish the newcomers. They were lucky because they got a complete tiny flat with kitchen and bathroom. We were lucky because Mrs Lilley proved to be a sound and very amusing character. We had no sooner handed over to her than she began furiously scrubbing down the whole place. 'It's too dirty for me,' she said with easy candour. Her toddler from the start addressed me as 'Bomb-bomb'.

Through Mrs Lilley we heard willy-nilly all the gossip of the village, how the different inhabitants treated their violently unwanted guests. There were stories of shocking unkindness and farcical human quarrels.

The legal minimum, we were told, was provision of a bed and access to water. One owner of a large house took this literally. She gave a mother with two children a dirty unheated attic containing a bedstead without bedding. I don't know where the water was, but the kitchen was forbidden. When the wretched and homesick evacuee asked if she might borrow a brush to sweep out the attic, she was told she should have brought her own with her.

Another woman gave two of her rooms, properly furnished, to a mother with a large family, but ruled that she could not and would not have them trooping through her hall. They were forbidden the front or back door and told to climb in through the windows. Had I been an evacuee I think I should have preferred this arrangement as being more independent and not all that inconvenient when you got used to it, like children playing house. But no sooner had the news arrived in London than the outraged husband came down and took them all back to the bombing. His wife and family were not going to be treated like monkeys. I hope they survived.

My Mrs Lilley was terrified of the country. She feared to take the five paces across her pretty little courtyard after dark. After a time, she asked with propitiatory apologies, if she might have her husband occasionally for a Saturday night. It was a matter that had aroused much feeling in the village. Women and children of course had to be saved. Men were for bombing. There was nothing in the Evacuation Order about having the husbands too. In a village widow's house a strange man was a figure of all menace.

Mrs Lilley herself did not give her man much of a character, but she looked to me well able to control the situation. She was allowed to have him whenever he could come down. One of her friends, on the other hand, when asking the same favour from her hostess was refused outright. The wife pleaded that you know what men are. If it wasn't her, he'd get someone else. Then, said her hostess, she must do what other people did — take a punt. It only cost two shillings.

'Just imagine!' said Mrs Lilley, incredulity all over her face, 'TWO SHILLINGS for *that*.' I have seldom heard more derisive contempt put into one word.

Mrs Lilley was the last evacuee to leave the district. She was permanently buoyant and Rabelaisian and got on well with everyone including Ivy Violet. I still hear from her occasionally. I was indeed lucky.

◇

Ivy Violet produced a gardener for me to replace the young one who had been called up into the Navy. Fred Broomfield had spent all his life as butler-valet-chauffeur to a Royal Academician living in this village. After his employer's death he had a total breakdown from which he was just recovering. He gave as a reference his old gentleman's daughter-in-law, who told me she would be glad to be rid of him. He had no manners, could not be taught to call her madam, and when spoken to gave answers such as 'Naw,' or, 'I might and I mightn't.' I did not feel my self-respect would be chipped by these naturalisms, while on Broomfield's side, hearing that I was a painter, he slipped consoled into his lost niche and remained as the basis of my life for twenty years.

Broomie, as he came to be called by everyone, had the face and bearing of a marquis in an eighteenth-century portrait, with the extraordinary added quality of innocence. I often wondered, looking at him and his fine hands, who his father was. Aristocrats may be born anywhere. He was untouched by baseness. He can never have done a mean

Above: Sir St John
Gore, from a pen-
and-wash drawing
by Elisabeth
Vellacott
Right: Broomie

thing. With so much innate nobility, a lack of subservience was natural. He had been through the First World War as a truck driver and had been badly gassed. His was not Gray's elegiac innocence. He had seen evil.

One of the Londoners who had retired to Hemingford Grey was Sir St John Gore, of Omdurman and Ladysmith, once a superior officer of the young Winston Churchill. He suffered from arthritis for which he took an erect disciplinary walk every day along the river bank. His rule was that he must touch the far kissing-gate at least with his stick before turning back.

With the unbridled pride of a discoverer or of a mother determined to show her new baby, I made him, clearly reluctant, come in to see my stony rooms. Thereafter he came nearly every day for elevenses. There was a schoolboy truancy and secrecy about his visits, because his hostess regarded Elisabeth and myself as neighbours to be avoided at all costs. For one thing I had had a brush with her about the right of my dogs to use the river path as much as hers. There were occasional fights and she wished mine permanently confined. I offered to shut them up every time she walked hers if she would telephone me before setting out, but this was indignantly refused. It would have been neighbourly. Consequently, if it happened that she and Sir St John walked along the river together, he and I were total strangers, but he would be here again at the first opportunity. He was a great entertainer, prepared to croak out whole acts of Gilbert and Sullivan, or deliver a first-rate homily from Polonius, which sounded for once quite convincing. He could have given that advice to a nephew and it would have been acceptable. His conversation was a joy — from accounts of his sister in London who would not use an air-raid shelter because she found a raid much cosier in bed with a novel and a cigarette, to far-fetched memories of walking with another young dandy along Piccadilly betting on the cigarette ends that they saw swept up off the pavement by the ruched petticoats of passing beauties. He had done a little painting and loved talking Art School with Elisabeth. He was a widower and for all his gaiety an immense sadness lived with him. He often spoke of his wife — 'that dear Lady, always so tired.' He made it sound the ultimate grace. One day he came in to me much shaken. He had been in St Ives, and there had seen, displayed for sale in the window of the one antique shop, his own familiar dining room suite, at the end of which that dear lady in ghostly memory still sat.

Sir St John also enjoyed Broomie's company and always talked with him. His name was too much of an unknown sound for Broomie, who shortened it to Singey and as such always addressed him. The familiarity seemed to be enjoyed. They would stand together in the garden, Broomie upright in his huge boots, his marvellously beautiful bald skull playing with the light, Sir St John thin as a clothes hanger in his ancient British warm, his boots shining like mirrors, Singey and Broomie to each other, man to man.

It was a long warm summer. The Padre used to bring down bathing parties. They undressed in the garden and hung their shirts and socks over the bushes while they bathed. I detested this, but could hardly oppose it. I had not then developed my capacities as a gardener. It is impossible now to imagine dirty small clothes hung on my roses that are treated with the greatest reverence.

There was one splendid creature who came to the bathing parties. His physique was the perfection of supple unexaggerated muscle. He was an athlete and a campanologist. The bell-ringing had perhaps given him his powerful arms. His face was smoothly sculptural and so strong one felt nothing at all could unsteady it.

I was seeing Sir St John off at the front door when this young man happened to be returning from a bathe. He had chosen to walk up the garden on his hands, legs easily in the air, and was accompanied by my young Alsatian Arno who in distraction was running round him, alternately licking his face and nipping his arms, to advise him, to warn him, that this was not how it is done. He should be the other way up! When he finally got to his feet he was emotionally congratulated by the dog, and I introduced him to Sir St John. Immediately under my eyes it became a true military occasion, as if he had been cited for an award. Sir St John's spectral form was in command on some remembered battlefield. It was momentary but startling. When he had dismissed the young sergeant he turned to me and said, 'That's the kind of fellow I always like to have in my regiment.'

If I could turn time back I would like to see an interview between Sir St John and the Padre, for my enlightenment by his old wisdom. But I do not think they ever met. Sir St John was religious both naturally and conformably, but not blindly so. He attended church regularly, but once told me that all his life he had taken a pocket book to church in which to write down anything memorable that might be said in the sermon. It had remained blank.

The Padre was often at the house. He used to write his sermons on Saturday nights sitting in the ingle-nook of the big fireplace to the accompaniment of Beethoven's Fifth Symphony, which he found necessary, and with everybody milling around. This is what I mean by infiltration. He could not control his ebullience or the words that came to his lips. For instance, there were some lengths of tree trunk lying in the garden that I wanted moved. With his usual helpfulness he brought a team of men to do it. It took three a side to lift one piece and as they staggered across the lawn the Padre went ahead and guyed the burial service. 'I am the Resurrection and the Life' — the words he said over the bodies of their young friends in the RAF cemetery. To a near believer it was profoundly shocking. I can see that to a total believer a ritual too often repeated may come to seem a charade, not to be respected as one respects the truth it represents; but parsons' jokes should be kept for gatherings of the Cloth.

Elisabeth had left the farm and now undertook the cooking for the supper parties laid on by the Padre.

Throughout the war we entertained air crews, or the parents of the dead, or merely the homesick, for lunch or supper most days, without ever receiving any extra rations except an occasional half pound of sugar from the Padre. We must have been allowed a widow's cruse, for we had nothing on the black market. Elisabeth had a genius for making something out of nothing and of course the table, when, as they used to say, they got their feet under it, looked more appetising than the Mess. There was always a concoction of some kind, and it was always edible. I can't imagine now what we ate, but there was a round object known as Village Pie which was organised by the Women's Institute and distributed once a week. We were constrained to eat it for a while but soon found it impossible. However, the pies were useful as a Friday treat for the dogs, bowled along the lawn to be coursed and brought down. Towards the end of the war when the buns obtainable for the coffee interval at the concerts had become too repellent, I discovered that there was a concession for wedding cakes. Thereafter we had a weekly wedding, the cakes being initialled in icing sugar with imaginary musical brides and grooms — A. T. and K. F. (Toscanini, Kathleen Ferrier) etc. The confectioner never questioned the likelihood of my catering for so many couples.

Various displaced streams of life flowed through the Manor from a Europe overwhelmed. We were on the books of the *Amis de France Libre* to receive for leave or convalescence whoever they sent. In 1940 Jean and Robert were our first Free French — two eighteen-year-olds from Le Havre. Jean was the typical sallow French schoolboy, unmuscled and melancholy. Robert was a dynamo of tragedy and passion, mad to be in action. He was the spokesman. His story could have come out of the New Testament. There were four friends who had decided to escape to join de Gaulle in England. Robert had arranged with the owner of a rowing boat to bring them across. The time and place were fixed. As the hour drew near, one came to excuse himself, saying, 'My father and my mother have begged me not to go. For their sake only I must stay behind.' A little later came another saying, 'I have been offered an opening in business, the chance of a lifetime, and therefore I cannot come.' The third came and said, 'I have just met a wonderful girl. I am in love, and therefore I cannot come.'

Robert therefore set out alone, and the only person to see him off from the quay was his small brother, too young to arouse German suspicion. He found the boat was to be shared by Jean and an English lady eighty years old. They and their boatman started across the Channel in the dark. I cannot remember now how long it took them. It cannot have been less than two nights and two days if the three men rowed in shifts. Of the intrepid old lady I know nothing. Probably they were not able to speak to each other.

We did what we could for these two inconsolables, who stayed only a week. I had an English visitor here at the time whose behaviour towards them has shocked me ever since. Robert wrote later from North Africa to say Jean had been wounded and invalided out, and long after, on the eve of D Day I received a telegram, written in French and so mangled that it was unreadable. It was sent from an East Anglian port, signed Robert, and he asked to be allowed to come for a night before . . . I think the rest and the address for my reply had been scrambled deliberately. No plea for a repetition of the message had any result. I could not answer it therefore, though as far as I knew he had no other friend in England. God knows what he found in France, his own death most probably as I never heard from him again. The first Free French soldier to set foot in France on D Day had his name, Robert Latour, and was instantly killed.

◇

To return to 1940, Vincent had a fiancée in Jersey, which was his home, now overrun by the Germans. He showed me her photograph — an exceedingly beautiful girl. His operational flights made it possible for him to drop tokens, handkerchiefs with his initials, etc., near her seaside home, and ultimately a message to wait for him on a certain beach. He contrived somehow to be flying alone on the appointed day, and actually saw her waiting there, but before he could land a patrol of German fighters appeared and drove him off. I got the impression that it was more a boastful romantic adventure than real heart-break, he was so much a boy. But the young are often more cruelly involved than their elders believe.

We heard a lot about the Padre from his flock. Although he was indefatigable over welfare work, always on the look-out for things he could do, such as seeing that those in hospital got their letters promptly, looking after anguished parents, helping those on leave to get away, he was unpopular because of his incessant scrounging — chiefly of people's cars for charitable purposes. He excused himself by saying he was God's Beggar, but it did seem to slot very easily into his character.

Vincent was particularly annoyed by him. The Padre never failed to see the squadron take off, nor to be there waiting when they returned from a raid, but when the crew, some of whom might be wounded, who had kept their damaged plane in the air minute after minute for what must have seemed a lifetime, at last were safely down and stumbled out of the plane, he would tell them off for swearing. If it was the take-off, he would be distributing New Testaments to read on the way out or in case they were taken prisoner. Vincent had thrown them back at him, saying they weren't going on a paper chase. He confessed this to me afterwards. 'I feel awful about it. It worried me all the way out, I know I shouldn't have said it. But when we get over the target you can bet I say my one word prayer all right. He doesn't think.'

The Padre also confided his difficulties. He knew he made himself unpopular, but felt that treading on people's feet was part of his job. I did my best to moderate

The author putting a record on the gramophone

his tactics, but probably his conversations were another stratagem for leading me to think on the right lines. He had got himself into trouble by a sermon in the station chapel on 'Love your enemies'. It caused a number of men to refuse Church Parade and the Padre was reprimanded by the CO. There were other aspects more suitable to preach about. 'After all,' he explained to me, 'I am an officer in the RAF and under orders like any other. It's a man-sized job here and I don't want to get sent away. But what am I to say to men who come to me in trouble?' What indeed.

One day Vincent brought the news that the squadron was to fly to Malta, not in a body but one by one. It was a dangerous flight because their Blenheims could only carry enough fuel to get them there with perfect navigation and no unforeseen difficulties.

Eric was among the first to go. His fiancée came to spend the night here and we gave him the best send-off we could. He was lost at the very end of his trip. Two nights later it was Vincent's turn. He came here to leave me his motorbike for Peter, gave me the most theatrically stylish and heartbreaking salute and was gone. He arrived safely in Malta, moved on to Egypt and was killed in action there three months later. Here is his last touching letter. Perhaps before he died he received the mail he so longed for.

RAF Headquarters
Middle East
Egypt
5 December 1940

Dear Mrs Boston,

Here I am again! I do hope you have received some of my letters by now. I have not had any at all sent here yet, they do take a time. I am quite sure I shall go crazy when one does come.

Give Elisabeth my love and ask her how the painting is

going. I just close my eyes and I can see the dining room fireplace, looking so very grand with its 'Wyton figures' keeping beautifully warm. I am sure it must be wonderful beside the fire these days. I have nearly forgotten just what a fire looks like, one made with logs and coal and things, not one made by incendiary bombs, which as you can well imagine, are very numerous.

Have you been having bombs at all Wyton way? I do hope not, if they so much as even chip one little stone of your most beautiful home, they will have me to reckon with. I heard recently that the old Squadron had left Wyton, do you still have fellows for tea, etc.? I did love it and it helps an awful lot when I think of the happy times I have spent at your home. I wonder how many years will go before I see it and you again.

Cheerio Mrs Boston,
Love to you all
Sincerely yours
Vincent xxx

P.S. I will be able to write a more interesting letter when I hear from you, but at the present there is very little to write about.   V.

These two were our first casualties. Later on we lost friends as fast as we made them till it became meaningless. For Eric and Vincent and three others in particular I mourn to this day. One of them has already become nameless, but their faces are with me in the house.

◇

In February 1941 the Padre organised the first gramophone concert. With characteristic drive he laid on an RAF bus to bring the men.

The music room was still unfurnished except for a couch and four small chairs. How was I to seat a busload? Rows of chairs facing the gramophone would kill anything. I collected all the single mattresses in the house and laid them on the floor round the room, with others propped up against the wall to lean back on. These were all covered with whatever I could find that looked harmonious, largely fur and sheepskin against the cold, and piled with cushions. The back seat of my car was found to fit exactly into the splay of one window with a mattress curved round the recess behind it. By this means twenty-five men could sit or lie at ease. My eldest brother, the artist James Wood, referred jibingly to 'Lucy's fur-lined Valhalla'. These divans, an improvisation inspired by necessity, were in keeping, but a very great labour, as they all had to be restored to their bedsteads in between the concerts. Wooden shutters made a perfect blackout, and when the room was lit with a multitude of candles it was so unlike anything to be found on an RAF station as to make the men blink with incredulity as they entered. Nevertheless, the most frequent comment was, 'It is like coming home.' I used to think of it at that time, looking round at its bare stone cavities, its visible age, as the pit out of which we were digged, but in any case, the house has of itself, noticed by everybody, an embracing friendliness for which there is no accounting.

Before the war, in my desperate Continental solitude, I had discovered music as a possible answer to all trouble, in that, if there were nothing else, it was enough. I was offering it on those terms with a fanaticism that might have been ridiculous but for the keyed-up emotions of war. It must have given me a kind of authority, since the oriental ease of the room never gave any of the RAF the wrong idea. Strict music was what they came for. In the interval we served coffee (real) and buns (horrible) in the dining room, using beautiful jugs and china. Elisabeth and I were always in our evening clothes. We gave the music all the ceremony and also all the ease we could devise.

After the first concert I knew I must have a better gramophone. I advertised for a second-hand EMG, stating what it was to be used for. Immediately I was rung up by

Listening to a wartime concert in the music room

Captain Toller (then unknown to me) who said his machine was lying at home un-used and he could deliver it that very morning. He brought his excellent EMG with its immense horn, and left it unconditionally for the duration, no questions asked. It was of course hand-wound, with thorn needles that had to be changed for every record.

This was a good thing. I doubt if a roomful of people would sit still and silent for two hours listening to the radio, but if someone is working quite hard to keep the mechanism going it helps to focus attention. The acoustics of the Norman room have always seemed to me quite

The music room, 1943: from a painting by Elisabeth Vellacott

extraordinary. It contains the sound whole while allowing
it to expand and explore.

The Padre attended the first few concerts, but when the
music was over and the audience sat on unwilling to leave,
he tried to turn it into a Christian debating society, sitting
in the centre smoking his pipe and giving leading
questions. This was intolerable to me and I told him so. He
might have answered that he was organising the concerts
and must be allowed some say in them, but he did not. He
might have been offended, but it was impossible to offend
him, he took nothing personally. However, he ceased to
attend concerts since he could not use them, but continued

to promote them and to frequent the house.

The first concert from which the Padre was absent was attended by someone very different — a corporal with nothing above the eyebrows and a policeman's boots and slow heavy tread. I watched him with surprise, he was so alien, unmusical and unsure — a fish out of water and conscious of not being wanted. I did not then analyse any further. The next week he was replaced by an officer who was highly intelligent, literary, artistic and musical, but far more pushing than a guest ought to be. Afterwards I said to Elisabeth as we talked over the evening, 'Who do you suppose that was with his foot in the door?' It was not long before we understood. However, C.H. was of our kind, able to understand our outlook and recognise our sincerity. He continued to watch over us for a long time, giving us I am sure all his protection and becoming an intimate friend. When after the war I met him again and thanked him for shielding us, he blushed painfully. It had never occurred to him that we knew all along that he was from Intelligence — there every day, almost living with us. But his friendship was real.

The concerts flourished. Once a week was not enough, so we decided to have a real highbrow evening as well, as several professional musicians came regularly. However, everybody came to both. They asked for what they wanted in advance and I always tried to get it. Two things I ultimately had to pretend I had broken, or we should have had them weekly for ever — the *Enigma Variations* and the *St Anthony Chorale*.

One night while a late Beethoven quartet was going on and on, a newcomer's disappointed enthusiasm burst out, 'Say, Missis, ain't you got no Handel? Give us some Handel, do now.' He was promised it for the next item.

Once or twice we had the honour of entertaining Dr Dykes Bower, organist of St Paul's Cathedral, then serving as RAF Adjustments Officer. One evening he came down in a state of rage that had to be given vent. The Padre was organising a Nativity Play — perhaps performed by the children from married quarters. He had the ill judgement to ask Dr Dykes Bower to play 'still music off' at suitable moments. Perhaps he thought it only tactful to ask the senior musician on the station, who might otherwise be hurt; or perhaps he planned it as a draw for the public, or as a way to coax Dr Dykes Bower to take more interest in the music of the Chapel. Anyway, the suggestion was most reluctantly agreed to, on one condition — that a grand piano must be provided. Doubtless the mess piano, frequently dosed with beer, was only too well known.

On the night, Dr Dykes Bower found himself in front of a harmonium, of which some of the notes did not play and others stuck down and had to be lifted by finger nail. It also had lost a leg, so that an orderly had been stationed there to hold it steady while the distinguished performer pedalled — furiously because its lungs were weak.

The official hour for the Manor concerts was seven p.m. The house was left open for all comers. Usually Elisabeth and I were just broaching our precious egg that was to keep us going for the evening when early enthusiasts arrived. The sacrifice of that egg, the taste of which was already in one's mouth, was cruel. Others came as their duties allowed throughout the evening and simply walked upstairs to the music. Sometimes it was two in the morning before they had all left. By that time Elisabeth and I were standing on the doorstep to which we had coaxed them, but still they talked in the bitter cold, unwilling to go back to something so unnatural as the station. During each concert above the music we could hear the droning roar of our bombers flying out overhead. From the absentees in the room we could guess who were among them, and as they flew immediately over the house their thoughts must have come down to us. If it was a summer's evening they would also see their mess mates on the river in punts, a mapped view of quiet and peace that they might be seeing for the last time. Late in the night we would hear the survivors limping home. They flew in a wide circle round and round the house waiting for the signal to bring each plane down in turn. Sometimes an engine sounded so bad one wondered if it could last out even one more lap and yet the ordeal was dragged out. Not till all were down could one think of sleep.

I have only twice in any concert hall before or since experienced music where the company listening generated such cumulative intensity as we did then. Although recordings were poor and thorn needles apt to fray, something necessary, relevant and alive came through. Perhaps it was the timeless enclave of the room when time was so short and there might be no tomorrow. I am sure the long past of the house was a resting place for those who had, as they said, no future. However, music has terrible hooks and when some pilot was present whose face too plainly showed what he had been through, I had to tread very delicately in choosing a record, lest association should suddenly undo him. It was safer to let him choose the whole programme as unobtrusively as possible, and the others always connived. There was one boy of outstanding personality whose face at that time I am glad to think his mother never saw. I used to wonder how he could possibly listen to the serene music he chose. He was killed in action as had to be, as he knew. The grief of mothers for only sons is beyond all other griefs, beyond endurance. They used to visit me after the war, filling out their sons' old letters with visits to places mentioned there.

The Christmas concert was always full. We decorated the room lavishly with evergreens and had a Christmas tree candle-lit. Everyone brought their memories and their nostalgias, and though there was no feasting or exchange of gifts there was a very strong feeling of festival.

The programme would be the Pastoral from Bach's *Christmas Oratorio,* the Et Incarnatus from three masses (the B Minor, Beethoven's *Missa Solemnis* and Mozart in C Minor), and then, as so many of the audience came from the North, all the Christmas parts of *Messiah;* 'For unto us a Child is born' gloriously rolling round the upper spaces of the room in irresistible rejoicing. When it came to 'He shall feed his flock', the soprano part was recorded by Isobel Baillie, the idol of the north country, whose voice was as unconstrained as a blackbird's. When she came to the repeat of 'Ye shall find rest to your souls', on the awaited high note of 'rest' her voice hung for a moment like a consoling star, and every heart in the room hung with it.

After that, rather shaken, we might have the glittering frostiness of Britten's harp solo from his Ceremony of Carols, and end with 'Jesu Joy of Man's Desiring' and Myra Hess's arrangement of 'Sanctify us by Thy Goodness'. Throughout all this the stillness and attention was so great it could be felt. But if now tired and relaxed they were still unwilling to go, we would finish for home's sake with the least hymn-booky carols, 'Lullay my Liking' and so on.

Towards the end of the war we acquired a new ghost. A late-comer was heard coming up the uncarpeted stairs to the music room door, outside which he waited for the record to end. When Elisabeth, as always, rose to open the door, every eye turned to see who was coming, but there was no one there. Thereafter this happened often, and in fact continued for some years after the war whenever I played to friends in the evening. We assumed it was the shadow memory, or haunting wish of a lost airman. One evening just before the concert I received the news that one of our regulars had been killed. Half way through, steps were heard up to the door. Elisabeth opened it, and in came the dead man. Everybody froze and waited breathless to see him vanish. He was a small nervous man, and began to fidget under such fixed deadly staring. He looked anxiously round, adjusted his tie, his socks, but remained with us. Nobody liked to say anything. It was someone else, unknown to us but of the same name, who had been killed.

Concerts, however, though they had these moments of extraordinary feelings, were lively. The majority of the audience were ground staff including WAAF, between whom a continuous interchange of comic loves passed under our eyes. Hands fervently held for a month would change sides and equally ardently hold another's. There was the WAAF who clearly came less for music than for the cushions, which she clasped to her bosom as a little girl does her doll, stroking and loving; and the hungry WAAF who asked for Bach because she found him so *nourishing*.

Sometimes the uniformed crowd was enlivened by non-military visitors. I had for instance a friend who, being temporarily homeless, made a long stay. She was young, vulnerable and warm-hearted, but just at the age when not to be sophisticated and not to be desired would be painfully shaming. She was also unhappy. An inexperienced girl when she first feels life's hook in her, behaves like a fish on the line. Her reactions are wild, this way and that, and in vain, the hook remains. Perhaps because it was so childlike and guileless, her posing was comically overdone. She was undeniably beautiful with huge agate eyes and a voluptuously perfect mouth. Her skin was like white satin and her teeth like pearls. She had a trick of opening her lips to smile while keeping every perfect tooth clenched against its perfect opposite number. Does this suggest a pocket Venus? She was a giantess. She had been attached to a theatrical company and staginess had gone to her head. She could not come into a room, she only knew how to make an entry with all her enthusiasm, gesturing and framing her face to rapture. She was not one of those who bend a little at the knee to be less conspicuous. On the contrary she seemed afraid of not making impression enough, overwhelming as she was. Every little opinion was emphasised with clenched fists beating on her knees, with her head first thrown back with her eyes rolling, and then bowed down, down, like Job receiving the last messenger.

Sometimes the curtain would be timed to rise, discovering her in an interesting position. When she overheard me on the telephone agreeing to receive some of the RAF, she would hurry to her room and come down in a sunbathing outfit and the largest Mexican hat, and be ready posed on the lawn, busy like Ophelia with her book, when they arrived. The unimaginable acreage of snowy skin thus displayed appeared to cause simple consternation. The men would take a wide circle to pass her, as if afraid she might jump up and chase them. She cooed like a turtle-dove when pleased. One could almost see her throat vibrating as if it were feathered.

At the concerts she wore a low cut black evening dress and many beads, and she heard the angels sing, gazing up with clasped hands. She was sitting once in the middle of a divan next to a small, dry, shy man. Though she was nineteen and he approaching forty, they looked more like a mother and her oppressed son. I forget what was being played, but it set her in motion. She rolled like a whale in good water, and sighed. Her neighbour glanced nervously at her, and shifted slightly further away. The music continued to wind her up. Her lips parted, with her hands over her heart she seemed likely to slip sideways in a sort of trance. He shifted again. I watched fascinated as Brahms — I feel sure it must have been Brahms that so swelled in her — relentlessly cast her towards the panic-stricken man, who fled, inch by inch, till he fell off the end of the divan and spent the rest of the evening safe on the floor.

Fortunately for the peace of the airmen they were never at breakfast with us. Our young giantess breakfasted in her nightgown — and I am writing about 1940 — with her heavy hair falling round her to the ground. She wore instead of bedroom slippers, stockings of wide green fishnet, in which her legs were like salmon.

One morning I was expecting young Mr John Allen the builder to discuss some outside repair to the house. As we walked by the big yew tree a cooing caused us to look round. High up in the branches among the play of light and shadow a very large fishnetted leg was hanging down. It was not easy at first to recognise it for what it was, and even more surprising to Mr John than to me. Then some way above it appeared the over life-sized face, dimpling like an elf, which with a shake released a fall of Melisande hair. Mr John gave no other sign than his wry trouble-expecting smile.

There was another occasion that perhaps amused no one but me. Until he was posted abroad Peter used to come home on leave, at first in rough hairy khaki with clumsy puttees and huge boots. Among the spruce and mostly rather small RAF types he looked, sprawled over a divan, like a fallen tree that had got there by accident. Later when he had his commission and was less rugged, he once brought a girl friend. No sooner had we settled down for music than, overcome by the candles, the glamour and the divans, she flung herself wholeheartedly onto his breast and lay there throughout the evening. The RAF to a man were shocked. This was not what they thought proper behaviour at the Manor. Peter sat it out with a face of studied espressionlessness that spoke volumes to me. I hoped that the RAF would reflect that in such circumstances there is nothing a man can do in public.

◇

The two dogs, Arno and Birkie, were always present, Birkie merely companionable, but Arno was musical with a marked preference for Mozart. He admitted without question anybody in uniform, quietly rising from his seat and crossing the room to sniff the hand of any newcomer. Only once, for some reason of his own, he growled, and what is more, in a pianissimo passage, for which he looked at me with that total apology dogs' faces can wear after committing a bloomer.

If, as often happened, some tired man fell asleep and snored, again Arno would cross the room and lick his face to a gentle awakening. He disliked the modern music of that time, such as Bartok, and with a reproachful dignity would walk out. He had his own seat in the music room as had all the regulars. Should it happen that while he was going round greeting his friends a newcomer unwittingly sat in his place, the man was soon disconcerted by finding a large Alsatian sitting rather haughtily on his knees.

Arno was very nervy in an air raid, but Birkie would bark defiantly at the sound of an enemy plane, and enjoyed immensely standing up at the attic window to watch the fireworks and bombs over Wyton.

Numbers at the concerts might be anything from thirty to one or two, but the maximum always had to be prepared for. The RAF bus to bring the men had been withdrawn and the numbers dropped sharply for a time. We had one particular faithful, Don Cleaver, a professional violinist. He was a reserved man of strong feelings and a glorious clownish sense of humour. He made it his responsibility that never should we keep open house for nobody. (It would of course have been desolating.) He came in all weathers and from whatever airfield in the district he was posted to. Once he even came on a snowy night from Bourn, cycling with one leg, the other being injured. My dormitory was not now for pilots, but for ground staff coming from a distance. We were fond of Don, counted absolutely on his coming, and if he was almost alone, that gave him a good chance to hear as often as he liked any violin solo he was studying. Had he lived he must surely have been a friend for life, but he was killed while being ferried from one airfield to another. The plane crashed into the Bedford Level.

The other five days of the week we entertained exhausted aircrews. If it was warm they slept in the garden or wrote letters. By supper time they were reviving, and half way through the meal they would generally become very lively and very funny, re-acting for us as farce their terrors over the target, even making us laugh at how they thought the rear-gunner (present with us) was dead. The rear-gunner always seemed to get the worst of everything and be the butt of all the gallows humour.

These men, who were generally NCOs, were a delight to me. They came from a cross-section of the people of the British Isles — a Highland postman, a Durham miner, a painter of flowers for Rowntrees' boxes, a Birmingham manufacturer, Welshmen and Cockneys. None of them seemed to find us strange or difficult. Elisabeth was good with all comers. Her laughter is irresistible, and at that time she was too shy to do anything but listen perfectly to all their stories — and produce her miraculous meals out of nothing.

In spite of all this activity, we both found time to paint, and I had begun to take the garden seriously.

◇

On answering the bell one day I found the Chief Constable on the step. He introduced himself with these surprising words — 'Mrs Boston? How do you do. When somebody is reported as a spy by every other person in their village, I think it is time the Chief Constable got to know her. May I come in?'

We had an amiable enough tea-party together. I confirmed that I had a son in the Royal Engineers, otherwise no questions were asked and only small talk passed. My impression was that he dismissed the village gossip, but there was a follow-up sometime later not altogether pleasing.

A rather girlish middle-aged woman, a little over-dressed as if anxious not to be thought dowdy, with the falsely hearty manners of a commercial traveller, arrived without warning, saying she had been asked by the Chief Constable to call on us.

'I am told you are very good to our boys in the RAF.'

There was something slightly 'off ' in the way she said it, but I did not get the significance. We brought her in and showed her the whole place, as I always did, but she seemed, for all her peeping, dissatisfied. Her conversation seemed to us inept to the verge of lunacy. She began by telling us how very easy she knew it was to get drunk. It even happened to her sometimes. 'You can't really blame a girl for that.'

All-girls-together is a manner I greatly dislike. Elisabeth and I sat in astonishment waiting for a clue. She seemed to be working to put us at our ease while feeling very much out of order herself, like someone whose gears won't engage.

She picked up the book I had been reading to look at the title, and dropped it as if it had bitten her. It happened to be the Confessions of St Augustine. She hopped up and down ejaculating jollities, and finally found herself looking down through the interior Norman window in the music room that gives onto the spare room. There she saw a double bed glittering under one of Elisabeth's sequin-covered muslin bedspreads.

'O!' she let out like a pop-gun. 'A fairies' room!!'

Now what could she have meant by that? At long last she went, saying at the door that she would be coming again, probably every month.

We were staggered, and rang up a friend who knew the district better than we did, to ask if she had ever heard of such a person. 'Oh yes, of course. She's the Welfare visitor, she keeps an eye on all the prostitutes.'

However, she also must have decided that we weren't somehow quite the type, for she never came again.

I was still amused, far from taking in that I was a real concern to Intelligence. Meanwhile the house continued its own mysterious life and from time to time sent feelers out from its darker corners, such as slight poltergeistic displacements, footsteps up the wooden stairs, wandering lights, voices, etc., but so much immediate and dramatic human life filled the place that irrational trifles did not get much attention. If Elisabeth and I were alone, there were urgent hammerings at night on a side door never used. The first time it happened I took the dogs and went to open, thinking some accident must have taken place and help was needed. No one was there, nor did the dogs bark or go chasing off after an intruder. They kept well behind me. After a few recurrences we ceased to take any notice. Then one night it was very persistent, leaving one door to go round and hammer on another. We shrugged it off and continued knitting. Eventually, because of his importunity, I went to the door, and found there a policeman, displeased by his long wait. He had come about a crack of light showing. 'And I have been knocking a long time.' 'Oh yes, we heard you, but we just thought it was our ghost. We get a lot of that.' As I said it, I realised the perfect idiocy of this when said to the police. I did not realise the insolence of it when said by a spy to cover comings and goings. Fortunately he was a junior and had not been given an official line on such an excuse.

Some, but not all, of our hauntings were traced much later to a local maniac given to midnight wandering. For choice, I would prefer the tics of an old house.

◇

I had two staunch friends in the village who stood up for me throughout, even speaking up at dinner parties where it seemed I was the topic that best got people talking. Through them I heard that the C0 himself had said I was so damn clever they couldn't find a thing against me. As the war went on they got hotter and hotter, but still couldn't catch me. That this was because I was innocent was apparently impossible to think. I myself was not worried in the least, knowing there was no case. This was foolish, as a case can easily be faked in the national interest. Perhaps I was spared because they hoped through me to catch my presumed accomplice. My friends were shadowed to and from the house.

There was a Warrant Officer among those to whom the house meant a lot, who came very often and to every concert. His job was secret. I was careful never to ask about it and I had no idea where he came from. He arrived by bicycle, so it must have been within ten miles. The dogs were fond of him, and one day, out on their own, they arrived breathless and wagging at his secret place. Do one man's bicycle tyres smell so different from another's that they can be traced far afield? Anyway Arno and Birkie knew what I didn't, and possibly even they are noted in my dossier for suspicious work. They may well have known a great deal. They may have shadowed the shadowers, whose presence they would certainly notice.

The only things that bothered me in what I otherwise considered a farce, were, first the insufferable insolence that the detective inspector who twice visited me contrived to put into the words 'Well, Mrs Boston, *and how are you getting on?'* I was nauseated by Intelligence's implied belief, when I reported that I had found German ration cards in the garden, that I had picked an officer's pocket. I most minded the blushing misery of a WAAF officer for whom I had an affectionate respect, when she faced me for the first time after receiving her warning. Clearly the thought was there that it was not absolutely impossible that I should be a traitor.

However there were people to whom, for no reason but their blessed trust, it did seem impossible, and to them I am as grateful as surprised. Nobody that I was meeting had known me before the war, or knew anything about me.

Elisabeth does not seem to have been suspected although she was here all the time and doing exactly what I did, except that she didn't wear a dirndl. Poor Austria! As much a victim of the Nazis as any other invaded country.

◇

By this time the Padre had been posted to Italy with the Squadron, and having lost him we realised how much warmth and personal interest had gone. His successors came occasionally to the house but seemed in comparison lifeless figureheads. Maybe they felt equipped to deal with unbelievers, but not with dangerous female spies. The Padre — he so filled his role that no surname was ever needed — was for a long time a prisoner in Italy. When I saw him next he had grown up. He cannot be left out of this story, so I must trust to his long friendship to forgive my account of his youthful exuberance.

◇

Meanwhile *Les Amis de France Libre* continued to send their very welcome men. Evidently no one had thought to tell them I was suspect. I did not have many, but they were wholly indiscreet. They clearly felt, as so many people say who come here, that it was 'out of this world'. Their tales were too good not to be dramatically told and they let themselves go. There was a handsome flamboyant fellow called Jean Meyer (according to himself high up in the Resistance hierarchy) who caused Elisabeth and myself infinite amusement. He had come from prison in Spain by the escape route connived at by Sir Samuel Hoare, whereby they could pass on to England as French Canadians.

Jean was very proud of his almost sole-less boots in which he had crossed the Pyrenees on foot. He used to make forays in St Ives, where with his scarlet kepi and roving eyes he captivated the shop girls. By lifting his foot onto the counter to show them the soles that had crossed the Pyrenees, he was able to extract all sorts of compassionate rations which he brought back in triumph. In France, of course, the black market was patriotic, anti-German as well as expedient. In the end, Jean did accept from us the fact that we simply did without. It says a lot for him that he could take that in without complaint or contempt.

Whatever the stagey charms he displayed for shop girls, with us in the house his rudeness was incomprehensible. He would only speak English and his was desperately bad. Not only was there never a please or thank you or excuse me, there were none of the polite gestures natural to all Frenchmen. I could not imagine what class he came from. His brusqueness was continually snubbing and hard to get on with. Nevertheless we couldn't help liking him. He was burning with patriotic and political passion. At this period we had many Americans coming to the house whom Jean would harangue in incomprehensible torrents of false grammar. 'How you think to Laval?' I heard as his final challenge. The American looked as blank as Americans can, and replied 'I guess we haven't thought at all.' Jean collapsed into his seat, and as I opened the concert with a record he had asked for, I could see the pounding of his heart under his tight tunic.

He listened avidly to French broadcasts, crouched over with his ear to the radio, still turned down so low that only a practised ear could hear. I think it would have shocked him to hear it loud. He had daily monosyllabic calls to his headquarters in London. The telephone is in my entrance hall, where one day he was telephoning in his pyjamas, which he treated as ordinary casual wear. Unfortunately they, like his boots, had seen hard service and the legs were so tattered as to be absent where they were most needed. As I saw two very shockable spinsters approaching the front door, I took a rug and wrapped it round him, saying, 'You will perish of cold like that.' 'Madame,' he replied, casting it indignantly away, ' I, I perish only for France.'

Broken English has many pitfalls. He was once apologising to us for the state of his thick black hair which had deteriorated under prison conditions in Spain. 'Till then,' he said, 'the most beautiful thing on my body was my hairs.'

It was only on the night before he left us that I tumbled to it that his rudeness was literally studied. He must have heard that the English had no manners, and was practising the supposed way of life with the language. Perhaps he hoped to be able some time to pass himself off as English in a tight corner. Anyway, on his last night he received a call from his closest friend and immediate superior, of whom he had talked much, of whom we knew both the real and the code name. For the first time I heard Jean talking his own language in his own personal manner, and here was the warm, easy, well-bred Frenchman whom we would have been so happy to know.

'Ah, mon vieux, quel dommage que tu ne sois pas ici. C'est un lieu delicieux, mais absolument delicieux, tu ne peux pas l'imaginer. Et ces dames sont charmantes. Fais ton possible pour passer ta permission ici.'

I heard from Jean after the Liberation. He held some post in de Gaulle's first government. He married an English woman. I do hope he spoke French to her.

◇

The last of our French guests was a fat, bald coarse man suggesting very crooked business in private life. He might have been fifty years old. He too had come via Spain under the assumed name of Douglas McPinton, his own real name being the one secret he kept. He brought with him as Mrs McPinton a wardress from Holloway gaol. She was young, plump and personable, and though strictly speaking he was abusing our hospitality by bringing her, I liked her. She was frank and tough, and not vulgar at all. She talked easily about her prison work and was so sensible and kind that she removed for ever the worst horrors of imagined imprisonment.

His part, requiring more courage than his appearance suggested, was to be parachuted into France on dangerous missions. Among other things he told us that when things got really hot he took refuge in the ward of a certain Paris maternity hospital. He was fat enough for the part, but his blue jowls must have been a difficulty. Presumably he always had to be giving birth with a gauze mask over his face when the Gestapo inspected.

For all his stories, as a visitor, he was too gross to enjoy. When I knocked on their door with the breakfast, the word 'Entrez' meant that a naked tableau of the two of them had been staged for me. At dinner when I was serving he would lean over the table and transfer the best pieces from the dish to her plate, 'Pour remonter tes forces', and look after himself in the same way, as if in a restaurant that he owned. But this was a trifle, more admissible in France than here. I have no doubt he was well equipped for the kind of work he had to do, if it was dirty work. I can less easily see how she could bear him, unless as a change from police officers and because he lived dangerously.

Others lived dangerously for whom I was more concerned. An aircrew was an inseparable unit. Often two or three would have liked to come to the concerts but one was unmusical, in which case none came, though they would all come to supper. When there were casualties, a crew had to be made up out of survivors who had not flown together before, all uneasy until they had knit into a new unit.

One night a crew came to supper who had just taken on a new rear-gunner — a real sacrificial lamb this time. He looked at most sixteen, a slight shy boy, over young to leave his mammy yet. He must have faked his age, but even so there had been a period of training. One couldn't believe he was actually qualified to fly in a bombing raid. The others clearly felt upset and protective towards him. 'Our new boy. He'll be going on his first flight tomorrow.' So this had to be a celebration party, however appalled one felt.

Two nights later I saw him again, and without the rest of the crew I wouldn't have recognised him. He had grown overnight into a solitary desolate man. He did not return from his second raid.

◇

In the field adjoining my orchard there was a training camp for Engineers. Every day they put up and took down Bailey bridges, banged about with grenades, or were made to cross the river on single planks and pushed screaming in by the officers to learn that water was not so dreadful as you might imagine if you had never been in it. Hospitality was offered as usual, but met with no response. The pub was infinitely preferable to both officers and men. I once brought a group of privates in to see the music room and the only remark, as they looked round at my divans, was 'Lor, missis, you ain't got no legs to yer chairs.' They were a noisy and disorderly lot, breaking into my orchard en masse like looters in an army of occupation and stripping all the fruit. I could never teach Arno that my territory extended beyond the moat. It was his idea of the right boundary. Also they were in uniform and so admissible.

Eventually the Engineers were moved on, leaving the meadow ruined by concrete floors, rubble roads and pits. So it remained until 1971 when it was finally cleared and levelled out and re-sown, a mere thirty years after.

In 1943 there was a camp of Non-Combatants in the neighbourhood, employed in sewage work in Fenstanton. They proved more our type than the Engineers, and welcomed hospitality as we welcomed them. They were intelligent and cultured, and their principals were private and well-mannered. Among them was the artist James Archer, whose beautiful drawing 'The Prodigal Son' was a parting present and hangs on my stairs.

The Non-Coms raised the number at concerts to the point of discomfort. Some had to sit on the ladder-like wooden stairs to the attic. I suggested that they should have a separate night, but there was an immediate outcry from the RAF. They did not want to be separated from these men for whom they had great fellow-feeling and respect. So we continued to overcrowd and enjoyed it. When, to our regret, they were moved on to some other labour chosen for the abasement of intelligence, their place at the concerts was filled by Americans. These continued until the end of the war and even afterwards, when short courses were arranged at Cambridge for men waiting their turn to go home.

We got on excellently together. They did not seem foreign, unlike the GIs one saw about in Cambridge, with their arrogant ox-like faces chewing the gum and their off-pink trousers tight over projecting bums. Those who came for music, when they sat round in the Norman hall, showed the 'melting pot' as a witches' cauldron giving off old European faces. Those with Scottish names looked like Raeburn portraits. Italians, Irish, French, Teutons and Slavs might at any period have passed through this house as travellers. They seemed more true to racial type than the hotch-potch English. They were shy and quiet, as if from surprise, and have left warm memories and lasting friendships. From one of them I later borrowed the name Oldknow for the family in my Green Knowe books. He wrote to me after the war with the endearing sentence — 'The old Manor is what every American wants and doesn't know it.' He took some of the most beautiful photos of the house that I have.

One of our English habitués at the time was in the photographic department at Wyton. His story (as far as I can now remember it, with apologies for technical howlers) was, that the Americans had, in a huge new building, the most up-to-date photographic equipment imaginable. The target photos brought back by returning planes were put in at one end and automatically went through the processing to come out at an office at the other end of the building ready enlarged. This took a mere two hours. Nevertheless, the British did it in forty minutes. An American deputation was sent over to examine our improvement on their system. They found our friend in an improvised dark room turning the developer *by hand*. (This allowed the selection of urgent photos for instant examination.)

Our primitivism knocked the deputation right back. Obviously it was impossible. I do not doubt that the British now do it the American way.

I never noticed the slightest hint that the Americans had been told I was suspect. By this time British officers were forbidden to visit me, except the one currently watching me, and all NCOs were warned. It is wonderful what a mountain of suspicion can be built out of nothing. I had once thought, with heartbreak, that I had left England for good, but I was back there, passionately identified with it, living in a house that had witnessed all its history. One looks back sadly. Who can feel love like that for a close network of motorways and continuous shoals of uprooted people? Roots are 'out'.

◇

The end of the war was celebrated in Hemingford Grey with dancing in the village street. I had a set of carnival masks left over from some pre-war party, which I distributed among my guests so that we could join in the jollity without my being cold-shouldered as 'that spy'. Every bright cottage window helped to illuminate the street, and showed its living room to curious eyes. This in itself was a dramatic raising of the curtain of blackout and fear. It was disappointing to see that no interior was individual, picturesque or cottagey as one had imagined. All down the street they were identical, like waiting rooms. Cottageyness has passed to the upper classes. There was a bonfire in the widest part of the road, round which we danced. The masks caused a small commotion. The wearing of one builds up an inner tension and excitement that shows itself in a freedom of movement and gesture that is in itself half way to a disguise. We were challenged, I was tentatively hugged, but heard no whisper of recognition.

◇

After the war I gave a Christmas party for German prisoners, thinking no one could be sadder than they, defeated and disillusioned. Except for one much older, despairing man, they were arrogant and odious, ungrateful to the point of sneering. Perhaps it was worth the effort for that one crumpled old fellow. Anyway one had to try.

After the Germans came the Latvians, who were in a temporary camp awaiting resettlement. I never met a set of men who more impressed me. They were mostly farmers with a strong dignified peasant culture plus an excellent State education. They spoke very little English (German and Russian were their extras), but mimed freely, so that conversations were dramatic and hit-or-miss, leaving plenty of room for imagination. 'In my country is many trees, high, high, black like blackout. When night is, bird big like man, live there, him open wings, very wide and fly. ' They wished to communicate, from their first visit brushing aside all their difficulties and our own shyness. They were all members of the Latvian resistance army, which was why they could not go home. The Russians had tempted many back with a promised amnesty, but those who returned had been rounded up and shot. The wives of those who refused to come back were allotted to mutilated Russians. The group who met here were markedly homogeneous, as bitter as sword-blades but courageous and realist.

I had two favourites who worked locally on a farm. They were brothers who at home had shared an inherited farm and lived together in the large farmhouse. They were both married and each had young sons. Of their families they had no news and nothing was too bad to be probable. The elder of the two, Martin, was a gentle character. He seemed stunned, as if half of him had perished. The younger, Alex, had a face in which every wrong, every sorrow, was savagely, consumingly alive. I have never seen a man so highly charged, especially when listening to music. His concern for his brother was to me almost unbearable. In my sheltered position I saw none of the horrors of war at first hand. I never saw a house go up in flames or ambulance men coping with the desperately injured, still less the condemned being rounded up. It is greatly to the honour of this house that men with faces on which the unimaginable is clearly *seen*, could come here and not find it alien.

These two Latvians, Martin and Alex, were much with me. I not only loved their company but they repaid hospitality by coming in the evening to scythe for me. They scythed superbly, meticulously, like Andrew Marvell's reaper.

They shared a semi-detached cottage with a third Latvian and I went to have supper with them. The place was spotlessly clean and orderly with an improvised minimum of furniture. They had found in a junk shop two oleographs of romantic northern views with forests, stags and blue lakes, which gave the room a continental look.

Their tiny kitchen garden was a model of skill and economy. As a refugee's first foothold the place was full of promise. They had a new life to make and it was going to have all the skills and values of the old one. It is bitter to have to write that the dislike and hostility of the English farm labourer to the Latvians' idea of work was so violent that they decided to try Canada. In England a man is not allowed to do what he can.

On Midsummer's eve I answered the doorbell late in the evening to find a party of Latvians formed up outside, carrying two large wreaths, one of oak leaves and one of corn and wildflowers. The men broke into song and I stood there embarrassed , wondering what was going on, while they went through many verses. Then Martin and Alex stepped forward and hung the wreaths round my neck. I had been ritually blessed with fertility. The oak was for the head of the house and the corn for the woman, so I got both. I was told the wreaths must be kept till the following Midsummer. I did keep the oak, hung in my dining room, where it gave off a delicious perfume for many months.

The Latvian group also gave me two handsome presents of traditional work, an elaborately carved wooden casket and a brooch of Baltic amber and hand-beaten silver which I constantly wear. From people in their circumstances these manners and rituals were very touching and a warming change from local suspicion.

Soon I had to say goodbye to Martin and Alex. I hope they knew how much good I wished them. For several years they wrote from Canada, steadily increasing their holding, though Martin was ill. Then the letters stopped. Did Martin die and was there nothing more that Alex could say? But it is natural for a correspondence to lapse, especially if all is going well. They deserved much.

6

The Garden

The war was over, the house empty. Peter was married and far away in the north. Elisabeth was back in Cambridge. Except for my two loyal friends, the village had rejected me and I did not care to accept any late overtures. My leisure was suddenly enormous and my energy at that time equally so.

Now is the time to talk about the garden. Nothing bores me more than other people talking about theirs. Gardens are like one's babies — why should other people like them? Nevertheless something that has been my fanatical occupation for thirty years must be mentioned. It is now an inseparable part of the Manor's aura, it flows clean through the house, it tempts you in, it tempts you out, and its scents compete with and complement the smell pervading the rooms from the wood fire.

I have to admit that the non-garden, as I first found it, was very beautiful. Rushes had invaded the moat and swayed as the moorhens swam. The lawn was covered with cowslips and an Elysium of small flowers. The big trees swept to the ground. I made an unconvincing resolve to keep my hands off it.

I kept the cowslips for perhaps twelve years, but it meant we had to leave the lawn uncut until they had seeded. In the end I had to yield to Broomie, who was too old to wrestle with rough grass. There are still a few, enough to take over if it ever goes wild again. One remembers how quickly wild flowers covered the ruins of London after the bombing, and, as I do not use weed-killers, I am aware all the time of the forest and wild flowers that would, if left, obliterate all my work in eighteen months. Any corner of the four acres that I fail to attend to in the year is snatched back by the wild. Holly, oak, ash, yew, cherry and elder and hawthorn have to be dug out of the borders every autumn. This I love. It would be awful to have won the battle. The seedling trees are always planted elsewhere.

When I first came to it, the house stood in its medieval context, almost unaltered — wide meadows all round it as far as one could walk in every direction, lanes bordered with flowers and over-arched by trees, the river running clean and free from any kind of motorboat, with a quietness all its own, quieter than even the lark- and bee-trilled meadows. In the village street the smaller houses had latticed casements with beautiful scrolled handwrought latches, now all replaced by Crittall windows. There were four half-timbered houses, all still beautifully kept, and some Georgian, but nothing new.

The quietness and isolation was unnaturally prolonged by the petrol shortage. The village had long since forgone its horses and stables which would have added such animation in the past. My milk however was delivered by horse and float — the lovely morning sound from my childhood went on, taken for granted, till suddenly it was gone. A rude and hurried van took its place.

What I want to evoke is the feeling I had at the time, not foreseeing the future, that the past of the house from the beginning still existed — the winds coming off its hay-fields, the clouds trailing shadows across the familiar woods, all the sounds of song birds, cocks, cattle and sheep, pump and bucket, axe and saw; the overriding tyranny of the seasons, the human fears and isolation, the deep passions and strong earthy loyalties. There was reverence for memory, and *et expecto*, the belief in a future. I was lucky enough to have caught it whole. I therefore know it and love it as no one else can, since that context has been wiped out, with its dignity and breadth. It was with feelings that included the entire view and its extensions east and west, up and down stream, with the past of the house leading up to this moment and beyond, that I began to make a garden.

During the war we had no petrol for mowing, so that lawns became hayfields. In June the blacksmith brought a horse-drawn haycart in, and he and his son scythed the garden and orchard. The contented horse between the shafts swished and browsed on the lawn while the leisurely rhythmic actions of raking and forking went on. It was beautiful to see and hear, and wonderfully carefree. Now the lawns are velvet and brushed in straight lines up and down, and when I recently opened the garden to the village my notice read PRAMS NOT ADMITTED. (Consequently nobody came.)

◇

I never made a plan of the garden-to-be, it grew little by little. The acre between the house and the river was where I began, because that was totally bare. It lacked even the moat that once crossed it, but on this side had been filled up. The six flowering cherry trees, flanking the cutting which brings the river water into the remaining moat, were planted first. They were as small as walking sticks and I thought I was planting them for the far future. I know now that cherry trees spring up almost over night. Those sticks, now thirty-two years old, spread wide and high beyond all expectation and now have passed their best and must soon be replaced. As a child one thought of trees as being permanent like the hills, but I have already outlived most of the trees here. The yews and the great beech still stand. One feels fairly sure of the yews, but the beech if it went would be a cruel loss. It is a presence that delights all my days. In one gale all the other big trees round the moat came down in the night, their crashing unheard in the howling wind. In the morning I was appalled to find the south boundary of the garden without any shelter or privacy. However, countless saplings sprang up to fill the vacancy and before long it was so thick that yearly we have to fell some. One comes to think of the foliage of the earth as rising and falling like waves of the sea, only in slow motion. The whole thing is on the move. I am constantly shocked by the impatience of gardeners who come to me for advice. 'Three years!' they say. 'We want something *now*.'

My second move was to plant sweet briar and honeysuckle all along the river path for the pleasure of strollers. But alas, old ladies with a little empty vase on a town mantelpiece cannot resist a little bunch, and there are a great many of them passing by. Every sprig within reach is torn off. It was a surprise to find old ladies so much more destructive than children. They browse.

◇

In the winter of 1946-7 we had the heaviest snow storm in my long lifetime. It began while friends from Cambridge were having dinner with me, snugly behind drawn curtains, and round a spitting fire. When they thought of going, the car was found to be almost buried. For three days we all shovelled, hoping to clear a passage down the drive, but it filled up as we did it. It was like trying to shovel away the sky. The flakes were huge, purposeful and giddy, fantastic to watch when we sat inside. They descended on the garden, and through their rising and falling play one could glimpse the steady disappearance of all known features. The frozen moat was filled up level with its banks, the big yews were glittering pyramids rising from the ground; drifts changed all the contours. When on the fourth day the snow ceased, we were confronted with a mysterious rolling landscape. Beyond the doorstep one did not know where the earth was. The smell of snow was piercing and vivifying, the glitter a warning that this was all mirage and enchantment.

The thaw brought an equally record-breaking flood. In our yearly floods the water seeps through the under-stratum of gravel to reach river level, my garden being well below the footpath along the bank. This time the Ouse overflowed its banks, making a savage little waterfall the whole length of the garden. The river forked, one stream going straight up the village street and one across my garden and over the fields to Fenstanton. It flowed across my front door step, but did not come into the house, where carpets were stacked on the dining table and upholstered chairs raised on bricks.

All the houses down the village street were flooded. The inhabitants went shopping in army 'ducks' boarded out of bedroom windows. The overflow from the moat cut off the road to Hemingford Abbots, so I was marooned alone. Milk and bread came through the flood by tractor. Broomie in waders reached me daily by walking along the top of my garden wall, through which, old and porous as it was, the water rushed as through a sieve. From there he sidled along the iron railings till he reached ground high enough for wading. This was a dedicated approach and I watched him fearfully. The water on each side of the wall was not deep, but it was fierce, and the wall might quite easily have collapsed. One house on the flood's cross country course was washed away.

In memory I seem to have been marooned for weeks, but in the end the banks gave way further down stream and relieved us.

My first excursion was down my drive in wellingtons. The water was up to their tops and thick with sewage, so one had to go slowly. It took me forty minutes to reach a point where I would wave to a friend making the same effort towards me. Even then we were not within shouting distance.

When the water was nearly gone, the whole population turned out to make up for lost gossip. It was a Breughel scene. Inhibitions had gone, as always in a catastrophe. Old women tucked their skirts into their bloomers, making

Above: the garden in 1943, looking north towards the river. A photograph taken by an American wartime visitor, J. Oldknow.

Below: The garden in 1973, with its six flowering cherries and eight trimmed yews bordering the path to the river

Another view of the garden

silhouettes more exaggerated than any toddler in nappies, and were wading round with unrestrained curiosity, looking into open doors to see the damage inside. Buoyant housewives were proud of their damage — flood stains three feet up over expensive wallpaper newly hung, and mud that deep that had had to be cleared out. Others were soured for years to come. All down the street it was the same; one of my friends had been kept awake all night by the sound of her parquet floor rattling on the bottom of her grand piano. She had a great county laugh like a unicorn's. Later there was of course an organised subscription of relief to flood victims. I was allotted two bars of carbolic soap.

It was my garden that had suffered. The gravel path had been torn up and hollowed into a river bed. The lawns were heaped with gravel banks and mud. The sweet briar hedge, through which the waterfall had poured, was left dangling from the iron railings, its roots in the wind, its bank of soil washed far away.

All this had to be barrowed back where it came from. Because it had to be done, I told Broomie to do it, a brutal order that shocks me now. He did it, single-handed, while the mud was still wet.

◇

The best known feature of the garden now is the topiary. In my youth I knew and loved Levens Hall, near Kendal, famous for its Elizabethan garden. One of the things that endears a garden to its owner is the number of plants in it that are memories of somewhere else, a margin full of references that are unknown to outsiders. In memory of Levens Hall I planted beside the path leading to the river eight seedling yews, meaning ultimately to trim them as simple cones. However the coronation of Elizabeth II gave me a better idea. On the eve of the event I set about cutting them into pairs of orbs and crosses and crowns.

It was a slow business to get the open arches of the crowns growing. For the day of the Coronation they had to be faked with newly cut yew tied in place. One bush had not produced the growth needed for either an orb or a crown. It showed a propensity to be a bird. Fortunately there was the Ampulla that it could represent. Later on I planted and cut a chess set nearer the house. None of these will ever be perfect in shape. Yew grows intractably and fast, presenting me with tough, thick branches where they can least be accommodated. Every year I have to do amputations that leave holes and scars. Should one be given to thinking in terms of a hundred years, by then the trunk will be nearly as thick as the present bushes. However, none of us can now think in those terms, even if we live in a Norman house. During the summer from May to October I have to trim the topiary every three weeks, by now using the long-handled edge-cutters to reach the crosses on top. They have a spicy scent when cut.

In spite of the disaster of the flood, and its recurrence in a mild form every winter, I was unwilling to waste such a situation. I began to build up beds above water-level. This was my five-year plan, during which time the garden was piled with hills of soil waiting to be barrowed, and marooned trucks, sunk up to the axle in the soft ground, frequently featured in it. Laborious building up has to be repeated every year, because the river sucks the bottom away. This is gardening lunacy. Soil comes high in my expenses.

These beds can never be high enough to make deep-rooting plants really happy, but there are now four such beds, each about thirty yards long, that contain half my collection of old roses, plus two similar beds for irises and two for Hybrid Perpetuals, in all eight long parallels from the house to the river – a forbidding thought, but the lines carry the eye irresistibly along to the distant view so that it is always part of the garden. Perhaps for this reason they manage to look as if they had happened naturally. Also the plants wanton, to use a Shakespearean word, and the discipline does not appear. I am a believer in straight lines as being self-evident and restful. I hate the aimless wiggle-waggle advocated at the back of most catalogues and generally thought of as adding space.

I try to have nothing in the garden that is not scented, though a few things creep in for intermediate flowering or difficult positions. Think of the year's scents, remembering each in turn – winter sweet, winter heliotrope, witchhazel, violets, polyanthus, pheasant-eye, hyacinth, wallflowers, azaleas, lilac, sweet briar, rosa primula, viburnum, honeysuckle, irises, roses, pinks, pansies, stocks, tobacco, lilies, chrysanthemums and many, many more. Of the old roses, each scent is recognisable as rose, but each is also unmistakably itself only. And yet there are many scentless gardens.

Scent is to me very mysterious. It is the most immediate of the senses, seeming to reach straight into the unconscious, unanalysable and profoundly moving. It can produce the same kind of awed delight as great art – something *other* has been reached. But it has this as well, that it flows on the air. We breathe it in and incorporate it into our bloodstream. Scent is bliss, and as far as we know, meaningless to us.

[For those whose sense of smell is not atrophied, a minority in the urban world, the scents most free on the air apart from those I have just mentioned are *Erica Mediterranea* (if you can grow it), *Cerasus* Joi-nioi , *Nicotiana sylvestris, Lonicera syrangantha, Cistus purpurea.* These all give off scent in clouds. There are deliciously scented tulips that can be smelled as you walk, but they are now almost unobtainable.]

I had tried to grow old roses in my contaminated garden in Cheshire, but they did not survive. Now was my chance, and I began my collection, spurred on by Sacheverell Sitwell's *Splendours.* Every year I combed the catalogues for something I had not got. G. S. Thomas, then of the Sunningdale Nurseries, used to produce an illustrated catalogue with verbal descriptions that were irresistible. He also very kindly procured various rarities for me which will never be available again. Alas, some of the best do not like it here, and when they are gone are gone forever. Such is the Archduchess Elizabeth of Austria. The Rose du Roi is another rarity, at present doing magnificently. I fear pollution is now affecting this garden too. Every year there are inexplicable sudden deaths among my treasures, and new bushes do not grow as they used to.

The old roses, by which I do not mean just vaguely 'Moss', but species, Gallicas, Damasks, Albas, Centifolias, Bourbons and early Hybrid Perpetuals, give me such acute pleasure that I cannot resist another specimen, but I do not collect in the strict sense. I have discarded many after trial because, though rare, they failed to please.

To anyone who knows the old roses, or is interested in English poetry, it is grievous to think how the word rose has been degraded, what it used to mean and what it means now. Leaving aside 'there is no Rose of Such Virtue' as being meaningless, roses not being considered, as they once were, as having virtue. I think of all the love poems.

Go, lovely Rose!
Tell her, that wastes her time and me,
That now she knows,
When I resemble her to thee,
How sweet and fair she seems to be.

This could hardly be sent attached to the stalk of Masquerade or Super Star, scentless, and lurid like a neon advertisement.

The earliest roses were a discovery, treated with awe as a supernatural happening. They were treasured in the temple gardens of the Medes and Persians. We know little about early horticulture, though Babylon was famous for gardens. The earliest rose we know of is the Red Gallica (*gallica officinalis*) which was a symbol of the sun in the twelfth century BC and deserves to be so, because of its rich cherry colour, dazzling like the rising sun. The flowers are about the size of a field poppy and equally ephemeral, but during their moment splendid and heraldic. It became later the Red Rose of Lancaster and as the Apothecary's rose was grown extensively in France for all the medicinal virtues with which it was credited. Among other uses the sharp scent was thought to repel plague.

The next earliest, 1000 BC, is voluptuously and individually scented and appropriately comes from the Temple of Aphrodite on the Isle of Samos. It is a delicate pink with more petals than the Red Gallica, but loosely put together, as it were experimentally. It has not yet learnt how to arrange its fullness and has the careless look of some wild flowers, such as meadow sweet. But somehow it had developed the overwhelming delight of the true rose scent. This is the Autumn Damask, presumably a mutation as it is unique in its perpetual flowering. There were clearly Damasks earlier still, flowering only once, from which it sported. It flowers here in my warmest corner, but often looks homesick for the Mediterranean. I can imagine it rampant in its own climate, a very distraction of love. It was admired and described in antiquity because of its perpetual habit, but in spite of the interest it aroused it has few direct descendants. There is the Rose of Paestum, mentioned by Virgil, with single flowers very like Red Gallica. Can Aphrodite have mated with Apollo? I scent some priestly mystery.

In Europe until the sixteenth century all variety occurring in roses was either by accidental seeding or by mutation. Deliberate cross fertilisation came with science in the late Renaissance. Till then the types were few and stable. In Gerard's *Herbal* (1597) only fourteen were listed. Consequently it is impossible to put a date to an early rose except for its first naming or its representation in art, as at Knossos. The Damask Celsiana, for instance, one of my favourites, is listed 'prior to 1750' but it seems to me to go back almost to the birth of gardens. As with wild flowers, one cannot think any human has had a hand in it. The Garden of Eden is its proper place. Maiden's Blush 'prior to fifteenth century' is very full petalled and almost formalised, but G. S. Thomas told me it could go back to the Romans. They were rose lovers and may have had some surprisingly developed forms, such as the Rescht Rose found by Miss Lindsay in Turkey. No other rose I know is so tightly and neatly packed with petals nor so deeply scented. It is crimson, about the size of a crab-apple and, like the Autumn Damask, perpetual flowering. One gets to recognise family likenesses in roses but I know of none that looks even distantly related to this.

Gallicas and Damasks are of nearly equal antiquity. Gallicas form dense spreading thickets and vary in colour from palest pink to pansy purple. Many are daintily or even dashingly striped. The best Tudor roses are among them. Damasks are rather taller, arching, pale pink or white. All are scented and flower prolifically. Chaucerian gardens would have both, also sweet briar (eglantine) and a hybrid Dog Rose x Damask which became the White Rose of York.

When in the seventeenth century rose breeding began, the rose changed from a discovery to a creation. Natural roses were small, often miniature. The aim would have been to get more petals and thus more scent and later more size. It was the plant itself that had to devise patterns that would fit more petals in. Different intricate and beautiful arrangements resulted that the breeders can never have anticipated, though they could stabilise them. Some make tight little balls like French marigolds, others flat saucers full of petals. The prettiest is a three-fold subtlety. The inside petals are folded forwards over the centre to make a button, the outer rows turned up edgeways to make more room, and finally those that can find no other space to breathe curl over backwards to the stalk to form a rosette. In bud these roses are like button mushrooms, which as they open develop hour by hour into ever more perfect formation, until having done all that was required of them, they vanish at a touch or a breath. I find them more moving than any modern words can say. They have come from so far, bringing a lost age and its secret thoughts with them.

The Centifolias (rose of a hundred leaves), seventeenth-eighteenth century, are familiar to us from the Dutch flower pieces. With great originality they achieved the shape of a brandy balloon, globular, incurved and hollow in the centre for holding the glorious bouquet. Unlike all previous roses they hang their heads, and their soft weight on one's palm is one of their pleasures.

During these two centuries thousands of roses must have been raised and lost, and hundreds refound and named much later. I searched present-day lists of old varieties for one which might have inspired Blake's 'O Rose, thou art sick'. There were no red roses listed of the right period that satisfied me for a 'bed of crimson joy'. Crimson roses, it appeared, as distinct from cerise or purple, only came later (with the exception of the strange Rescht Rose recently discovered). But last year I received a postcard reproduction of a Dutch painting of appropriate date, and there was a true crimson rose looking a perfect ancestor for one of my much later hybrids.

In the nineteenth century rose-growing passed over to the French. They produced many great beauties of wonderful style, but in exploring the possibilities of Gallicas and Centifolias I sometimes wonder if they didn't go too far. Some of the later larger flowers burst out of their buds like tight-laced ladies above their corsets, the opulence exaggerated with frills and flounces. Then I think of the elaborately draped and tasselled drawing rooms full of rustling ladies, and all those vases. No lesser roses would do for them. Many are heliotrope too, a gentle elusive colour that was much appreciated as the large families were nearly always in half mourning for someone. These silky heaps of petals were full of scent.

Concurrently, after 1800 a totally new line was being developed from the neat little scentless China Rose that flowers perpetually, and the Wild Tea Rose of the Himalayas. These Asians were newly discovered and imported. Hitherto all roses except the few Autumn Damasks had finished by mid-July. The original cross between a China and a Damask happened accidentally from adjacent hedges on the Ile de Bourbon, which thus gave its name to a new kind. The first generation was splendid, combining fully the Damask scent and the China habit. Mme Pierre Oger and La Reine Victoria are superb examples, but others are sometimes scentless, sometimes hardly or not at all perpetual. They had to be crossed again and again with Chinas to ensure this quality which was the overriding aim.

The results of crossing with an entirely new strain produced plants vastly varied, throw-backs, absolute novelties, side-lines and failures, some larger than anything yet seen, some jewels of precise perfection. About this time also some of the new dark red roses conjured up a velvety texture new to the genus, that we now take for granted in roses of that colour. 'Old Velvet Rose' is a name applied to the Tudor-shaped Gallicas, but that is a sheen to the eye rather than a texture felt by the finger tips, or if one is smelling it, by the lips.

By the turn of the century Gallicas and Centifolias were relegated to cottage gardens. The Hybrid Perpetual and Hybrid Tea were everybody's roses. The Tea Rose scent had taken over. It is very delicious, very refreshing, but it does not make me exclaim with Wordsworth 'Dear God!'

This is where my collection stops. The age of discovery and the age of creation have passed. The modern rose can only be called an artefact. Large and pop-smart like hats in a shop window, once rained on they are as tatty as roadside litter. Still newer ones are fadeless and rain-proof like plastic, which they might just as well be. Also non-stop flowering like non-stop talking can become a bore. As for scent, blindfolded you would know they were vegetable, though perhaps uncertain between banana skin and apple-peelings. The old roses have a perfume that fills the senses, evocative and resonant like music.

Breeders are trying now to get the scent back, occasionally succeeding, but the public has lost the idea, and perhaps even the capacity to recognise it.

Gradually the compulsion to add one more new and ravishing scent has crowded the vegetable garden off the map. At the same time the unknown quality of bought vegetables makes home-growing essential. This is a quandary and dooms my rose collection for the future, when greens will certainly be put before my spreading prickly eccentricities.

It comforts me that while pigeons voraciously strip my little remaining vegetable plot rendering labour void, no wild creatures but caterpillars and aphis are interested in roses, and against these a multitude of tits work diligently. I did once see a squirrel sitting on the wall nibbling a Tea Rose, but apart from that charming peccadillo the squirrels have been resident for fifteen years and I can't see that they do any damage at all. It is true that I feed them copiously so they are not driven to forage. One baby developed a liking for chewing geranium stalks, like a small boy with liquorice, but he grew out of it. They are grey, but not to be despised for that. Their elegant poses, antics and leapings add vivacity and entertainment.

I had great difficulty with the inner garden behind the house. The moat is a square with the corners rounded off and the lawn a crooked segment of it. It was an awkward shape without focus or vista. The young trees planted by my predecessor — medlar, tulip-tree, mulberry and Judas, four telling names — were placed where the eye could do nothing with them, and became more and more troublesome as they grew, which they did mightily. When I have to confess to these murders I see that it is found unforgivable. The young mulberry went first, with hardly more regret than for a raspberry cane. Years later as I felt my way towards a shape, the by then rather splendid tulip-tree was slaughtered with prayers and apologies. The Judas was spared until its prostrate branches lay like anacondas all over the lawn. Then I visited the Cambridge Botanic Gardens and chanced to see the expanse of ground laid waste by the sprawl of their Judas, which I learnt was only twice as old as mine. My whole inner garden would hardly have held it. The hard conclusion is, Judas trees are beautiful up to fifteen years old. After that they must be felled, and one can start again with a young darling. The medlar after its twentieth year ceased to bear, and aged about forty it conveniently died. It has taken me thirty years of feeling my way, felling, planting, obliterating, re-shaping, to coax the inner garden to an instantly acceptable and endlessly interesting shape. In fact when I come out in summer in the late reluctant dusk for a last breath and the last bird call, there appears to be some mystical ballet of trees going on, stilled only because I am intruding!

My brother James looks on all this with a disapproving eye. He finds gardens vulgar and the more professional the vulgarer. He asked me how I could bear to waste my time on something so ephemeral. I was stung, because I had thought myself concerned with a very long span.

'Ephemeral compared with what?'

'With Art, for instance.'

The west side of the house: 'yew trees hug the building'

Well, the Lascaux caves certainly outdate most things, but works of art are as vulnerable as anything else. The Manor, which is the heart and reason of the garden, has an awe-inspiring past and as much of a future as anything can hope for in this blindly destructive present. Over it the sun and the moon have circled day and night for 850 years and the seasons pass in a drama on which the curtain never comes down. It is the contrast of movement against the comparatively permanent that so delights me. The small annual flower on its thin stalk opens to the early summer, lasts perhaps a fortnight and is gone till next year. (I am thinking of *Nemophila maculata* — Nobody-loves-me, most delicate and endearing.) Others may flower for six weeks, or a cherry tree live for forty years, and they are all adjusting themselves to each other, climbing through, or colonising, or moving outward towards the sun in perpetual change. If at last I begin to sense the house itself as ephemeral, I feel I am painfully growing up.

◇

I have mentioned Mrs Butler whose food-hatch passed through the shaft of the old privy. She lived in Papworth St Agnes in a house very nearly as old as mine, and like me had devoted herself entirely to it though she only rented it. She lived there quite alone with no outside help. I was taken to see the house which in late Norman times belonged to the Manor, Hemingford Grey. It did not in any way resemble mine, having been extended and 'modernised' in the fourteenth and fifteenth centuries.

Mrs Butler was older than I, and so had had longer to develop eccentricities and to detach herself from current living. For instance, in her large bedroom there was a stone fireplace with the ashes of a fire on the hearth. I said, how lovely to go to bed in such a room by firelight. Did she always give herself this luxury?

'Oh no,' she said. 'Only the first night I came here.' So the ashes had been there a quarter of a century. Much could be said about Mrs Butler, who was charming,

intrepid and ferociously passionate about her house, but it
is her garden I want to talk about.

One turned out of the lane to enter a wilderness — not
in the eighteenth-century sense. An immense barn had
been burnt down during the war and left as it was when
the fire died out. The ruins and all the ground surrounding
it were overgrown with towering hogweed and thistles.
The one-time drive led to the back door, with the moat a
few paces from it. A steep shingle of tins led from the door
into the water. The expedient — very likely reluctant at first
— of instant disposal had grown into a habit without her
noticing the gradual result. She showed the moat with
pride.

There had been no less than three serious fires during
her tenancy. Mrs Butler had repaired the fabric of the
building at her own cost, but the terrace in front of the
house had hardly an unbroken flagstone and was littered
with masonry and heaps of rubble, overturned urns and a
broken sun-dial. It was furnished with two light iron chairs
and a table, such as one sees on casino terraces, but
squashed beyond use. There had been steps down to a
garden, but it was impossible to tell where they ended
among the nettles.

From the terrace one overlooked the grounds as far as
the lane, with a tiny village in the distance. There was no
sign of any hedge, nor border, nor path. No once-valued
trees or shrubs marked an outline of what might formerly
have been.

Mrs Butler led me round among the weeds and brambles
with confident equanimity, displaying her garden in which
she took pleasure, while explaining that it was more than
she could really do. She had not pruned her roses or got
round to tying up the dahlias. She drew my attention to
them with a wave of her hand. I used my eyes hard and
saw nothing. It was a weird and ghostly walk and pierced
me to the heart in case I was seeing my own unavoidable
future.

On my return I asked Broomie if he knew that garden.

He said he had known it very well at one time, a very beautiful place, excellently kept.

I invited Mrs Butler back to see me, for we had too much in common. I was nervous lest the reality of my garden should waken nostalgia in her and invalidate her dream. In the event, I had the strange feeling that so much solid green-blooded growth, such sappy flowers whose heads have a palpable weight, such fixed demarcations of where one thing ends and another begins, such rooted trees which if you walked into them would give you a nasty knock, were simply gross — undesirable, usurping imagination.

Mrs Butler had come in her own car. She looked very 'County' in purple hand-woven tweed. Her exterior was contemporary and practical. I do not know, of course, what she saw. Perhaps she had known the Manor before my day and simply saw my garden as not being there, the position reversed and I the dreamer. Or perhaps it was only on her own premises that she needed her extra-sensory powers.

Some time later she sent me a parcel of bulbs 'out of her garden'. They were beautiful white colchicums which have multiplied, and now, in their season, transfigure the autumn garden here.

They seem to be real.

In all my garden labours for twenty years Broomie was my companion. We often worked side by side, being lucky in having the same natural pace, thoroughness and silence. He was a little older than I , and suffering more from wear and tear. Sometimes when I asked him if he would do one of those clearing jobs that are back-breaking, he would say, as firmly as briefly, 'Naw'; but later I would find him tackling it. I knew that his refusal must mean physical distress so that I often took the harder jobs myself.

Mrs Broomfield had been cook in the other house when Broomie was butler-valet. They had only married after the old master died, though gossip said she had wanted him all her life. They were a perfect couple. I sometimes had tea in their cottage which was really countrified, warm and comfortable. It was glorified with some of the RA's pictures and some of mine, and little views of Hemingford before even I had known it. Among Mrs Broomie's cherished china on a shelf was a small terracotta statuette that I had thrown out and Broomie had retrieved, for whose nakedness she had knitted a maroon pullover, an indication of her determination to keep his thoughts in order.

Their conversation, unlike the kitchen talk of Ivy Compton Burnett's novels, had absorbed not a parody of the vocabulary and authority of the drawing room, but perfect manners and an easy interchange. She would have made an accomplished hostess. She could feed the conversation at the right moment or pass it over to him, and neither ever interrupted the other. Mrs Broomie was plump. Her Sunday blouses with a large brooch at the throat were the perfection of kitchen style.

Very occasionally, in a crisis, she came in to cook for me. When this happened, Broomie would show off.

'Hurry up with that barrow now. I'm waiting,' he would say to me as she went past.

'Fred! Fred!' would break from her. '*Your lady.* How *can* you speak to her like that?'

'Look sharp now,' he said to me with a wink. 'Get moving!'

It was a daring game he greatly enjoyed.

One of Broomie's jobs in his previous situation had been to go round the garden or grape-house and pick his choice for a still life, which he then arranged. The RA had but to come down and paint. Broomie would have liked to do the same for me. He was disappointed that my painting had given way under pressure of so much else, though I still did it occasionally. He tried to tempt me, bringing for instance a bunch of pussy willow, assuring me it would make a lovely little picture and I would only need black and white. He had been used also to drive his master up to Burlington House and knew many of the contemporary

RAs. Since his breakdown he was afraid to drive a car. He had also lost weight. Once he must have walked behind a real butler's protuberance because his good Sunday suit hung round him in stiff empty slopes. He was the Vicar's Warden and very low church. When a new vicar was inducted Broomie had, *ex officio*, to carry the Warden's rod in procession round the outside of the church. This lay heavy on his conscience. 'Them sticks' he thought were not right, popish in fact, but he had been forced to do this thing. He shook his head in grief. His eyes were as blue as forget-me-nots.

7

The Start of a New Career

I often went into Cambridge for shopping in my ridiculous rust- and moss-covered car, which slept out in all weathers and was in every way neglected and abused by an owner with no feeling at all for machinery. I never failed to call on Elisabeth, whose minute house was by the Round Church. Her basement kitchen was a centre where everyone met, dropping in for coffee one after the other. She has a genius for making and keeping friends and is the warmest of hostesses. Almost everyone I know in the south-east I met originally through her. Her friends were great givers of parties. Nan Youngman and Betty Rea, Elizabeth and Cecil Collins, Jan and Zoë Ellison, Eileen Mitchell and her then lodger Bryan Robertson, Dr and Mrs Youngman, Lady Taylor, all gave memorable parties. It is tempting to describe some of this artistic circle.

Nan and Betty at that time lived in Papermills and made it a lively focus for Cambridge talent of all kinds. Betty was an elemental of great force, and no expansion of jollity and exchange was too much for her. Now Nan is alone in a charming cottage too small for parties on such a reckless scale. She is as real a person as ever lived, reliable and judicious and a perfect chairman for difficult committees, but in private life she puts herself over as a clown. Nothing that she says comes out untouched by her very individual dry humour, and it is the distinguishing flavour of her pictures. It is the kind of humour that with laughter calls out love — a quality of all great clowns, and like them Nan seems to hide a basic melancholy. She is as orderly as a cat. Her studio, where all pictures are neatly hung, not in heaps in corners, shows no sign of how they are produced, but displays instead rows of carpenter's tools, each hanging in its proper socket, sharp, oiled and rustless. Nan is ozone.

Jan Ellison, half French half Dutch, is a sculptor and also a potter. He was in his youth, in the Mounties and in Paris, as glamorous and handsome as only a Frenchman can be, and is now very splendid, like a worn columnar piece of Gothic sculpture.

He is brilliant at arranging exhibitions, having worked for a long time for the British Council in Persia. He works with ferocious enthusiasm, sparing himself not at all. He would move mountains, and eddies of exploded inertia surround him. His force has a kind of despair about it. Yet he is the most fluent, persuasive and gay dancer that anyone could wish to move with. This lovely ease and freedom of mind and body in space, moving like the spheres, must be a quality of the spirit, rarely found and to be reverenced. Jan has the tenderness of a child, and is as wilful and as subject to crashing disappointments. He is infinitely outgoing, without deception or conceit, and therefore he is loved.

His wife Zoë looks like an El Greco Madonna, but seems to have opted out of her own life through lack of confidence, and chosen to come on stage in a discreet minor part. She is by nature so candid that she can only speak simple truth, and perhaps therefore has shut her lips for ever. But out of this secret thinking sometimes a laugh explodes that pulls everybody up short. She is a most gifted potter. Everything that leaves her hands is a formal poem. These are her thoughts. I wait impatiently for each firing. Almost all that I drink out of, eat off or put flowers or birds' nests in, is from Zoë.

Elizabeth Collins is an imperial figure, adjusted to

welcoming, a born hostess. She wears striking clothes and huge stunning hats and seems also to wear a ritual mask, behind which is X, a complete mystery. This may be because her face has more power than is needed for the life she seems to lead. She should be seen from afar in some great drama, Clytemnestra, or Dido, or St Helena. She is multiple. Her pictures are brilliant and delightful, but tell nothing of herself but her brilliance and delightfulness.

Bryan Robertson was very young. He began with no advantages but his remarkably fine eyes and eager intelligence. He was riding the colt of his rearing and sidling ambition in a gale of laughter and friendliness, as mercurial as he was single-minded. He has made his name, first by his achievements at the Whitechapel Gallery, and since last year has charge of a gallery in New York State University. He now has great presence, as is fitting. It was a privilege to share with him his youthful high spirits.

When I lunched with Elisabeth in Cambridge, Bryan Robertson was always there, and usually Jasper Rose, then an undergraduate, came in for coffee. He is a huge man with a voice swelling like the grand organ, there seems no limit to its volume. Had he been a prophet the walls of Jericho would have crumbled without need of trumpets. He sings old ballads admirably with careful lightness, but if for a moment his concentration wavers a note escapes of natural power and has to be checked down again. Nature has given him a lion's mane and an aquiline face — not just any eagle, but the ferocious monkey-eating eagle. Yet he is the kindest of men, and as he says himself, timid. As an undergraduate he painted spontaneously and his friends snapped up his pictures. Painting then became his absorbing passion. He was the first hairy young man in Cambridge. His black hair was thick, wild and long, and though for formal occasions he was clean-shaven his blue-black chin sprouted by the minute. His nose and hair were usually streaked with primary colours delivered unconsciously in the wilder strokes of his headlong painting. His appearance shocked all Cambridge. He once painted his own portrait almost life-size, full length in the nude, as the Wild Man of Borneo, for exhibition in a local gallery. In spite of his unconventionalities he was chosen as Proctor and was a very good one. When Jasper is in the vein, he can be excruciatingly witty, non-stop for so long that one can't even get the laughs in because the jokes are *in stretto*. When not in the vein he tries and tries and won't give up, and that is not so good. While still up at Cambridge he married Jean, a tiny bright-eyed robin or mouse, who is really an indomitable character quite up to him. After they had been in America a year she came back a stylish beauty with a lovely air of confidence. Jasper too was cleaned and trimmed in God's own country. He returned to find all Cambridge long-haired, dirty and slipshod, and was painfully surprised. He is now Professor of Art History in Santa Cruz and Provost of his college. He and Jean come over in the summer with their two brilliant sons. Jasper with grey hair and a trim imperial is now a fit model for a public statue of a benevolent notable, though in the flesh still lit with flamboyance. When we get together there is only unconstrained warmth and nonsense as before. He is an excellent mimic and puts on other characters so easily and often that sometimes I catch myself thinking, 'It's all right. *That* was not him. This is the real Jasper now.' Once in Elisabeth's garden in Hemingford, to the astonishment of all her neighbours, he gave a demonstration of lectures on the Nude delivered one after the other by a dry elderly English pundit, a metaphysical German, a Russian-Jewish art collector and a Texan in his first gallery.

◇

In Hemingford Grey the war was over but post-war life had hardly got going. Ever since my evacuees left I had had a series of tenants in my tiny annexe, at first friends from the RAF, but later strangers, most of whom were as bad as a tiresome illness. One could never imagine in advance what they would do to exacerbate. Fortunately they were all very temporary, it was an *échange de maux*. At last I had a couple whom I could meet on an equality and whose company I enjoyed. It was as if I had been cured of shingles or toothache, and creative energy was released.

Every day was mine, whole and unbroken from dawn to dark. I was myself again and the spell of the house strong on me. Since one supposes stones and mortar cannot of themselves exert influence, I am always left wondering what it can be to which I respond personally and inescapably. I suddenly thought that what I felt so strongly I could surely write down. This produced the novel *Yew Hall* which I kept hidden for many years. For a plot I had used the characters of my valued tenants, sometimes using their very words. I did not think my mixture of obvious truth and wicked fiction could ever be shown them. I had immensely enjoyed writing it, and had proved to myself that I could put down what I wanted to say, though it now seems to me too profuse in words and enthusiasm.

I paid my first tribute to Broomie in *Yew Hall*, but it is far too slight to do him justice. With every year I valued him more. When, four years after writing it, the book was published, I gave a party for everyone who had in any way helped me by criticism or encouragement. Ann Faber was present and Francis Jeffries, ex-RAF, who had introduced me to her and so started my career. Bennett Johnstone and his wife Lucy were there. I had painted a portrait of her while she read the manuscript. I had intended the four characters in the story to be present, but 'Arabella' and the twin brothers could not come, so Broomie, present in the socially easy role of butler, had the toast to himself. I can still hear with pleasure the warm cries of 'To Broomie!' To my surprise he gave a polished speech of acknowledgement, as if used all his life to after-dinner speaking. It must have been as unexpected to him as it had been to me (I had never imagined the hostess could be toasted) but I had found no words at all. Broomie could barely read. He said he was no good 'at scripture', by which he meant anything in print (it may have been lack of spectacles as much as lack of practice), but he was a wonderful example of wholeness achieved without education.

I had no sooner completed the writing of *Yew Hall*, like a poem to celebrate my love of the house, than the place suffered a cruel blow. The large meadow that flanked the moat, hitherto inhabited by a few calves, was taken over by the National Playing Fields. The mechanical leveller roared round the field for days, turning up first the village gas main, which followed it like a writhing snake unnoticed by the driver till his return journey, and then the roots of my trees, from which top soil to the depth of two feet was removed without consultation leaving the broken roots exposed and turned heavenwards.

I was able in the end, after much battling, and when the damage was already done, to establish my right to both banks of the moat. I thought to encourage good relationship by making my boundary as attractive as I could, but from the first day until now it has been trampled down, broken up and defiled with litter openly and defiantly. I had begun by putting up arches all the way along to make a pergola of roses, but these were all smashed down the first week. At first I ran burning with anger to defend my property, but this only caused boos and jeers whenever I walked round my own garden. As the only alternative to scolding, I then went every match day to stand on my side of the fence and field the ball for them whenever it came over, to eliminate the need for them to break the fence down in order to get in. This produced sniggering mirth, as of course it must. What could be more ridiculous than an old lady fielding for the local toughs? There is no answer. Two mutually exclusive ways of life share a border. The silence that was so full of meaning for me is shattered by the brainless screaming of men and children from which there is no escape. There was from the beginning one enthusiast with a particularly obnoxious voice which over-shouted all others. His language was filthy — which of course is all right in its place, the football ground, but hideous in a garden where remoteness has become an art. I endured him with repulsion for perhaps ten years, but now his voice is heard no more. The children used to copy him, not in mockery, but in serious practice for adult life.

The proximity of the Playing Fields is a 'worsenment' of the Manor from which there is no recovery. The beautiful garden on the Norman south front is untenable at weekends, every spring evening, and during the whole of the school holidays. The very fact that it is so beautiful makes the disturbance unbearable. Only in the early morning quietness falls on it with the dew. I had been here ten years before a nightingale nested in the garden. It had not been here a week, singing all night in the tallest elm by the river, when the grand finale of the first football season took place. The nightingale has never been here since, but it is something that once in my hearing that ancient and most moving sound rang over the garden. I never slept among nightingales again until many years later when I went to stay with Oscar Watson in his tiny cottage at Chandon, on the Loire. There the night was alive with them as the sky was with stars. They sang even round the railway station as I was waiting for the train to take me home.

To those for whom what I am preserving is of no value, my embittered defence of it can only seem selfish and anti-social. It was dejecting to find myself, now that I was no longer a spy, forced into the position of public enemy number one in the village, again a position from which there is no escape since as encroachment from every side continues I must always be the *animal méchant qui se défend*. For the sake of the house, to raise friends for it in need, I began to show it to as many people as possible, inviting passers-by of all kinds, anyone who paused to look over the garden wall. It has been a great comfort to me, feeling it so desperately vulnerable, that the place is responded to with excited delight by almost every stranger. I have no confidence now that either its fame or an army of friends can save it. One has to be content with seeing it while it is still, in part, there.

I felt that nothing could console my rage and grief at having its integrity violated by the Playing Fields, but just then an article appeared in the *Cambridge Review* which put the position in perspective, and ever since has helped me with a wry grin to tolerate it. I would like to quote it almost in full.

RAGERIES DE GROSSES PELOTES

Association Football is an old game in England — perhaps the oldest British sport — for it was played here before the coming of the Romans. According to one historian, and there is much evidence for this, the game always suffered royal animadversion. Thus Edward II, in 1314, issued a proclamation forbidding the game as leading to breaches of the peace :

> Forasmuch as there is a great noise in the city caused by hustling over large balls (rageries de grosses pelotes) ... from which many evils might arise which God forbid: we command and forbid on behalf of the King, on pain of imprisonment, such game to be used in the city in future.

Only a scholar would question the surmise that *grosses pelotes* meant footballs. It may be a matter of some shame to the Englishman long proud of his legendary public good order, but it is a delight to the sportsman, to discover that this injunction was ignored. Edward II, properly from our point of view, as a lover of the game has observed, was dethroned and assassinated. In 1389 Richard II passed a Statute (12 Rich.II.c.6) forbidding throughout the kingdom 'all playing at tennise, football and other games called corts, dice, casting of the stone, kailes, and other such importune games.'

The frivolous absorption of Englishmen with such riotous disports was a source of continuing anxiety to our rulers, but we must be grateful for the popular refusal to abandon the game.

Henry VIII's great Cardinal could effect little change, and 'foote balle', according to Sir Thomas Elyot, continued to contain 'nothinge but beastlie furie and extreme violence whereof procedeth hurte . . . ' Though still castigated as a 'useless and unlawful game' and an 'idle practice', Association Football – though bearing close similarity to its later bastard offspring Rugby Union – was more than thoroughly rooted in the Elizabethan era. The Bard reminds us occasionally of this. Thus in *The Comedy of Errors* (Act II, Scene I), Dromio of Ephesus laments:

> *Am I so round with you as you with me*
> *That like a football you do spurn me thus?*
> *You spurn me hence and he will spurn me hither:*
> *If I last in this service, you must case me in leather.*

It also seems that some of our more sophisticated modern tactics were not unknown. Thus in *King Lear* (Act I, Sc.IV):

LEAR. *Do you bandy looks with me, you rascal?*
OSWALD. *I'll not be struck, my lord.* (Striking him.)
KENT. *Nor tripped neither, you base football player.* (Tripping up his heels.)

However, Elizabethan football brought daily its 'Dooley' tragedies and worse, for the game was played with typical Elizabethan violence. The finding of a county jury in the Good Queen's reign reveals the attitude of the law, for on a certain day in 'Ruyslippe, Co. Midd.,' the accused:

> with unknown malefactors to the number of one hundred assembled themselves unlawfully and played a certain unlawful game called foote-ball, by means of which unlawful game there was amongst them a great affray likely to result in homicides and serious accidents.

A few years before Shakespeare's death the following resolution was entered on the Manchester Lete Roll :

> That whereas there hath been heretofore great disorder in our toune of Manchester, and the inhabitants thereof greatly wronged and charged with makinge and amendinge of their glasse windowes broken yearelye and spoyled by a companye of lewd and disordered persons using that unlawful exercise of playinge with the foote-ball in ye streets of ye sd toune breaking many men's windowes and glasse at their plesures and other great enormyties. Therefore, wee of this jurye doe order that no mannor of persons hereafter shall play or use the foote-ball in any street within the said toune of Manchester . . .

There is thus little doubt that football was around, not organised, though certainly widely played, in the seventeenth century. Its effect might certainly have weighted the criminal statistics unduly.

JERRY WEINSTEIN

◇

In the interval between writing *Yew Hall* and sending it to the publishers, I had written the first of the Green Knowe books, partly because I was hard up, but more to people the place for myself. I do not know how anyone can judge of what they write unless they are writing for themselves.

An unexpected delight, to me the most rewarding part of my subsequent career, was the immediate acceptance by my son of the suggestion that he should illustrate *The Children of Green Knowe*.

I can draw and paint what I am actually looking at, just as I can describe what I experience. I am a reporter but have no pictorial imagination. Peter has it, and he can magically draw what I can only think. It makes a most happy partnership, but how he makes time to do it is painful for me to imagine, since his own job often keeps him at work all through the night.

The books were submitted together and both were accepted by Faber and Faber. At first they wished to put *The Children* in their adult list, but as I insisted on Peter's drawings it was ruled that pictures were only for children, so I became a children's writer. I did not at the time realise what a step down this was.

Yew Hall got a stinking review from John Betjeman who thought I was being serious when I was being ironical, but *The Children* was well reviewed in the *Times Literary Supplement*. I received in Cornwall a telegram from my neighbour, John Peters, then at Cambridge University Press, congratulating me on the review, which I had not seen. This was the only pat on the back I got for it from anyone and established him in the top category of friends.

◇

In 1952 my nephew John Hemming wrote to me. I had scarcely seen him since he was a boy, when he professes to have been terrified of me, though I tenderly revered him even as a child. He wrote now with extraordinary prescience to say that he had met a girl of whom he felt that she and I were somehow going to be very important to each other.

I went to meet them on Cambridge station. At the end of that reportedly mile-long platform I saw my nephew approaching accompanied by a child's legs carrying a large blue hydrangea plant. Behind these globular flowers when we met was a little being who took my breath away. She was not the child she looked, but still young enough to be embarrassed and overawed by the possession of glorious globes of her own. She had brassiered them up so high that her rounded face and hydrangea-blue eyes appeared to look out between them, like a prehistoric figurine. With her expression of frightened innocence she made a picture for some as yet unwritten folk lore.

Parted from her plant which she presented to me, less hunched and with her long neck freed from anxiety, she was so angelically beautiful, so vulnerable and so un-placed that I immediately gave her a local habitation.

Wherever I took her, people caught my eye with loving surprise that in this shabby post-war world there could be anything so fresh and new. What was so touching about her was not innocence in the usual meaning of ignorance. It was that, in spite of the comic sexiness of her get-up, she had the far greater vulnerability of a delicacy almost austere. She had caught, as one catches a disease, the idea that glamour was essential to a girl, and had tried to conform by making for herself out of bits of cast-off material, stylelessly as for a charade, very off-the-shoulder blouses, out of which her slim adolescent shoulders and neck rose with the startled look of total nakedness, the more so as her skin was so transparent that not only her eyelids but her whole body was imbued, from young veins and from reflections, 'with blue of heaven's own tinct'. Add to this that she carried her head with an aloof dignity, and that she was incapable of making any movement in the nature of shrugging, flouncing or snuggling, and the would-be glamour was seen as the perfect foil for its transcendent opposite.

John had been right. Caroline has become for me the daughter I so much wanted, and she inspired my next book *Persephone*. She married John and they live in Cornwall, hence, much later on, *The Sea Egg* featuring her two sons. Perhaps no one but she loves this house as much as I do, and she adds to its serene gravity a charm and wit that seem to be of its lineage.

The house is a great sorter-out of persons, because what it offers is so unexpected. People have quickly to re-adapt themselves to it and the phoney are exposed. Bright talkers become as drunks, pouring out nonsense and finding no *point d'appui*. But to the vast majority of English people it is like the grass of a hillside under one's feet.

◇

Made confident by the double success of my first two books and feeling that I was getting the hang of writing and could now take a long step forward, I wrote *Persephone*, taking Caroline as a model for the heroine. It took two years to write. I still think it far the best I have written, but it was rejected by almost every publisher in England and by Harcourt Brace and others in America. It lay in oblivion for thirteen years.

I was shocked by *Persephone's* failure, which I could not understand. I returned deflated to the idea of Green Knowe. I had been repairing the old patchwork curtains hanging in the dining room, in which every piece of material was pre-1803. As one turned over the folds, it was easy to pick out the clothes of the whole household, young, adult and old, everyday and best, master and maid. It grieved me to have to cover any of them up, but a hole is no use even historically. Out of this study of ravishing hand-printed muslins, cottons and cambrics − the quality of the materials themselves was a joy to the eyes and fingers − came the idea for *The Chimneys of Green Knowe*. The theme of blindness had occupied my mind ever since I came to the Manor, as if it belonged to the house. In imagination I connected it with the Crusades, but the only fact I know is that Elizabeth Gunning who lived here as a child, had a blind son by one of her ducal husbands. There is no evidence that the boy ever stayed here. It was an interesting mental exercise to try to imagine the house from the standpoint of a child who could not see it.

◇

It was after the publication of *The Chimneys* that I first met Margaret McElderry, then of Harcourt Brace, New York. She did me the honour while in England of coming here to see me. I went to meet her at Huntingdon station, and among the crowds pouring out of the train we singled each other out at a distance and both laughed. We have laughed ever since, with pure pleasure.

She is like a figurehead riding the great waves, if one could imagine a figurehead that constantly dissolved into jokes and always imagined itself to be at the stern. She is a driving force as sensitive as a gramophone needle and by nature self-effacing and shy. All her movements are big, buoyant and dancing. I have a photo of her emerging from the sea on Nantucket as a goddess of high spirits that the Greeks never thought of. She is composed of opposites that all somehow pull the same way, making a strength and charm quite individual. Her nose, for example, starts from her face as if she were descended from the Duke of Wellington, but having begun in this grand manner, it then changes its mind and tucks itself into her face in the most demure feminine curve, an enchanting joke. It would take an American Solomon to find a metaphor for her eyes. They are not melting, still less are they questing. One must have seen something like them in majestic sculpture. They are set so rightly in the original architecture of her face that looking at her you know exactly who she is, and that she will always be so.

She is gloriously American, with that great warmth they bring to everyone they meet, till one has to wonder, since it can't always be sincere, if it ever is. With Margaret, it always is, and one must be content with one's millionth part. (I did once see her socially stumped. It was a great relief to me.) We meet here every two years for the shortest two days there could be, but I have never seen her on her own ground. She has an iron will and must be formidable at her desk. I have however seen her winding up a week's business trip in Brown's Hotel, expertly and precisely packing her many cases while the telephone rang continuously and people pleaded for last-minute interviews. When she actually left, the management and all the staff formed two rows to bow her out and she sailed forth, leaving me feeling like waste paper after royalty has passed.

In all these years of friendship with Margaret, she has never seen my roses. There is at least one nurseryman who sells them in California, Ben Tillotson, giving luscious sexy descriptions of each, but I do not know if even this sells them in any quantity in the States. One would expect to find a few in New England in odd neglected corners, but even in this country they are harder and harder to get as mass selling is the only profitable business. It is not too much to say that most modern roses disgust me, yet every year I try some of the novelties for late flowering, and one or two get a stay of execution, and perhaps live to be lovingly accepted.

It is obviously an eccentric passion to demand that roses should have historic and literary meaning and a whole world of associations and values as well as their beauty and that particular unsurpassed scent that strikes into and opens out the brain. It is rare that I find anyone who shares it with me as important, not just a preference or a gimmick. I wrote in *An Enemy at Green Knowe*, for children to read, of the old lady fighting on the side of the angels, 'her roses seemed to her the clearest sign of the essential nature of life'. What can children think of such a statement if they have only seen Super Star?

8

Comings and Goings

Elisabeth's house in Cambridge had become such a general meeting place that she found it hard to work. She decided to move into distant quietness, and bought a site in the corner of a large orchard only five minutes walk from me. Peter designed the perfect house for her. The elevation is an equilateral triangle of light wood just lifted off the ground by cantilevered wings from a central base. The building of it was a pleasure to watch. It was a long hot summer, and when the open framework was set up like a bird cage golden in the sun, the workmen, stripped to the waist and burnt to the colour of the wood, clung about it whistling like canaries. They were the same men who had worked on my house, but one of the foremen had then been the boy-who-held-the-nails. The studio fills the major part of the triangle, with windows on all sides and in the roof, yet it feels like a private interior, not at all like a greenhouse. Elisabeth at first complained that it forced her psyche into a triangle and made her feel peculiar. For a while she drew only triangular trees, of which I have one picture in my house. Her nearness has made it possible for me to have first refusal of all she does.

We must have more in common than anyone would suppose, since her pictures are the only ones I ever want to hang in my house. (I have my own there, as by right, and naturally my colour sense goes with my own decor.)

I want almost every drawing Elisabeth does and have over the years made a collection of them as money allowed. I particularly love her rock formation drawings. Her soft pussy-cat movements and mysterious but insinuating smile would never lead one to expect drawings so sharp, exact and unflinching, of the fractured throw-ups of the earth's crust. Over these frightening realities she contrives to lay the strange light that both penetrates the sea and reflects up from it. Her mountains out-Wordsworth William. When she draws a valley, over the immense immobilities she can bring the subtlest and most ephemeral atmospherics, up-currents and down-draughts, gleams, shadows and rain-mist, all in transit.

In these drawings there is never a human being, but her paintings are by a different person. In them people cluster in a kind of perpetual enigma, escaping, confronting, standing aloof, clasping in despair, being led by the hand to somewhere undesired. All is strangeness and hostility, and yet the composition of all these separates is superlative. I never cease to wonder at it. I do not understand her colours, which are perhaps deliberately uncoordinated in order to maintain a dream-like non-world.

It looks in 1971 as if she may be moving into another style, or going back to take up an old one. During the war she did a painting of a bread queue which was factual, funny and gay, with children racing like butterflies round the patient, heavy crowd in their sour old coats. Movement round the immovable again. She has said for a long time that people and landscape can't go into one picture — a difficulty I don't understand. Where else is one but on earth, even now? But she has struggled with this for some time, with a series called Inside and Outside, in which the people are in rooms, highly-coloured, and the landscape or townscape is silver-grey like the photo of a dream. Or, if she has concentrated on the view, figures may be furtively hurrying off the edge of the canvas, or the figures and the scenery painted in two entirely different styles. Now at last in 'The Outdoor Sleepers' humans and the earth are come together as one, and in the painting of her brother Phil, warming his stockinged foot before the fire with a door behind him open onto a hilly view, he is entirely at home in both worlds.

Elisabeth is always in deep and secret thought about painting. She never misses an exhibition of old or new, and yet remains in what she does, undeflected from her own extraordinary intuitions. And she will not say a single word about them.

◇

Some time in these years I met Jim and Helen Ede, of Kettle's Yard, who subsequently donated their house and collection of pictures to Cambridge University. The resulting friendship must have been instantaneous, for I can no longer remember when it didn't exist.

Jim is idealistic beyond what some people can take, and with it quite inflexible, under a loving modesty of manner. He is tall and slender, an immaterial dandy with an unparalleled genius for setting disparate works of art and objects together, so that everything is bettered by his combining, like a wit among wits. He is exquisite in everything, but never precious, never static or closed in. His perfections of arrangement are always changing and taking in more, appearing at rest but always liberating. His house makes mine in my estimation drop suddenly from what I thought it was to a barbarian's cave strewn with gnawed bones. I have fallen over backward trying to keep it large.

Helen has the sturdy frailness of a mountain flower vibrating in the wind. Her face has suffered none of the humiliations of age. She is perfectly beautiful in the same way as when she was young, but has become dis-embodied, a psychic appearance, and thereby a graceful act.

In contrast with this withdrawal of the flesh she has a Highland voice as big and bounding as the sea and as caressing. Her laughter is like the smack of a wave. Listening to Helen is one of the joys of my life.

It was Jim who had the idea of bringing parties of undergraduates in May Week to see my roses. Surprisingly to me, they enjoyed it, and I did so immensely because for a long time I had met no young people. It has continued every year with greater numbers and a wider spread of the net. It has never yet been wet on 'Jim's day'.

I have a Damask Rose called Hebe's Lip, in smelling which Jim quoted, 'Oh might I drink from Hebe's Lip!'

I replied that of course he might, and brought out a bottle of Hock. Since then I give when possible select small parties who choose their own globular rose to drink from. It is rather a dribbly business, the roses leak, but utterly delicious; also long drawn out, the process can't be hurried. One thinks of Chinese drinking poems, and of I.A.Richards sitting in the shade of the beech tree wearing one of my large straw hats, emerald green.

◇

I was emboldened to start giving garden parties myself, guessing at the weather and telephoning everybody at the last moment when I thought everything was just right. I am particular that the roses shall be perfectly displayed, every dead head and deformed leaf off. On every bush, among its innumerable roses some half dozen, because of their position on the bush and the angle at which they face, are inevitable eye-catchers. These must never be cut or the whole vista will lose sharpness. In filling the house with roses I only take flowers from the back or those that face awkwardly or have some modest trick. They can be just as perfect.

Once, seeing the garden in perfection, I arranged with a professional photographer to come and take rose portraits. The evening before his visit I gave a party. As I was seeing the guests off, one of them arrived breathless with a real armful of roses saying, 'I just couldn't resist. It can't matter to you, there are so many.' She had picked every one of my eye-catchers as she walked round. A cow would have eaten the very same ones had she been loose in the grounds.

Apart from set parties when I change my persona, it is my fancy that everyone who comes into the garden — especially the inner garden and the hidden corner of that where the Norman front is wrapped away from view by big trees — shall enjoy the feeling that this is a secretness where other people don't come. Although I now show people round every day, I cherish this illusion, and I see that it holds good for them. They step out of the ordinary into the extra-ordinary, into an ordered profusion that seems effortless, existing like woods or moors, private for the person seeing it.

The success of this mirage has unexpected side effects. I once agreed to receive a girls' school from a very good address in London. Two bus loads came, and as each girl stepped out she dropped me a pretty curtsey. Their headmistress came with them, a would-be maternal figure, and two of her staff. I was impressed by the good manners of the children, and when I had shown them the house, hearing that they proposed to picnic in a field I relaxed my stringent rule of NO PICNICS and suggested they might prefer the garden.

It was in the month of May, in full nesting season, bird song woven into the air. The girls were delighted, and having been given their rations they split off into small groups of friends to different parts. The headmistress then with her staff joined me at my garden table and settled her plump person comfortably. 'I have told the girls they can do their little doings in the bushes. I didn't think you could mind.' She was like a nanny who thinks that so long as their dear little panties aren't wet, all is well. But these were girls of eleven and twelve. If her staff had not been with us I would have given her an unexpurgated rendering of my thoughts, but their presence in the ensuing embarrassment would have been too much. I could only notice with wry amusement the breaking of bushes as un-ready girls burst out, chased off by the gardener who thought they were after birds' eggs.

◇

I have an affectionate respect for the English middle-aged working class, or whatever euphemism is now in vogue. I love showing them round. They are almost always friendly, natural, well-mannered, appreciative and without envy. What they say as they go round is always the same, even to the tone of voice. It is almost as stereotyped as bird song. Half a dozen clichés cover the whole range. But they welcome pleasure and expect it and express it. The visitors that I don't like are those who, having got themselves invited inside the garden gate, then keep me standing there for half an hour while they tell me about somewhere else, and stand in my house with their eyes shut for better visualising while they describe Anglesey Abbey. One however I loved. She was very old and frail and on a Bank holiday was conspicuously alone. I brought her in and learnt that she lived in a caravan on a caravan site and had no living relatives. She had once had a little Regency house, and as she sat having tea with me her thoughts came alive for her. She closed her eyes and conjured up each room in her house and everything in it. The desk stood there, the chintz couch and nice little rug in front of the hearth, and so on, with curtains, ornaments and pictures, a deeply loving inventory. I asked her if she had any of these treasures now. 'Not in a caravan,' she said. 'I had a little garden with a lilac tree by the gate.' For about an hour and a half she was back in it. I thought she might have visited me again, but she never did.

I once turned out, with passion that took them entirely by surprise, a party of young people who had no manners at all, and once only I have refused to take in an unexpected party. I had finished a hard day's gardening at seven in the evening and had come in at the back door too tired to make myself any supper except tinned soup. I carried the bowl with attention fixed on it to avoid spilling,

into the dining room, surprised to find it so dark. A sudden
thunder cloud? I put the soup down and raised my eyes.
The three large windows were all blacked out with faces
pressed against the glass, noses and lips flattened. Some
were on tiptoe leaning over shoulders, others crouched to
look under elbows. Such faces look hideously sinister.
Their eagerness suggested devils come to fetch me away.
I pulled myself together and opened the french window.
'Good evening. Who are you all and why are you here?'
Before I was even given an answer half a dozen had
already nipped in under my arm and were examining the
contents of the room.
'We have come to see the house.' I explained that it was
a private house.
'We know that. That's why we didn't come inside. There
are two bus loads of us, come from Bedford.' Why hadn't
they tried to make an appointment? 'It was just a sudden
idea. We've heard *such things!*' This was voiced as a lament.
I was too tired for generosity. I gave them the run of the
garden, closed the window on them and went back to my
soup, now cold.
Another day I admitted a Lincolnshire Church Treat in
charge, as I found out too late, of a fulsome Minister. He
tried to push himself forward as the focal point of the
excursion and buzzed round me like a fly, resting here and
there on my arm or hip. When at last I got them all
shepherded back to the gate, he asked my name. 'Boston,'
I said, and then, to emphasise that it was not Bostock, 'like
the Stump.' 'Boston,' he said giving me a squeeze, 'Boston
perhaps. But there the likeness ends.'
I give this the prize as the silliest thing that has as yet
been said here, but there are runners up. A chaplain from
one of the Cambridge colleges once confided to me in a
sacred whisper, 'Young men's souls are *so exciting.*'
Visitors of every kind come in this casual way off the
river bank, often very interesting. There are many house
visitors too, for whom willy-nilly I have been forced to
learn to cook. My brother Frank has come from the

beginning for all Bank holidays and Christmas. He is a supporter in all trouble, a willing nurse when I am ill, a financer when I am low, a generous bringer of bottles and a sprightly washer-up. He likes lots of company. When he laughs, it takes him like a punch in the midriff, he doubles right up. Elisabeth is good at provoking this well-known and much enjoyed contortion.

◇

Broomie's wife fell ill, and after many months lying at home, she died. He was desolate, but touchingly allowed me to give what comfort I could. Every morning when he came for the day's orders while I was breakfasting, he stood poking a log on the fire with his foot, his face turned away from me, while tears fell on the hearth stone. Another day was beginning without her. Nothing was said, but presently he would have a cup of coffee and we would discuss the garden as usual. I don't think I ever saw his teasing smile again. He kept his cottage immaculate as she would have wished it, and there he sat alone. Apart from his church duties and what he called a 'crazy game of dominoes' at the pub on Saturday nights, he had no life but the Manor garden.

Often when sightseers left the garden after walking round with me, Broomie would say, 'Them's no gardeners. They never said a word to me.' It is a sad fact that very few of my visitors ever do speak to the gardener, unlike the old-fashioned gentlemen who used to visit his late employer the RA, to whose manners Broomie was accustomed. Complete strangers of course don't know if it's one's husband in his old clothes or the two-hours-a-week man, and so are nervous. Americans are better. They will take a chance. As Broomie had nothing else the lack of courtesy hurt him.

I had Broomie for several years more, working on as usual till one day he told me he wanted to see a doctor.

He was sent to the hospital for examination and came back shocked and shaking. I asked him how it went.

'Awful. They didn't half make me sweat.' He was to go back at the first vacancy for an operation.

He died after a mere week in hospital where I visited him every day. The ward sister was hateful to him throughout, taking it out of him in every way, especially if I tried to speak for him, he being too modest to complain for himself. He died unconscious and I rejoiced as if I personally had been reprieved from what might have been his fate had he survived.

His coffin was brought to the village church on the evening before the day of the funeral, and left there overnight. When I was told this, I took flowers and went along to soften that loneliness. It was dark and my flashlight was dying. It lit only a yard before my feet. I did not need it along by the river, which gives off a light of its own however dark the night. Not a soul in Hemingford Grey was stirring. My footsteps rapped sharply as they followed the bobbing circle of light along the narrow overgrown path to the church and across the churchyard. Already at the porch a creepy chill struck me, as if the place were dangerously taboo except on Sundays. The door was not locked and the latch clattered, breaking into the heavy silence within. The closed air was suffocating with the smell of damp, of hassocks and hymn-books, of humans in Sunday clothes. At once repellent and familiar, it combined with the known shapes of the pews to suggest powerfully everything that keeps out of sight.

It simply never occurred to me that there must be an electric light switch somewhere by the door, nor, had I thought of it, could I have brought myself to advertise my presence by illuminating all those windows. My business was as private as any thief's.

The torch picked out the stone slabs at my feet and then the base of a pillar, the back of a pew. I kept my other hand outstretched lest I should bump into the font or upset a table piled with prayer books. I realised I should have to find Broomie by hand. Advancing into the over-charged darkness, I too-suddenly found myself touching a light wooden box. I am used to important oak coffins, heavily encrusted and loaded with brass. This might have been something delivered from a factory. The scantness of it in the dark under my hand was horrifying. Could this be my Broomie, in a box cut down to the least millimetre? I laid the flowers on it and wept bitterly from shock in that Stygian place.

I still had Ivy Violet Lander, digging herself in and making the house more and more her own. She excused her lateness one day by saying that she and Mr Lander had been having 'an up and a downer'. In my ignorance I took this to mean an unexpected bout of conjugal love, but I believe it means a cat and dog fight. She, like Broomie, had now lost her mate. I knew little about him except that he also was a bantam, and that he and she had shared one table knife for twenty-five years before I gave her a second. When he died she showed no outward sign of grief, but her little house was empty and in mine there was always something going on. She could not keep away. There was loyalty and devotion certainly, and money had nothing to do with it. It was impossible to pay her. If I gave her more money, she at once made more work to do. If I gave her a Christmas present she gave me one worth ten times as much. She once gave me a load of coal.

She had a large head for her diminutive body, made larger by a tremendous mop of white hair. Her smallness was an obsession with her. There was no topic of conversation that did not immediately connect with it. She was not a breaker, but whatever loss of treasures occurred was caused by her jumping, duster in hand, to flap at them. She had large, bright grey eyes, a nose like a big toe and was always joking. After a severe attack of Bell's Palsy her face remained twisted to one side, which did not distress her in the least, and it also left her blind in one eye and almost totally deaf. Later on she grew a bristling white beard. In spite of her witch-like appearance, it was always obvious that she was the good fairy. It was impossible not to respect her.

Her working clothes were my cast-off best, hanging to her ankles and dirty beyond what one could bear to imagine. Her best, for whist drives and Bingo, were cheap and new, and she covered herself with Woolworth jewels. She rode a bicycle so much too big for her that she could not reach the seat, but stood on the pedals and went furiously at a wobble.

Her childhood must have been very hard, judging by her habits of economy. She took all left-overs home, even one tired lettuce leaf was worth retrieving, and she finished off anything left on our plates or in our glasses. She had a horrid little song to the effect that you need never want for marmalade while there's orange skin on the street. She never learnt that water from the tap was more expendable than water brought from a pump down the yard. She saved every drop in sink or bucket till it was thick and black. Every day she did a dozen things I could not bear.

Nevertheless, she took the work of the house right off me, and kept its floors and furniture in a high state of shine, all the time watching over me, on the look out for more she could do. She would even stir my tea for me. I think she would have liked me to be paralysed so that she could find scope for her boundless helpfulness. She talked often about her holidays, but never took them. I think she only raised the question as a lead for me to say I couldn't do without her. If I pressed the matter and said I would manage somehow, she wept.

Owing to her deafness, she could not receive the compliments of people going round the rooms while she was at work. She took a great interest in my family and my near friends, who ranked as hers, and never grudged the extra work they caused. Total service with total equality was her notion. On one occasion when Sir Martin Ryle was visiting me, he found his way into the kitchen to talk to her. Afterwards I said to her, bawling as one always had to, 'You've just been shaking hands with a very famous man.' 'Have I?' she replied wiping her hands on her clothes. 'I wonder what he thought of me.'

Apart from the loss of Broomie, whose face I had blessed every time I looked at it, I was now faced with the loss of my garden and my way of life. For months I struggled on with a drunken old-age pensioner and a firm of mechanical gardeners, who for a crippling price would roar over the lawns for an hour with huge machines that could only cut squares round circular beds and left long tufts at every corner, so that the end result was uglier than if it had been left uniformly long. I was in my late sixties, but still vigorous enough to hope I might maintain a rearguard action and keep much of the garden recognisable, if not as it should be, but the prospect was harassing.

However, the happiness promised me by the house where I first saw it still held. The young gardener who had laughed with Ivy Violet over Mrs Merryweather and her precious carpet, turned up and offered himself for the job. He was now a sturdy forty-five-year-old who had been in the Navy during the war, then on the Railway, then ditching and hedging on the airfield. He knew little about gardening when he came, but is very intelligent and has eyes to see why I want what I want. He is infinitely honest, patient and tough, and is now a second Broomie.

9

A Snub of Success

My next book was *The River at Green Knowe* and for the writing of it I took to the river again after many years, exploring it by day and by night.

I discovered to my grief that the Great Ouse, as I remembered it, had gone. The water was discoloured, the water lilies extinct. On one stretch the caravan site came down to the water's edge, all lit up at night. At Huntingdon bridge the smell of the water was unbearable, in Hartford the back gardens came down to the bank with gnomes and gardening to match, as if no river was there. At Houghton Mill the huge elms round the mill-pool had all been felled. On the left the field was full of cars, on the right the edge was trodden down by the summer's multitude, the broken rushes full of cigarette packets and chocolate wrappings. At Hemingford Mill the surface of the water was carpeted by ice-cream cartons.

It was slightly better downstream towards St Ives where there was still an osier bed, and along the back of the town total dereliction and decay had their own charm, having once been beautiful — inspiring by comparison with gnomes. Only the full moon at midnight gave back to the river its old dignity, its worshipfulness. Even the moon since then is no longer aloof. In spite of all that is said, it seems to me a contraction to bring everything within reach, not an expansion.

A photo in *The Times* of Guy, the gorilla in the London Zoo, triggered off *A Stranger at Green Knowe*. I spent many hours in front of his cage and was given the greatest help by his keeper and only friend, Laurie Smith, both in formal introduction to the magnificent creature from the keeper's inner passage and in the supply of information, addresses and books. During Laurie's three weeks' holiday I saw Guy's despair, and actually witnessed, awe-struck, the tragic dance, like Samson praying for strength to pull the place down, of which I wrote in the book. I described this to Laurie on his return. He told me gorillas had been reported as doing this but that he had never seen it, and if I had, I could think myself extraordinarily privileged.

I wished to dedicate *A Stranger* to Laurie Smith, but the Zoo authorities refused their permission on the grounds that my book was 'entirely against their principles'. Odd that the useful supposition that animals actually prefer captivity can be elevated to a principle.

The subject to me was a big one. It had to contain the whole force of my belief that all life, not merely human, must have respect, that a man-centred conception of it was false and crippling, that these other lives are the great riches of ours. In particular I wanted to make clear my immense admiration for this creature so vulgarly shuddered at, and that there was no cosy answer to the wickedness that had been done to him.

This book was awarded the Carnegie Medal. I was not very excited by this, because it seemed to me unlikely that a really wonderful book for children would be written every year, and as the same writer could then never receive it twice, that left one as the best in a period of twelve months after all the notable writers have already been excluded. It did not strike me as a dizzy peak. However my publishers wrote ardent congratulations, and letters from the awarding body of librarians wrote awesomely of the 'supreme award'. I was gradually coaxed away by such professional shibboleths from my common sense. I began to feel perhaps I had done something good, and that it was arrogant to depreciate an award. And not only one's vanity but one's proper pride as an artist longs to believe in recognition.

When however I was officially told that I would have to attend a conference and make a speech, before a thousand delegates, with press, photographers, spotlights and flashlights, I felt I would know better how to face a firing squad. I had never made a speech in my life. Even announcing to thirty friendly airmen what record I was about to put on had made me blush. That was the nearest I had ever come to public assertion and the sound of my own voice.

For months my spirits were crushed by this looming catastrophe. I was too proud to funk it but felt I might very easily die on the platform. An old lady having a stroke among strangers did not strike me as a good end. I wrote my speech, a harder problem than writing a book, and learnt it by heart. I took tuition in speaking, ridiculous as it now seems. I went upstairs alone once or twice every day and projected my voice, carrying the all too familiar and perhaps meaningless words into the upper air of the Norman hall. I have forgotten now what I intended to say, but I think it was very passionate. Every day I felt iller, till at last I went out to my fate.

A special train was run for the conference from London to Llandudno, stopping at every main junction to take in more librarians. Each platform was packed with them as the train drew in. I discovered to my surprise that all librarians look alike. When seen in the mass, all facing the same destination, their conformity was total. As the train filled up I realised that whatever it was they all had in common, I was conspicuously without it. Cold looks, implying that I was improperly using their special train, chilled the whole long journey. I comforted myself with the childish fantasy that it would be different if they only knew!

The Naples of the North was an invigorating surprise. I had convalesced there as a child and had remembered nothing but the pier and the hotel lift boy who obligingly took me up and down all of one wet day. I had failed to notice the great semi-circle of homogeneous architecture enclosing the bay, which on this later occasion shone like blue silk. I had been given an address which proved to be almost the last hotel on the esplanade. There I met the three wardresses for my execution or bridesmaids for my marriage to the public, whichever way one chose to think of it, all children's librarians. Eileen Colwell was one, a famed storyteller who has never outgrown the appearance of a very bright eight-year-old, but is capable of organising anything and getting round anyone. In spite of the difficulties she had with me she has remained a most valued friend. Another was Virginia Haviland, an onlooker from Boston, Mass., and the third was my official sponsor, who may well have been on the selection committee. She was to introduce me to the meeting next morning.

The conversation opened with apologies that there had been some mistake about the hotel booking and they had been forced to accept the only empty rooms in the town. They had allotted the best one to me and the three of them were under the roof in the servants' quarters. As there was no service it was understandable that these were empty. We went out to a better dining place, and it was there in a rosy light over coffee that I innocently and nervously asked if they thought twenty minutes was about right for my speech. There was a pause for consternation. Then Eileen Colwell said, 'There is no time allotted on the programme for a speech from the recipient.'

'But I was told it was obligatory.'

'I myself am only allotted five minutes for introducing you,' said my sponsor. 'So how could you have twenty minutes?'

All the effort and strain of the last weeks had keyed my self-control up to go through my performance, but not to be so meanly punctured. I lost my temper and hit the table till the cups danced. I poured out my rage at the wasted time and nervous exhaustion, the nights of fear. With rage came adrenalin and I knew I could address thousands without turning a hair, that I was in fact all agog to do it and mad at being defrauded.

It was at this point that Virginia Haviland declared herself my passionate ally. She thought, bless her, that people were there to see and hear the recipient, that they would *want* to hear what I said. Virginia and Eileen were, as I found out later, the only persons at the conference who took any interest in me or my book. It was all, as I was quickly learning, a blend of eyewash and sales promotion. It was agreed that I could just rise and say, 'Thank you.' 'A couple of sentences would not be too much.'

My bedroom, when I retired fuming to it, was found to be on the ground floor facing directly onto the pavement of the esplanade. The window curtains had been torn down by the last occupant, perhaps in a hurry to depart. I complained to the management in vain. It would need a ladder and they had no one to do it. I had therefore to undress in the dark. The room was so small that if my suitcase was on the floor I could not pass it. There was nowhere to hang anything up, nowhere to put anything down. My clothes I threw on the grubby bed and spent a sleepless night.

In the morning I confronted the serious operation of dressing for my exhibition to the assembled thousands. It had to be done in full view of the esplanade at close quarters, and presented unimagined difficulties. The bathroom of such a place was not to be thought of. There was a wash basin set in the angle of the bedroom wall smaller than I would have thought could be on the market. It fitted flush against the walls without a ledge on which one could lay a toothbrush and would just accommodate a hand in the scooping position. Toothbrush, sponge and soap had to be on the floor. A lot of bending and rising went into the exercise of washing.

Once out of bed, one could put the suitcase on it and so pass to the dressing table. This had a swinging mirror of which the adjusting screws no longer held. It had taken up the horizontal position for good, reflecting the floor. Nothing I could devise would raise it. Any consideration of one's face would have to be done lying down underneath it, a very unsatisfactory method. Hair had to be arranged by guess work.

By this time I was in a philosophical state. The hotel breakfast was an interesting education in how some people take their holidays. After the meal we walked the length of the esplanade beside a sea so still it could only manage a ripple like a fleeting secret smile. But we had no time for the sea. The Pier Pavilion at the extreme opposite end of the bay was our objective. Outside it I was introduced to the young illustrator who was also being medalled.

'Are you the other one?' he engagingly asked, passing over a generation and my ill-groomed appearance. 'I can't tell you how glad I am to be with you. I've never been made to feel so small in my life.'

'Me too. We've been made fools of.' We went in together like a couple of children among brusque grown-ups.

The stage of the Pavilion had last been used for a drawing-room comedy and the set was still there. Against this background we were placed together at the end of a row of chairs and left there as if in our prams for a very long time. I watched the auditorium filling up and searched the gallery for photographer's equipment or spotlights, and the floor for a table for the press. There was neither. I wonder who had thought up that particular torment for me.

Finally the functionaries filed in to take their places, though without any welcome for us, and we all stood up for the entry of His Worship the Mayor. He talked with outrageous vulgarity for half an hour about the amusements, amenities and funfairs of Llandudno and the excellent hat shops and hairdressers where the ladies would want to enjoy themselves while hubby was at the conference. I think he can never have read a book and probably didn't know or care what particular conference he was opening. Last week it had been Labour and the following week was perhaps the British Dental Association. I wonder if they all got the same speech. Why not? I thought of my chosen words for which there was no time. With relief we all stood up to see him out.

There followed perhaps an hour of reading the minutes, the schedule and rules of the conference, and paying compliments to retiring members. The Head Librarian of the British Museum was awarded a certificate of good behaviour by proxy — he was wisely not present — and then our two sponsors said their pieces. I was assured that my book was really quite up to the required standard. We received our medals like school children and said our brief thanks, and all was over for us. While the other business continued we compared our medals with incredulity. Mine was almost exactly like one I got for swimming the mile when I was eleven. His was not even as adult as that. Of course the medals were only symbols, but of what?

Later I sat beside the President for the official luncheon. It was clear that children's books were so far below his interest that he had neglected to inform himself about this last unnecessary addition to them. Beyond saying he believed I had written a book he risked no conversation at all to my side, having some easier neighbour on his left. It was an excellent meal and I gave it my attention.

I stayed on an extra night to hear Alfred Duggan lecture, and cadged an introduction to Margery Fisher. Though I had sat for two and a half hours exposed to the gaze of all the delegates and it seemed reasonable to suppose they knew me by sight, yet as I moved about Llandudno, entirely populated by librarians attending the same lectures, sitting by the sea or dining in hotels, not a single person risked a smile or murmured congratulations as they pushed past, or showed the least desire to meet me. It was like being ostracised at a family gathering. I asked Eileen Colwell if the great majority were adult librarians and if children's writers were objects of aversion and contempt. 'Alas,' she said, 'that's just it. It's what we are fighting against.' I returned home with, I thought, a good funny story against myself, of total debunk. I hope I shall never be so naively taken in again. I had not thought I was much, but I had failed to grade myself as low as the opinion of the conference placed me.

Some months later I was invited (by the machinations of Eileen Colwell) to give the redundant speech to a gathering of exclusively children's librarians—a small lecture room full. This time I was treated with all the friendliness due to a visitor and ally. I had defiantly expanded my speech to forty minutes, and though the notes shook in my hand so that I could not read them and I must have appeared to be waving to a departing friend, I let them have it in full, and found to my guilt and shame that I could hold an audience motionless and breathless, and that this was fascinating and vulgar, degrading to the speaker. I have never wanted to do it again.

I very much dislike prepared or repeated speech and am increasingly depressed by my rôle of guide to people wishing to see the house, when I have to say the same thing every time. If someone who has already been here accompanies a newcomer, I am always prompted, 'Do tell him about . . .', and I find an incident that was once true has become with telling both dead and abhorrent, and as if false. I lose much for myself by telling other people. Similarly, after nursing a friend suffering from a nervous breakdown whose refusal to admit the existence of any joy had worn me down, I asked John Peters to carve for me on the main tie-beam a quotation, that for years had vibrated in my head unspoken, VOCATUS ATQUE NON VOCATUS DEUS ADEST ['Whether called upon or not, the god is here']; since when I cannot think it, for shame at having failed to realise that a factor moving in one's thoughts is more vital, more powerful, than when it is exteriorised. This of course applies also to my writing. I can never again see hoar frost with surprised rapture since I put it into words in *Yew Hall*.

10

A Notable Wedding

At three o'clock one morning I was woken by the telephone. It was Margaret McElderry in New York asking whether she might be secretly married from my house during a business trip to England in a few weeks' time. The name of her bridegroom, Storer B. Lunt, though famous in the book world of New York, was new to me. He was there with Margaret and we met and welcomed each other over the phone. I promised with delight to do all they asked. But secrecy was to be absolute. This caused me to receive some very funny looks from my son whose suggested visits were forbidden with no reason given. I could see him wondering what his mother could possibly be up to.

Margaret arrived first to discuss arrangements. The secrecy was not for reasons of high romance, but because they were both so well known that the obligatory guests would have run into preposterous numbers. They happened to have six great friends in England at that time, and that was to be all. Margaret suggested a caterer, anxious that I should not be worried, but I thought that for so small a party I could manage. I stuck to it that in this house it was better to be personal than grand. The old place however had a joke of its own in store for us.

The bridegroom arrived the day before the wedding. He is American in the grand tradition, generous, genial and open. He read English at Cambridge, England, and has travelled much and is at home in all countries, yet has kept and enlarged that total innate American-ness that to me is more bafflingly foreign than any other nationality. Margaret on the other hand is Irish expanded to the full in America.

The wedding arrangements led off with a farce of consciences. By law one of the couple had to have been resident in the parish for three weeks. We asked the rector if the usual custom of parking a suitcase in a house would satisfy him. Certainly, he said. It was the legal formula and perfectly all right. My land lies on the boundary of two parishes, but on the wrong side of the line. I asked my great friend Lady Hemingford if she would house the suitcase for us, but she thought Lord Hemingford would not approve of a lie even if sanctioned by the law. However my neighbours on the right side of the abstract line put neighbourliness before righteousness and amiably took the suitcase in.

This had been three weeks ago. On the day before the wedding Margaret and Storer went to the canon to get the marriage licence from him, only to find that he had not received it. He again was all furtherance and kindness and they understood him to say they could go ahead and that it would be all right. On the way home they called on the rector to explain the situation. Now it was his conscience that was stiffer than the canon's. He ruled that the wedding was out of the question without the proper paperwork. They went off then in much distress to the Registrar in St Ives, to find that he was on holiday and had left neither address nor deputy. They pursued him to his home address in Cambridge and there they ran him to earth after much dashing around, and the preliminaries were put right.

Margaret and Storer had been driving all day since breakfast and they arrived back at the Manor laughing and exhausted. I am sure things are more regularly managed in America, but they refrained from saying so. They had hired a car for the occasion and were lucky in their chauffeur, a young artist who drove whenever funds were low. He was both a charmer and a perfect help to them and to me.

After this agitating tour of two counties, they discovered in conversation over tea that, though they had brought with them a vast supply of champagne, in my simple country life I had never needed, and did not possess, ice-buckets, let alone ice. It had never occurred to me that you couldn't get married without ice-buckets.

The bride and bridegroom set off again to fishmongers, to caterers, to hotels, all round the district for another two hours, but at last ice-buckets and ice were laid on. Again, this was rural England and they took it as they found it.

While they were about on these errands I had been busy preparing in advance everything possible for the wedding feast. My kitchen tables were all spread with covered food, polished silver, glass and plates. I was just thinking of sitting down for a minute when the kitchen ceiling collapsed, followed by a deluge of water. A pipe had burst in the bridegroom's bedroom. The mess and havoc can be imagined, but miraculously little was broken. While I was ringing up for a plumber with very little hope of getting one, Ivy Violet without so much as an exclamation went instantly into action, setting basins under the leaks, mopping up and clearing away. The anguish in my voice proved enough to bring a plumber. The visitor's room was stripped, wainscots pulled off, the floor boards wrenched up to that ominous sound of splintering; the pipe was mended and everything put back, dried and made ready for when Storer should come in.

The kitchen ceiling gaped with a ragged spidery hole up into the joists, and Ivy Violet was hard at work re-washing every dish I possessed as gaily on the spot as if it were the war. I decided to move the champagne glasses out of the way into the Norman room. I was half way up the steep and winding stairs with a large tray bearing all my treasures, when all the lights went out. I managed not to drop the trayful before I reached a landing where I could put it down, jangling but unbroken. It proved no worse than a fuse which I could put right, but in my fumbling round in the dark I had smelled gas. It was strongest in Storer's room.

Nowadays, after centralisation, it may take three weeks to get anyone from the Gas Company, but at that time it was still local and very ready. Their man found that the plumber in putting back the floor had put a nail through the gas pipe.

This also was put right. By the time Storer and Margaret returned with their ice-buckets, Ivy Violet had got the kitchen back as it was before the accident, except for the smell of gas, damp, dust and plaster. The wedding was on.

All went smoothly from now on. The guests, Charles and Mrs Gregory, Alan and Paula Schwartz, Professor Basil Willey and Mrs Willey were on time at the church. There was only one slight hitch. Margaret in place of a hat had put a velvet band round her head as token covering in deference to St Paul's wishes. It had a tendency at unexpected moments to shoot forward over her eyes. In the middle of the service when the rector said 'Let us pray' the bride was heard to say *'Oh damn!'* as she was blinded again.

Our rector prefers the New English Bible, so hated by me that I no longer go to church. In the marriage service, in the lesson familiar to us as beginning 'Charity never faileth', we were all startled to hear the simple statement, 'Love is never rude. ' Certainly it is impossible to imagine Storer and Margaret being rude to each other. Nevertheless, those four words remain inescapably ridiculous. When we met in the vestry to sign up, I asked the rector what it was in the old version as the new had put the other out of mind. He could not remember, nor could Basil Willey who, I then learnt, was partly responsible, having been one of the translators. We looked it up afterwards, and I have to admit that 'doth not behave itself unseemly' also wakes comical lines of thought. Basil sent me later his extremely amusing and instructive essay 'On Translating the Bible' which won me over to his side in so far as we could suffer together.

On our return from church the unmanageable headband was thrown away, but retrieved by Ivy Violet in memory of the wedding. Her white hair was as thick and unseparable as a fleece, and the velvet band sank deep and firmly into it. It was worn every day ever after.

For the wedding feast I had acquired an elderly ex-college butler. When he arrived, the old and soupy state of his tails, waistcoat and knees, and his out-trodden shoes made me blink at the thought of having him in the house, and his face suggested a jemmy in his pocket. Nevertheless, on the job, in moving, how express and admirable! In action how like an angel! He was omniscient and omnipresent — and perfectly used to fallen ceilings, perhaps quite common in college kitchens.

Champagne and laughter were unloosed, Margaret as always was most vivacious and enchanting, even more so on this occasion among her chosen group, all as much Storer's friends as hers. Meanwhile in America the news was out and cables began to arrive. One read 'Tis a consternation devoutly to be wished'. There was laughter, but I have never liked to ask whether it was a howler from the Telegraph Office or an American chestnut on the lines of the traditional chamber-pot jokes at French peasant weddings.

Meanwhile in the kitchen the artist-chauffeur washed up, a glass of champagne beside him and another by Ivy Violet who has never forgotten him.

The newly married couple set off for Ireland. I was told, I can no longer remember on whose authority, that as neither was English the marriage was not valid outside this country. But what of that? It would only make our good intentions funnier.

11

More Books and More Friends

The little annexe continued to house a stream of changing tenants, most of whom became friends. I am hard to please, in fact an impossible landlady, requiring that their life shall be invisible and inaudible and that they ought to be glad to be here. There have been enough who were. In 1960 or thereabouts, T.A.M.Bishop, the palaeographer, became my last and permanent tenant, something dreamed up by my guardian angel to keep me contented for life. Nobody could be more easy, more generous or more interesting. Often we do not even catch sight of each other for weeks. He is utterly absorbed in his work and receives no visitors, nor ever joins in the constant entertainment of my house, but nonetheless there exists between us a strong and even affectionate respect. Never did two people annoy each other less.

Mr Bishop gave me invaluable hints in the writing of *An Enemy at Green Knowe* and appears, alas very impersonally, in the story as Mr Pope.

◇

The genesis of *An Enemy* was more obscure than that of the other books. It had come accidentally to my knowledge that the Playing Fields committee were proposing to build a pavilion to be used regularly for dancing, on the edge of the moat nearest to my living-room windows, perhaps thirty paces away. The plan showed that all the windows faced my way, directing the noise full at me. The committee explained that this was because if the windows faced the field they would all be broken. A line of public lavatories was to edge my garden path and the overflow from the septic tank to go into the moat. This had been passed by the planners a whole year before I heard anything about it. It would have made this house uninhabitable.

I took all possible defensive action, hundreds of visitors signed my petition and all my friends were called on to help, which they did enthusiastically, but in the end the house was its own defence. It is too precious to be treated like that, and influential protectors arose. Planning permission was cancelled and the pavilion re-sited at a bearable distance. Lord Hemingford I think tipped the final decision with a tactful joke.

The original Enemy therefore was the committee of the Playing Fields, and the fight to preserve the rare from hate and contempt was against them.

Conveniently for me, there was among my acquaintances a lady of learning who served well as a model for the witch Dr Melanie D. Powers. I have known four women who strike me as likely dangerous witches, two of the dominant and two of the sweet malicious type. I could say 'I know you by the way you walk', but not in the sense of the Negro spiritual. I can be happy for hours sitting in a crowded place watching the way people walk, far more tell-tale than their faces and gestures.

Some critics have complained that though in the book evil is infiltrating, powerful and very largely vulgar, there is nothing to pit against it but 'niceness' and some gibberish spells. Nevertheless the great invocation proclaimed during the eclipse of the sun contains the words:

Be Thou what Thou art and what Thou willest to be.

Omnipotence could not be more clearly and tremendously

expressed and loved. The words of course are not mine. They are taken from *The Key of Solomon*.

About this time the Bodley Head, out of the blue, for I had had no connection with them, wrote suggesting a monograph for their series about children's writers, and asked who I would like to do it. I was extremely pleased by this tribute, and suggested Jasper Rose, recommending him as a wonderful humorist. He delighted me by accepting, and took me more seriously than I had expected, though about my personal appearance he was as funny as I could wish.

This gesture from the Bodley Head was so unexpected that it gave me a strong sense of gratitude and obligation, so that when they asked me to write a book for younger children to go in their Acorn series, I was glad to try. *The Castle of Yew* is recognisably of Green Knowe extraction, though a branch line.

Kathleen Lines has always been of the greatest help and encouragement to me. She and Judy Taylor and Margaret Clark became very much my personal friends, so much so that when later Margaret asked me to speak at a meeting of the Children's Book Circle, I accepted for her sake what I would not do for anyone else and delivered my second talk, this time comparatively coolly. The friendship between us has continually strengthened, and I am happy that work of mine is in their hands.

Most of my books are an immediate reaction to something personally felt. The idea of *The Sea Egg* was triggered off by an egg of Cornish Serpentine sent me by Caroline Hemming in memory of Kynance Cove, where she and I had revelled in the sea. Peter and I went down to Cornwall for a holiday to think it out. Daily we absorbed the waves, the seals, the rocks and the cliffs. I particularly wanted to show Peter a cove half way between Land's End and Nangisel. It was a wide semicircle, high and sheer, sea-sculpted all over with meaningful but mysterious figures crowded together as on the front of a cathedral. I had previously spent hours marvelling at the carvings and trying to give dramatic interpretation to a staggering natural monument. When we got there, the whole cliff face had fallen into the sea since my last visit. There was nothing left.

I was prevented from writing for a long time after this by having to nurse an old friend with a nervous breakdown. As everybody knows who has had to do this without help in their own house, the exhaustion and despair of the patient eventually reduces the nurse to a like state. At last, after eighteen months, my friend was well enough to leave. At once I sat down to write, and all the normal joy that had been blotted out for so long burst out and bubbled up. It is a short book, written straight off in about three weeks, but wholly happy, thinking only of the sea. Just as it was published, the *Torrey Canyon* blotted out Kynance under black oil.

The illustrations Peter did for *The Sea Egg* seem to me quite perfect, though the rocks are those round Land's End, not Kynance, and are described by me in *Persephone*.

◇

The latter part of my life here is very different from the beginning. Then I knew nobody locally and owing to the spy-scare had lost the expectation of knowing anyone. My time was all my own, to spend as I wished, and I was never at a loss. Now it is difficult to get half a day to myself. The common sightseer takes most of my time, but apart from the distinguished circle opened to me by Elisabeth, the happy truth is, that if I could have selected who I would have to live close round me in the village within a few minutes' walking distance, I could not have chosen better than chance has given me. I find, with surprised secret triumph, that I can make friends for myself.

Among the first of my friends was Oscar Watson, with whom I stayed several times in France. He was formerly with Cambridge University Press and is now with Larousse in Paris, though his heart and home are in the Loire country where he runs a pottery. Oscar is a pulsar, an output of concentrated energy. Do not imagine a small confident man full of 'go'. His limbs are long drawn out and his face and head are like a precise elegant blueprint of nervous, intellectual and emotional tensions finely adjusted to carry as much as the system will bear. And like such a mechanism, Oscar is vulnerable. His dynamism has worn him away to a skeleton of steel, his hair, long before his time, is snow-white and fly-away as in a Blake drawing. His laughter is a sudden choking paroxysm that makes huge blue tears well up out of his eyes and run down his face, so that his conversation is muffled by his having continually to mop them up, but not a word of it should be lost.

Oscar is tyrannical to be with, because he does not admit that anything physical or material is beyond one's powers. Mind over matter is absolute, so that after a long train journey down from Paris, he once, without hesitation, carried a wardrobe on his shoulders from the station to his cottage, a mere two miles in a snow blizzard, and arriving there late at night laughed unto tears because in his absence mice had nested inside his mattress and had eaten through all the blankets.

The first time I stayed with him he set me to digging rose-beds, a delightful and proper occupation for me, but it was with a medieval spade as illustrated in *Les très riches heures*, with a five-foot pole for a handle. I remember it as having a heart-shaped wooden blade, but can hardly John believe it.

The ground to be dug was an overgrown road, once the *Route Royale*. This was at his first house in France, a simple shelter divided into three tiny rooms, their doors opening direct onto a vast meadow with the river beyond it. Water had to be fetched from a considerable distance and the nearest shops were two miles away. It was the most perfect holiday I have ever had. It was really medieval country, ruled by the seasons which are dramatically extreme, and crowned by the *vendage*, but it has no time.

Man can die philosophically if only his earth is immortal.

In any picture gallery of my friends, Peter and Diana Gunn must appear. Peter writes mostly about Italy and lovers of Italy and lovers of lovers of Italy (as Byron's sister) and is encyclopaedic about it. Diana writes poetry, novels and criticism. They are both wholly professional and may *not* be visited or spoken to on the telephone, hardly even be thought of, during their rigid working hours. Nevertheless, their life is a series of crises, calamities and setbacks of every kind, desperations and passionate throwings overboard. Crisis must be a quality of a person, as luck is said to be. It seems to be the Gunns' natural and inevitable climate in which they are at one or rather, take it in turns. Nothing less than having to report the worst will drag a letter or telephone call from them. In their much desired, rare visits they arrive like comets, brilliant, presaging and travelling on.

Diana is the only woman I have ever seen who fulfils my idea of a Great Beauty of the Edwardian kind, the sort to electrify the Opera House or a grand ball in the season. It is the type that comes of a long line behind it, incorporated in it, utterly unlike the rubbishy animal beauties of today. She is as tender and delicate as she is diamond hard and unyielding. She is tall and very thin. Her golden feathery hair is like the crest of a bird, and she carries her head with natural pre-eminence and looks down her exquisite nose in a way one can only enjoy. Ironically, her life is one long bitter contemptuous fight against Edwardianism, hitting and hitting herself and wondering why it hurts.

Peter seems perfectly fitted to live in such a battlefield. Perhaps he needs it to give scope to the breadth of stretch in his character, or to lacerate an underlying inertia. He is always at work and yet looks lazy. His large indigo blue eyes, that look as accepting as mirrors and as secret and unaccountable as lakes, dominate a face in which no other feature is in itself compelling, its bone structure is fine and regular but reticent. His speech, movements and gestures are all reserved, but he is blessed with a sympathy for and understanding of women, very rare in Cambridge, and can make an old woman remember what it felt like to be twenty-five, without her feeling silly or ashamed.

It was after I had been staying with Diana in their house on a bald mountain above Swaledale that I wrote *Nothing Said*, in praise of rivers and waterfalls. Of course the Manor was woven into it too. It was my own garden that suffered a summer flood, the tree on my river bank that fell. It is the slightest of books, plumped out with an extra number of enchanting drawings by my son.

Then there are Charles and Madge Howard, both artists, now alas settled in Italy. They are the Sun and the Moon. Madge has hair like snow and skin like snow in a faintly pink sunset. She dresses often in white wool and gives off a kind of gentle effulgence. She is delicately clear cut and very quiet, also now, owing to arthritis, bent to a crescent.

Charlie's face is like the ripe side of a peach, and his smile is such that you could hold out your hands at him to get warm. He has a special gift not of letter writing but of postscript writing on Madge's letters. Any words he puts down come off the paper to you as the whole man.

◇

I am now a grandmother and the house is filled with children every Saturday. My daughter-in-law Di already had two little boys when she married Peter, and now has two girls, of whom the elder, Kate aged three and a half, seems to me myself reborn.

After so long in undivided control of it, I had come to think of the house as a kind of museum for children. For years I had been adding to it things mentioned in my children's books as being here, which, till I chanced to find them, had been imaginary. Friends also continually send me missing items made or found — the wicker birdcage, the picture of 'The Frigate Woodpecker in a Storm', a racehorse shoe, the name board for Feste's stall, a flute, a box of sea-treasures, ivory dominoes, etc., so that visiting schools could see the books come true. I have not yet succeeded in getting a harvest-mouse's nest, badly needed for my collection of nests. Very recently an enterprising schoolboy, Philip Foale, has undertaken to make a doll's house replica of the Manor.

Each item had formerly a fixed place, and the loss of any of them I would have felt as a calamity. All this static museum stuff has now been swept away. The objects are desirable toys, strewn all over the house and lost or broken one by one in a torrent of irresponsible life. I do my best, but the epoch of possessions has gone. They are the least destructive of children, but for the young everything is kaleidoscopic, it must be broken apart and reformed every minute. Also they don't enjoy anything they have to take care of. They do not have to take care of their imagination, the vital element of which toys are only the used and discarded tools. They are now old enough to have Green Knowe books read to them and to fill out the characters with all the power of their own feeling and fantasy. I am amused to find that Green Noah has left the page and truly prowls the garden, that Terak the giant has been *seen* lying by the river. They are enchanting in themselves, they love the house and everything in it and round about it, and every little enjoyment or game is ritually repeated every week.

Ivy Violet touchingly adored children, but had never had any of her own. Her deafness cut her off from my grandchildren, while her toothlessness and bristly white beard gave her a goblin look, straight out of the pictures in a fairy tale — the sort of face that might peer round a mushroom. The children were wary when she tried to coax them. It was sad that she got so little response.

As she aged, she became an obsessive worker. She could not stop, except when she sat down and fell asleep, when she might sleep for a day and a night. Then she would not know what day it was, nor whether it was dawn or dusk. She would come pedalling madly along on her high bicycle and I would hear her little goat's feet running along the entrance hall. All out of breath, she would hang her red coat, that looked as if it had seen years of dirty warfare, on the tin-opener fixed to the wall, and begin work all in one movement. Every day, year after year, I took the coat off the tin-opener and hung it on the hook provided for it. She would watch me sideways round the broom handle and say, 'If I had to give you sixpence every time I hung it in the wrong place, you'd have been rich by now.'

Often I would urge her to take it easy, not to get so out of breath. 'I don't believe in wasting time,' she said, going off at a run carrying the heavy Hoover. Her legs were like matchsticks.

Watson the gardener told me that once, when I was away, he locked up the house long after Ivy Violet had finished work and was on his way home when he thought he had better make sure all the lights were turned off. He went back into the dining room and there in the dusk something caught his eye. It was Ivy curled up like a cat asleep in the armchair, having been overtaken by one of her twenty-four-hour naps. She will certainly share with me the privilege of being one of the Manor ghosts.

Indeed one day she never came. We did not worry, but just laughed and said she'd fallen asleep. The next morning also she was absent so I sent Watson round to her cottage — he always treated her with the greatest courtesy and helped her by sweeping her chimney or heaving coal as if he were a nephew — to see if she was ill. He found her bicycle propped against an open door, the wireless on, and Ivy lying on the sofa, dead. Her last ride standing on the pedals had been too much for her, her last sleep endless.

For several days afterwards the house seemed to be full of her pattering steps and all the little mouselike scratching noises associated with her (she had always done a great deal of her cleaning with a *penknife*!). I could hardly drink my tea in expectation of her leaning over me to stir it properly. At the same time, the house and the future seemed empty of love. All that devotion snuffed out.

12

A Chapter Requiring Superlatives

During the war I had found a companion for music, not as might have been expected Elisabeth, whose tastes differ from mine in that she is free from my basic melancholy. She is major to my minor. We go to many concerts together but never with a feeling of sharing. I believe she hears something different. She is more musical than I and certainly more original. However, my companion from the old war-time concerts appeared to want every note as I did, both in my beloved music room, that shell of sound, and in King's College Chapel, the Royal Festival Hall, the Raphael Gallery, Glyndebourne, Bath or wherever we could go. We listened as one person and if separated listened for each other.

Sometimes, listening together here to some special broadcast, I felt the house was built of music, permeated through and through with it, held in place by it. I caught myself realising that this that I was hearing was *now* (the present is a tense I am seldom aware of), as much a part of the house as its walls and arches, a high moment in its history to be taken in by it and kept. I offered it these ranges of being to be remembered as a sign that I had been in it.

For sixteen years I accepted as permanent the freak of mutuality in listening that had given me a companion — and then I lost him, as human beings do lose one another,

The author in her music room, 1973

suddenly and without foreboding; and with him music was taken from me. The mechanism of listening was broken and for many, many years, until now, the perfect acoustics of the Norman room have tingled only with silence.

I fought against my inability like a right-handed person learning to write with the left. Contemporary music was interesting if not addictive, and there were things never heard before that could be listened to, though I could only bring half a mind to bear on them. Caroline Hemming, on her rare visits, proved to have the other pair of ears I so needed, but that was perhaps for one hour in a year.

I met through Brian Jordan of the Cambridge Music Shop the young composer Ian Kellam, then teaching in St John's Choir School. He took me to hear his opera *Circe* performed by the boys, and I was immensely impressed by his control, his awareness and quickness of ideas and his unbounded friendliness. He is at the centre of a web of live fires sparking off in all directions. He put me into a fever of excitement by suggesting that he should write an opera from my book *A Stranger of Green Knowe*. Being totally ignorant of the crises and fluctuations of a musical career, I thought this was a new kind of life opening for me, when something new was badly needed. I put everything else aside and wrote the libretto, feeling sure I had done it well. Several years have passed since then and it has remained for many urgent reasons an unfulfilled idea, but an idea that Ian nudges occasionally as one might push a Halma man one square forward on the board. Something may come of it some day. He says the whole opera is in his head, ready to be written down if wanted. One scene, a long solo for Ping, was actually written for a commission, but at the last moment the performance was cancelled because of rehearsal difficulties. This was a blow to both of us. Meanwhile the toe of my slipper if not my foot was wedged into the door of a new interest.

At last in 1969 I accidentally heard, coming from the upper floor of the Cambridge Music Shop, a record of breath stopping sounds. *Who* was doing that? This was my introduction to Alfred Brendel's playing, and in pursuit of his concerts and records all my difficulties vanished. The Muse had turned her face to me again, for I also about this time met the harpsichordist Mary Potts. I had long wished to know her for the insufficient reason that I much admired her nostrils, which I had seen inhaling music at a concert in the Edes' house, Kettle's Yard. Being so unusually delicate and definite they promised the same qualities in her personality.

It is from my friendship with Mary that this chapter stems. We listened to Brendel together whenever we could. She took to the Manor instantly and began to devise ways to bring the tomb-like non-music of the so-called music room back to life. She took me home with her and played to me on her exquisite Tschudi. Christopher Hogwood came here and suggested bringing a portable harpsichord to play for me, but before he could do so, Mary had somehow, in a conversation in Edinburgh, persuaded Colin Tilney to come and sample the acoustics of my room.

Undeserved honours are frightening, but it was not I who had suggested this. I thought of my narrow twisting stairs and remembered how when the BBC were here to televise *The Children of Green Knowe*, six strong men had got stuck there with the rocking horse, their heads poking through the rockers and between its legs, and could neither move up nor down, while plaster fell round them. What of a musician with his greatest treasure? There was a danger of gasping temperamental rage. However, I comforted myself, he will not be as stupid as the BBC's team. If it can't be done, he won't try.

I need not have worried. When I heard the van brushing through the branches that overhang my drive, I went along to meet it. Through the half-open window of the pausing car I could see a smiling Renaissance-type face suggesting a livelier Raphael. I was startled by his youth, but found later that he was supernaturally timeless, and indeed it was like meeting one of the errant gods. I experienced then and there the shock of contact with total intelligence. I have rarely met what I now use the word genius to stand for — something different from high talent, brilliance, originality, megalopersonality or inspired nonconformity. All these can be eccentric, even lop-sided, but genius is concentric, unforced and of sublime clarity. I would like to think that life moves towards the production of such human beings, but I believe the old tree throws off its miracles at random throughout the ages. At least we see, to our great enheartening, what it can do.

First experiences must be treasured in memory, because their illuminating power is gone like a flash of lightning. The second hearing of a piece of music is never like the first, because it has lost the element of surprise. Afterwards it can be absorbed, possessed, called up again and again till at last it becomes subjective — the very opposite. This applies also to the first meeting with people. Surprise is truly from without. I do not know why we should be ashamed at sensing that the scale of values is rocketing. (All this while the van is pausing on the drive with the harpsichord, detached from its legs, lying on the floor covered with an eiderdown, and the baby asleep in its curved side as if they were intimately related.) We left her there while Colin and his wife Hilary went round the garden. They walked hand in hand, making it look like the Elysian Fields — but before doing so he had darted into the house for a quick look at the stairs, and could not long be held back from the business of the day.

The Norman room was of as much interest to him as a concert platform, no more. We chose a position and placed the trestles, then he and Hilary drew the instrument out of its heavy wooden case and carried it naked and murmuring up the stairs. With as much inching backwards and forwards as it takes to get a car out of a parking place, but without hesitation or fuss, it was juggled up into position, the most difficult entry, Colin said, it had yet had to make. The delicate creature had then to settle down after the journey, and be adjusted and tuned. Hilary found the room so frightening she could not stay in it, but

The dining room, where all the books were written

slipped away for a walk with the baby. This shows that though my interpretation of the room is the authorised version, it is not the only authentic one.

Mary, Elisabeth Vellacott and I settled down to listen. At the first vibrating notes the stones of the building began to tingle. The house seemed to me to come alive joyfully as in the Resurrection. The arches filled with sound, the whole shape of the room caressed and held the music. Nothing had been lost in the intervening years. But this time it was no gramophone with its frayed or fluffy needle, but sparkling, vital, spontaneous sound. Having once begun, Colin played continuously. I sat where I could watch his hundred faces. It was as if the faces of artists throughout the ages were contained in his, but unexpectedly more painters and poets than musicians. Even a young Rembrandt peeped out in a turbulent moment.

After perhaps three and a half hours of mounting excitement (he was introducing me to Frescobaldi), he really took off in a roar of swarming notes, passionately interacting, reforming and flying off, so that my ears were incredulous of what they were hearing and the only possible reaction was blissful laughter. Mary was standing to turn over for him with a kind of mad smile. More Frescobaldi followed, cooler, more deliberate, subtle and teasing. Then Colin stood up, suddenly very white, and said to me,

'I don't know what your programme is, but I'm tired.'

'My programme would be drinks at once and supper as soon as I can put it on the table.'

'But I shan't play so well after supper. Anyway, we'll see.'

But he could not stop. I collected Hilary and the baby and brought the drinks. He played on undisturbed while the baby tried the sound of everything hittable within reach, and finally settled to a merry tattoo beaten with candle ends on the floorboards. Then Mary played to Colin, but by this time I was downstairs nursing the soup.

After supper the entrancing child was put to sleep in my

granddaughter's cot, and we did indeed have more Fresco-baldi. Hilary joined us, finding the room less terrible by candle-light. The furniture had been pushed around to house the harpsichord, so the room was less beautifully balanced than it should be. If a harpsichord were permanent everything would be rearranged to do it honour.

It was a wrench to see the magical thing taken away. The baby was not laid in the instrument's lap for the return journey but slept in Hilary's arms. It was very late when they left, and a white mist was rising over the flat lands.

What thanks are possible to a departing visitor who has brought such gifts? I told him it was the loveliest thing that had happened to me for fifteen years.

'I would like to be able to say the same to you. But I did enjoy it,' he replied with the beautiful honesty of his eminence.

I shall hear Colin again I hope in concerts and broadcasts, but this occasion was unique for me, and like all really memorable experiences, it leaves everything open for more.

Postscript

by Peter Boston

Lucy continued to live at the Manor until her death. She still managed four or five hours' gardening a day well into her nineties. For the last eight years or so she lived entirely alone in the house, after the tenant of the annexe had departed.

She continued to have frequent visitors and small concert recitals. If she was feeling lonely she would be found at the garden gate on the river bank talking to passers-by, whom she would often invite in on the spur of the moment to look round the house and garden.

She corresponded (rarely and rather painfully) with Harold until his death in 1969.

In her ninetieth year I suggested that she might now feel sufficiently mature to be reconciled with my stepmother and, after only a little hesitation, she agreed. Barbara duly came over and I think they both felt better for the exorcism. Since then she also met my half-brothers and their families on several occasions with evident pleasure.

As the house has no heating, apart from ruinously expensive electric radiators and the open fire in the dining room which requires constant stoking and much humping of coal and logs, we were naturally worried about the problems of a nonagenarian living there all alone. I did eventually manage to persuade her to have some night storage heaters installed and some very expensive electric wiring was carried out in preparation. However, at seven o'clock on the morning when the heaters were due to arrive, she telephoned me to say that she would rather die of cold in the twelfth century than be warm in the twentieth, and would I please instruct the men to take the things away.

A little later, Diana, my wife, proposed to her that we should come and live in the annexe so as to be on hand to look after her comforts, cook her meals, etc., while leaving her to live undisturbed in the main part of the house. She thought about this for two or three days before saying 'Well, it's a very generous offer and I am most grateful, but I think not, really, because it would get in the way of my social life.' She was then ninety-six, and almost blind.

Shortly after this she mentioned to Diana one day that she thought (quite unjustifiably, I may say) that I did not much like one of her frequent visitors and suspected that I might have the idea that they were lovers. I was encouraged to see that it is never too late for the spring of youth to flow in the human heart!

She suffered a stroke on the 1st of March 1990, which left her paralysed and barely able to speak. Thereafter, until her death, the dining room where all her books and patchworks had been created was where she was looked after by Diana with the two gardeners, George Watson and Robin Wilson. She also received wonderfully sympathetic help from the local community nurses, all of whom were immediately aware that they were looking after a rare spirit of fierce independence.

Without the ability to converse, her last three months were largely spent in listening to tapes of her favourite music. Colin Tilney was tireless in sending her tapes from Canada of his new renderings of the Well-Tempered Clavier, and he was only one of four devotees to cross an ocean to make his farewell. Margaret Faultless also came and played her violin at Lucy's bedside, to the latter's intense pleasure: an event magically recorded in paint by Elisabeth Vellacott.

Having bidden farewell to all her favourite friends from several continents, she quietly gave up the struggle on the 25th of May, 1990, aged 97½. She had been in no pain and had not uttered one single word of complaint or self-pity during the whole of her paralysis.

Hemingford Grey, February 1992